Dream Encounters

Dream Encounters

A Memoir Based on One
Woman's Dreams over a
Period of 50 Years

Margaret Honton

Frankalmoigne

Frankalmoigne
Petaluma, California

Copyright © 2021 by Margaret Honton

Printed in the United States of America.
Typeface: Caslon Book BE 11/13.5.
Cover photo: Stein Egil Liland.

Library of Congress Control Number: 2021936552

Publisher's Cataloging-in-Publication Data
Honton, Margaret, 1932 – .
    Dream Encounters: A Memoir Based on One Woman's Dreams over a Period of 50 Years / Margaret Honton.
    p. cm.
    Includes bibliographic references.
    ISBN 978-0-9856423-4-1
1. Autobiography–Women authors. 2. Autobiographical poetry, American. 3. Dream interpretation. 4. Near-death experiences. 5. Reiki (Healing system). 6. Poetry-in-the-Schools Program. I. Title

BISAC OCC006000. Body, Mind & Spirit / Dreams.

For All Dreamers Who Carry Through

Asleep and dreaming, we are in pursuit of freedom in those areas that have eluded us while awake. The relationship between freedom and truth is the driving force of our dreams. They are an ever-available ally in the struggle to get at the truth.

– Montague Ullman, *Appreciating Dreams*

Contents

Prelude: Underscoring Premises 1

1. Sorting Roles and Works 6
   Play-Acting • Facing Crowds

2. Rehearsals and Rehashals 11
   Preparing for an Event • Reciting after an Event

3. Death a Fact of Life 29
   Requiem Mass • Three Tragedies

4. Genesis of My Creative Child 35
   Giving Birth and Nurturing • Extraordinary Girl Child • Distorted Boy Child

5. The Dreamer as Artist 43
   The Artist's Milieu • Motifs • Appreciating the Artist Within

6. Challenges from Childhood 59
   Cleansing or Purging • Cleaning up Messes • Shouting

7. Coping Strategies 69
   Swimming and Diving • Singing

8. Wayfaring 84
   A Back-Story to the Dream Stories • A Pilgrim's Journey

9. A Rude Awakening 93
   Competing • Solving Problems

10. The Give-and-Take of Dream Notes 103
    Recording Notes • Images and Feelings • Motifs and Themes • Dream Cycles

11. In Awe of Dream Animals 115
    Evolving • Transforming • Giving Solace

12. My Love of Flying 137
    Modes and Vehicles • Flying for Adventure •
    to Escape • to Orgasmic Heights • to Spiritual Realms

13. Opposites in Play 148
    Yay/Boo Pairings • Behaving out of Character •
    Paradox in Waking Life

14. Anxiety Dreams 154
    Taking Tests Forever • Undergoing Telltale Deaths •
    Being Unseen/Unheard

15. Nightmares 178
    Threat of Rape • Mayhem and Murder

16. Bedtime Stories 190
    Household Tales • Parodies • Whodunit

Interlude: Consulting Mirrors 199

17. Erotic Encounters 204
    Almosting It • Engaging in Sex Play • Enjoying
    Foreplay and More Play • My Playmate Lover

18. Here Comes Everybody 223
    Personal Myths • Vignettes

19. Me and My Shadow 229
    Dark Shadow • Bright Shadow • Collective Shadow •
    Foreshadow

20. A Hitch in My Get-Along 242
    Recognizing Trickster

21. Hello, Long Time No See 248
    Negative and Positive Male Aspects • Negative and
    Positive Female Aspects

22. Goodbye: God Be with You 259
    Letting Go of Children • Marriage • Home

23. New Levels of Awareness 277
    Reassurances on Physical • Emotional • Mental •
    Aesthetic • Integrative Levels

24. Wrestling with Religion 285
    Honoring Liturgy • Rejecting Tenets

25. Precognitive Dreams. 296
    Coincidences • Warnings

26. Beyond All Boundaries. 302
    My Near-Death Experience • Comparisons and
    Contrasts of Lifetimes • Therapies • Reiki

27. Anniversary Dreams. 314

28. One Template Laid on Another 321
    Being Mentored • Projecting • Healing

29. Epiphanies 331
    Illuminations • Ecstatic Openings • Numinous Dreams

30. And Let Perpetual Light Shine 341
    Preview of Death and Dying • The Journey Home

31. Angels and Guides 353
    Messengers • Counselors • Visitors • Advisors

32. The Interrelatedness of Dreams 366
    Tripping the Light Fantastic • Night School •
    Graduate Courses • Final Exams

Postlude: Reckoning the Bottom Line. 381

Addendum A
    Themes and Motifs Not Discussed in This Book 384

Addendum B
    Citations in the Order of Appearance 386

– *Prelude* –

Underscoring Premises

I write from the vantage of two lifetimes: one beginning with my birth in 1932, the next beginning with a near-death experience in 1990. Bridging the two, like an overpass to the multi-lane road of life, is a very long span where I've heeded directions and other signs posted in my dreams.

Yes, I am now 89, still blessed with dreams and nightmares and the ability to record them. And yes, my dreams highlight a spiritual journey. The theme of journeying is a favorite in sagas, myths, and ballads from ancient times to the present. The theme of spiritual journeying is implicit in liturgies, labyrinths, and pilgrimages, and is basic to this memoir. The trail from birth to death—as charted in journals, memoirs, biographies, documentaries—has been of unceasing interest to humans. To these genres I add dreams that highlight my personal journey.

In the early 1970s my daughter Monica and I signed up for a weekend workshop on integrating dreams into waking life. We learned about types of dreams, how to record them, how to honor them in highly individual ways, and the benefits of using them as starting points for meditation. These practical steps led to group interaction, when a few of the participants' dreams from Friday night and Saturday night were examined and appreciated. By the end of the workshop, we were motivated to look for spiritual messages within our dreams.

In the new millennium, when I told Monica that I wanted to compile in a memoir what seemed most valuable in my dreams, she warned, "You may conclude that there is no conclusion." When I told my daughter Cathy about this endeavor, her immediate response was, "Don't let the book get all sweet and sentimental; keep some of the nitty-gritty in." Similar advice came from a volume that I was reading, Thomas Moore's *Care of the Soul*: "Often care of the soul means not taking sides when there is a conflict at a deep level. It may be necessary to stretch the heart wide enough to embrace contradiction and paradox." In fact, almost from the start of writing dream notes, I allowed conflicting images, feelings, or arguments to have their say, trusting that meaning would eventually come through from unconscious to conscious awareness.

In compiling this memoir I have stayed close to the raw material, the dreams themselves. *I have made no additions but many deletions.*

That a single dream could well have been included in two or more very different sections is an indication of how interrelated all the dreams are. An example of this is a series of encounters entitled "Vignettes of Three Men Approaching Me," which in its entirety, along with my reflections on it, could have been included in section 17, Erotic Encounters; section 18, Here Comes Everybody; or section 23, New Levels of Awareness. In this dream I observe that "the first man is forgettable, the second man not a good kisser. With the third, I lessen the distance between us. He is a good kisser and pleases me" (Jun 13, 2020). These dream encounters occurred during the fourth month of sequestering in the Covid-19 pandemic, by which time I was feeling an extreme loss of physical contacts.

For comparison, here is a dream from the eighth month of sequestering, when I was seemingly facing a void; it had qualities of a vision and reassured me on the emotional, mental, and spiritual levels. I include excerpts here:

Nov 27, 2020
Images That Would Do Credit to Dr. Seuss

> I look out the ornate door of a large house (or possibly a resort hotel) where our family are staying. I see a very large truck piled high with goods—so high that they are held up there by tarpaulins with grommets. Now comes a larger truck with a larger load. Now comes a huge truck with goods piled sky-high. It's a slow-moving caravan, like a circus parade, except the colors are muted, to sepia.
>
> I call to my children, "Come! You have to see this!" They take their sweet time and miss the event. Oh well, the fact is, I am the one who is enthralled.

> There's something wonderful about the caravan, its procession, and the abundance. In the tremendously high piles of goods, there are many wrapped parcels, each with bar-coding. If a customer wants a sweater, the driver of the truck can locate a parcel of sweaters readily.

REFLECTIONS:
1. That the goods are piled sky-high suggests a spiritual dimension to the abundance. I am awed by the procession, feeling as if the truck drivers high in their cabs are princes in full regalia, traveling on their prized elephants from one exotic place to another. Or the Magi traveling to Bethlehem on camels laden with gifts.
2. My allusion to illustrations by Dr. Seuss carries a tone of playfulness within a learning experience.
3. The call to my children is a call to my Child Self: Look at the abundance in life. Imagine that each of the parcels reveals a positive memory. Unwrap those memories to lift your spirit.

In this memoir, I have included some dreams in their entirety; but for a greater number, have relied on excerpts. Throughout, the *modus operandi* of dream groups was utilized: If a dream is exceedingly long and wandering, or if its scenes are completely disjointed, choose the scene that carries the strongest emotion. Even though a great many allusions, quotations, and references appeared in my morning reflections, I have included only the most pertinent.

The title *Dream Encounters* suggests a plurality of people in my dreams. Certainly a multitude of characters was available for illustrating my journey. Some have identifying tags, while others are simply strange bedfellows. For most of the persons, I have used first names only; for a few special ones, their surname, too. A principle regarding inclusion or exclusion of persons in this memoir was given to me in a dream in which a Voice from on high declared, "Whoever is important by his presence is here. Whoever is important by his absence is not important."

Because my children's names occur in several dream excerpts, I list them, their birth years, and given names here: Angelyn 1952, Cathy 1954, E. J. 1955, Monica 1957, Joe 1958, Chas 1961, Maggie 1962, Stephen 1964. Each has unique talents; all have earned one or more college degrees and pursued a career. Three are world travelers, and two have marriage partners from far-flung countries (Japan, Argentina). All have a wide range of interests, and five have a family of their own. I am tremendously proud of all my children, admit to being in awe of them sometimes, and am unceasingly grateful to them for enriching my life.

Another name that recurs in dream snippets is Maureen. She is my sister (born 1940), who lived with us for a few years after she graduated from high school and who has remained important in our lives.

There are some major exclusions in this memoir. First, because three of my siblings and all of my children are alive, I have omitted dreams whose primary focus was on them. Second, even though my husband of 33 years (and ex-husband of 19 years) died in 2005, I respect his memory by omitting all but a very few statements that reference him–Edward (born 1930). Here it suffices to say, echoing Jane Eyre, "Reader, I married him."

Year after year I consistently recorded nine nights of dreams each month, with anywhere from one to seven dreams per night. I stored those records in boxes and kept them through three changes of residence. For a very conservative estimate, multiplying 9 x 12 x 50 years = 5,400 annotated dreams for me to sort through. Of greater interest to me than quantity, however, was the *span* of each dream theme: the period in which it developed, peaked in intensity and frequency, and then tapered off. My having recorded those spans was an aid in outlining this memoir.

My dreams are artifacts of personal progress, or lack thereof. The most obvious successes relate to performance in music and in drama. Although progress is shown in other areas, too, my focus has been on my personal journey, not on the tremendous societal changes in the United States during the past half-century. The dreams selected do touch on a few major issues such as racism, sexism, ageism, economic disparities, and the tyranny of insurance companies.

Well aware that memory is not based in chronology, I decided to compile sections of this book in *lifeline* order and entries within each section in *sequential* order. Collectively, there are examples of two dozen almost universally recognized dream themes, including nightmares.

I propose that you look at my dreams as if looking within one gallery after another of an art museum that has arranged a retrospective. My sincere hope is that the images and themes challenge you to savor your own dreams, learn to appreciate nightmares, and apply the wisdom of both to everyday concerns.

– One –

Sorting Roles and Works

Although my purpose in beginning to write dream notes at age 40 was to solve immediate problems, I also hoped to discover, or else design, a spiritual way that would sustain me in the years to come. My purpose in reviewing the dream notes almost 50 years later was to discover what has, in fact, held my abiding interest and helped me become more fully the person I imagine myself to be. To achieve these goals demanded a great deal of sorting–in my sleep life and my waking life. Here is an early example:

Nov 29, 1977
Sorting Roles and Works with a Young Man

> I'm sharing a room with a young man whose name is not Bruce. I tried that on him and got no response at all. He's sorting clothes [roles], trying them on.
>
> I'm working at a large desk, pounding away at an antique, upright typewriter, then alternating with an electric typewriter that has whole words written on certain keys: he, she, said, ice cream, dear, EJ's initials, Monica's name. Sometimes, when my back begins to ache, I stand up to type.
>
> The young man asks me about my poetry writing. I'm surprised because the stuff I've been working on is prose–the recent essays. I answer, "Sometimes in the Poets-in-the-Schools Program I show kids my scribble sheets and other drafts." I proceed to gather a fistful to show him, but drop them every which-where. Now food or something that stains is all mixed in.
>
> We are on hands and knees, scrubbing the floor, floorboards, furniture. This may be when we begin to take interest in one another as male and female. I wonder, How come a man and a woman are assigned to the same room, especially when they don't even know one another's names?

There are two beds in the room—a great double bed and a single bed. I decide to change the sheets, but there aren't enough fresh sheets to redo both beds. Obviously the double is the one to redo, and we can share it. Can we? Why not? Because this is a casual encounter? Oh, really? Then maybe we'd better do some more conversing first.

FEELINGS:
Frustrated by unanswered questions.

REFLECTIONS:
1. I wonder if I go ahead sexually in dreams only when I'm semi-lucid and realize anything goes.
2. There were three dreams in a row, which I dubbed "Sorting, Passing, Surviving." On waking, I feel "caught between the devil and the deep blue sea." Actually caught between doing, with rising resentment, and not doing, with increasing apathy.

Back in the 1970s I could not have guessed that four of the themes in "Sorting Roles and Works" would recur so often that eventually they would be included in a memoir. Those *themes* were Sorting, Writing, Cleaning Up Messes, and Almosting It.

If "Sorting Roles and Works" had come a year or so later, I might have been astute enough to recognize several recurring *motifs* because they would have been entered already in my concordance: partner, keyboard, fresh sheets, and ice cream. Also, I might have asked more questions relative to the dream itself and to how I could apply its suggestions in waking life. Possible examples: Since this person is not my dear friend Bruce, who is he and of what importance to me? How do I feel about dropping my pages? What antiquarian concept am I pounding away at? What modern concept are son EJ and daughter Monica expediting in my life?

Another dream about sorting soon occurred; excerpts included the motifs of sharing a room with an unidentified male; aligning as opposites; shedding assigned roles; embracing one another. I incorporated it in one section of "A Series of One-Acts," the first and last stanzas as follows:

> They share the same conventions,
> same hotel and suite of rooms,
> yet a curtain comes between them.
> Not just a scrim this time, she thinks.
> He shuffles, actor/agent Ought-Ought-To,
> around the chair-rich room.
> The collar of his trench coat conceals expression.
> She paces, Oh-Me-Oh-My, muffled in a London fog,
> unable to communicate . . .
>
> As Muzak swells, the background very forward,
> VIPs form a queue that wends through the hotel
> and weaves through all the same conventions.
> The couple align themselves as opposites
> in the chair-rich room.
> Now they shed their outerwear,
> becoming part of the commotion.
> He moves, she moves, toward the same musical chair.
> They flop, it collapses and enfolds them.
> They cry so hard they laugh, and the curtain goes up.

The sorting of roles and works in my dreams continued apace and prompted me to build a concordance of motifs and themes for easy reference and eventual understanding. I called that effort *Opening Night*.

In the 1970s, when I devoted so much time to dream work and play, I often asked myself, *Where do I go from here?* Within a year of consistently writing dream notes, I developed a three-part format for processing each dream: notes written during the night; feelings (emotional and sometimes physical) written in the morning; then reflections on both. I wrote a title with an identifying marker, so I could refer to it again if I wished. Later, when my dream concordance was well underway, I often added a fourth step to this format: entering motifs and themes, each on a separate page of that looseleaf notebook.

In only a few instances have I charted dreams numerically. As I was developing my concordance, I was focused on understanding the dreams, not on quantifying them. Yet, when son EJ asked about crowds in my dreams—specifically whether the number of crowds changed over the years—I was able to make a chart for the first decade of dream notes (1976–1986). In that time there were 46 crowd scenes, covering a wide range of activities:

- from academic faculty to construction crews
- from a crowd at a potluck to a spread for hundreds
- from crowds of Christmas shoppers to people haggling in a bazaar
- from chorus lines of dancers to a demonstration by 200 square-dancers
- from a motley group of singers to a symphony chorus
- from a gang of hoodlums to a crowd of people with gold bikes
- from a revivalist tent-meeting to hundreds of pedestrians held back by police
- from my observing a ballroom of dancers to floating above a crowd of thousands

Often a crowd included unrelated persons, such as Santa Claus with Julius Caesar, and the juxtapositions offered comic relief. Occasionally participants in the crowd had the same activity, as in a dream scene in which clowns tumbled out of a midget car, Mickey Rooney waved from a little red roadster, and Morgan Freeman drove Miss Tandy.

Have the crowds diminished since I moved away from Columbus, Ohio and the many activities and stimuli there? They doubtless have, but I quit counting.

For the first four years I did keep track of the number of nights I dreamed per month (twenty!) and I checked sporadically after that. By July of 1979 I estimated "at least 1,000 dreams recorded, more likely 3,000 when counting several dreams on one night." Now, in my advanced years, I am amazed that I had invested so much on an experiment that was without guidelines. Recently, when finalizing the manuscript for *Dream Encounters*, I read a statement by G. William Domhoff, the originator of the Dream Bank at UCSC, that gives me solace relative to the time I've devoted to dreams:

> We have shown that 75 to 100 dreams from a person give us a very good psychological portrait of that individual. Give us 1,000 dreams over a couple of decades and we can give you a profile of the person's mind that is almost as individualized and accurate as fingerprinting.

All right, here are hundreds of dreams and then some, from almost five decades—a "psychological portrait," if you will, and certainly an exercise in trust.

– Two –

Rehearsals and Rehashals

Almost every night I've had a rehearsal scenario preparing me for the challenges of the next day. Back in the 1970s, that included communicating with my computer, struggling with lines that resisted me, performing onstage, and outdoing contenders for contracts. All these themes appeared in the following poem, which I transposed from dreams:

Getting Through the Night

Scheherazade was adamant about the suspension of disbelief; she required this from herself when everything took place in her mind, but she felt even more strongly about it when she let others in.
– *Whatever Gets You Through the Night* by Andrei Codrescu

11:30 p.m. Residue
My new computer's icons dance around the screen . . .
I try to open my eyes, to delete those contrary images . . .
but calendar pages fly off the wall, land on my lids
heavily . . . film noir.

1 a.m. Recapitulation
Red cubes & green cubes
of institutional-strength Jell-O
slip, slide, bounce, defy my determination
to manage them or anything.
There's Dream Whip squirted high and low.
There's no control and no consolation.

2:30 a.m.   Recurrence of Conflict
I've been waiting all day in an unemployment line
to see a publishing rep. about my manuscript.
It's a grand hotel we're in—with chandeliers,
red carpeting, hostesses, and a maitre d'.
I go up a spiral staircase, only to be told,
"You're in the wrong line."
So, down and around I go, through a dim corridor,
to an annex like a cheap motel, to a grungy room
where John Lithgow ("Third Rock From the Sun")
is packing off the last supplicant.

One look at me and he exclaims, "Oh no,
not tonight!   Come back in the morning."
   I can't.
   "You mean you won't."
   I've been here all day, and tomorrow I am busy.
   "Too busy for breakfast?" Too weary.
   "Too busy for lunch?" I don't do lunch.
He gets more smarmy with each invitation.
   "Too busy for sex? Or you don't do sex? "

Now two other contenders appear, discussing
"expectations: what does one expect of a castle?"
I suppose they're talking about a castle in chess.
But no, about "a fortress with its keep," and how
"surrounded by a moat, the castle has feet of clay."
They don't know it's actually quicksand.
They don't know how fast I am sinking.

4 a.m.   Recollection in Tranquility
At a writers' conference overrun by men,
I'm downcast as representing women.
Yet I defy gravity and hold to my center.
I've been writing poems sufficiently sexy
they invite folks to read between the lines
and fill in the blanks at their pleasure.

Each evening, in a natural amphitheater
with greens as complex and more indelible
than a pastoral scene in a tapestry,
I reach out to the audience, and they to me.

5:30 a.m.   Receptivity–Dream Encounters
An Olympic medalist has given me a water-ski.
I don't know how to use it, but I tote it anyway
to the warm-water pool at the YWCA.
No lifeguard on duty, though, to show me.

I swim for several laps, until my reverie
is interrupted by a group of three-piece suits
standing around the pool, talking about
their expectations. The walls echo profoundly:
"We do not expect strangers in the water.
You violate company policy."
I see red . . . and before I leave the Y,
smash the glass of the fire alarm.

Going home I see a prof in a red VW
and a poet in a green BMW
hot-rodding on Pueblo Boulevard.
There's just no end to competition.
In the mail is a blurb from my literary agent:
"MH poems more dreamlike than dreams."
I smile at the ultimate compliment.

7 a.m.   Reconnaissance–Here Comes the Dawn
I'm in the Roman Coliseum, struggling
with lion after lion, title after title.
In the grandstand there's a commotion.
I tremble . . . thumbs up? or thumbs down?

There are two functions of rehearsal that I address in this section. The first *is preparation for a future event* such as a speech, a dramatic production, or a musical performance. Usually, rehearsal dreams prior to an event showed my distress over finding no parking place or being at the wrong venue; taking the wrong place on stage or being there on the wrong night; at a loss without my purse, shoes, or pearls; missing my score, notations, or entrance cue. Yet in waking life I never lost my belongings or suffered those indignities, if only because such dreams provided a checklist to consult before an event.

The second function of rehearsal is *recitation of a past event* for an audience. Typically, a hero elaborated on his conquests, a bard memorialized epic events, or a sportscaster provided a replay of a major competition. In my dreams, this looking backward most often focused on hospital experiences, which for me had epic proportions.

In my active years, rehearsal dreams expressed frustration and sometimes fear. An extraordinary dream (circa 1975) dealt with an array of rehearsal concerns and was the basis of the following poem:

Out of the Limelight

Pacing the aisles in Lincoln Center, I note
a canvas curtain instead of red velvet,
unwieldy as those plywood panels
around construction sites
warning WORK IN PROGRESS.

I can see only silhouettes:
the maestro, four soloists in a line,
and a chorus of two hundred
on risers for the occasion.
How odd, my not standing front and center,
blowing kisses, bowing graciously.

I am keyed to the amazing sound—
a major work, and tantalizing.
The stage manager yaps at me,
"What are you doing, hanging around?"
I'm in no mood to perform tonight.
He mocks, "Is that right?"

He says something about "intestinal fortitude"
and threatens to kick me out.
But along comes a photographer from *US Today*,
asking me to pose. "Just for the back-story.
In the darkroom I'll compound your features
with a psychedelic form of art."
Defacing is an art?

No time to argue, the curtain has parted,
revealing everyone in formal attire.
Sweet heaven, what's kept me unaware
that this is a premier?
I've abdicated a premier!

Now there's a fluttering in the wings–
a woman in a designer gown, retro
except the colors are parrot bright.
Something's not right, she seems only half there–
ill or drugged, limp and heavy.
The stage manager flaps and mouths at me,
"Put her down somewhere!"
I drag her to the green room, to a beat-up sofa.
There she wilts onto the cushions and withers
like a castaway bouquet.
Who am I not to revive her?

In ruminating on the subject of rehearsals now, in the new millennium, I infer that rehearsal dreams may well be in the category of "classic" dreams. They reference so many situations: auditions, interviews for jobs, presentations to superiors, plans for a trip, preparations for surgery. An example of the latter occurred in 2010, prior to surgery for a hip replacement. The dream showed me unprepared and toughing my way through an event; the reflections on it concerned readying my belongings as well as my body for the possibility of death (which I always do prior to surgery).

Jul 25, 2010
The Apex of Frustration Relative to Performance

> I realize I should have left 20 minutes ago for a performance at a cathedral. I go up to my bedroom to hunt for my black formal concert dress. Amazing—the dress fits! I can get into it, but first I have it on backward. Getting it on right takes much time and effort. I can't find shoes that can be paired, but finally a pair of black sandals. Each of these steps takes an inordinate amount of time.
>
> I haven't rehearsed the music, intend to sight-read it when I get to the cathedral. Late indeed, but the procession hasn't started yet. I say to the person next to me, "Well, okay, I'll just lip-synch." Instead, I use the word "mumble" on various notes, as if singing the lyrics for the first hymn (or whatever . . . this may be a cantata). I'm smiling, but the person next to me isn't amused.
>
> Three women start the procession, one of them possibly a nun, the other Gertrude Kuefuhs [a music professor]. There's much confusion overall. The light keeps changing—sometimes from wall sconces, then from candles, then a skylight that dims when clouds pass over. I've forgotten to bring my glasses and can scarcely read the notes, far less the words.

FEELINGS:
Frustrated, compelled; frantic, unimportant yet committed; amused by the absurdities.

REFLECTIONS:
1. I've been rereading Robert Moss' *Dreamgates* and paying attention to dreams that are a preparation for death. In this context, the black gown, which women in Symphony Chorus refer to as a shroud, is "fitting," thereby a reassurance about death.
2. Even though in the dream I'm 20 minutes late (which could refer to the 20 years since the NDE), I am unusually adaptable in every scene. A new element here is the absurdity of dressing formally and then showing up unprepared.
3. The inadequate and changing light = my desire for enlightenment, also my desire to lighten up. These resonate with tasks I've

been doing recently: measuring all my framed collages and packing many for storage; organizing my manuscripts—represented here by the musical score—and other works on paper for Cathy to deal with after my death.

INFERENCE:
These tasks are not just busy work, they are appropriate as rehearsal for death.

Relative to the second function of *rehearsal*—the recitation of past events—I include here a poem based on events and emotions in my waking life that reappeared, with gusto, in my dreams:

Resumé

Sometimes I think I have lived my whole life
in a basement apartment with one window,
one door, and a violent man overhead
slamming his wife against the wall.

Sometimes I think I have lived my whole life
in the sub-level car park of the State House,
stifled by the hot air of politics overhead
and carbon monoxide exhaust where I'm stalled.

Sometimes I think I have lived my whole life
as a migrant worker in a tomato field,
in the daytime worn to a shred,
by kerosene lamp too tired to protest.

Sometimes I think I have lived my whole life
in a closed-blind teachers' lounge,
where nasty gossip, though unsupported,
heaps higher than the mandated tests.

Sometimes I think I have lived my whole life
in the sweatshop of Globe Knitting Mill,
fluorescent lights sizzling overhead,
machines pulsating through my burning feet.

> Sometimes I think I have lived my whole life
> as Everywoman in fear of the dread
> Rumpelstiltskin or drug dealer
> intent on abducting her child off the street.
>
> Sometimes I think I have lived my whole life
> mundanely, an uninspired Cinderella
> with nary a thought in her head
> of a prince or a steed come apace.
>
> Today I am sure I have lived my whole life
> in a Rorschach test—misleading, misled,
> seeing through a glass darkly
> and wondering: *When* face to face?

Subsequent dreams, particularly those featuring windows or mirrors or resplendent light, partially answered that question about a face-to-face encounter with the Divine. Such dreams not only helped me see more clearly how I could deal with contemporaneous issues, but also gave me glimpses of an over-arching plan.

Chief among rehearsals of past events in my dreams has been my early hospitalizations. Many of those dreams were so vivid and painful that they seemed to be actual flashbacks to the original event. I do not claim that they were re-enactments; neither do I dismiss the possibility.

In an early draft of this book, I thought that *hospitalized* would fit under the aegis of nightmares. But I soon realized that it must be treated in a special way, due to the great number of dream notes, their intensity, their complexity, and their dramatic turn for the better.

In the first decade of my note-taking there were 66 hospital dreams; in the next five years, 30. There occurred a gradual shift in emphasis from my being incarcerated to my studying and working with energy in healing ways. That was due to my waking-life participation in classes, conferences, certification programs, and healing weekends for about three years. Then, in the years following a near-death experience, I focused on the healing art of Reiki and continued to explore other healing modalities as adjuncts to Reiki.

The fierce dreams from childhood that I still recall were nightmares about hospitals. I was terrified of anesthesia, that anyone would have such power over me. I was afraid of letting myself slide into sleep each night, supposing I might never wake up. There were fever dreams, too, in which I reached for a glass of water but was prevented from having a sip. Some distortions that I could not get out of my head included a sledgehammer, a butcher's meat slicer, a drill, and steel tubing.

I now believe that my parents meant well when saying, "It's only a dream." But, dear goodness, if only they had let me talk about a nightmare, they might have alleviated the cause of it.

I was fearful of nurses who demanded that I do things I was not capable of, especially the night nurse who patrolled like a policeman; subsequently, they were memorialized in many nightmares as my nemesis, Big Nurse. Factually, I was blessed with two doctors who cared for me over several years: Dr. Hill, a pediatrician, and Dr. Doran, a surgeon. I can never thank them enough. The first dream in this series speaks to that caring relationship, but the next two dreams are less realistic:

Oct 4, 1975
Stroking Is the Beginning of My Cure

> The doctor comes to me, not me to him. He asks me to follow with my eyes the path his finger takes. He does some gentle loops, to which I gradually adjust, then a stroking motion, very relaxing [maybe hypnotizing, I just thought of that]. I feel the sensation of being stroked, even though he doesn't touch me.
>
> Now I am stroking a green cloth of very fine material. It has a wonderful weave that I can stroke in several directions. I fold it lovingly and later put it against my cheek. Like moss or grass, textured more than velvet, with the softness of angora. This is the beginning of my cure. I know where I am, in a sanitarium, and why–to get in touch with myself and eventually with others. To love myself more, so that I can be loved and offer love. And I know the doctor cares.
>
> We walk hand-in-hand away from a beautiful house. I sense I will never revisit that house, and I'm saddened.

> Now I realize that "all the houses are one." That isn't true imagistically, but they have the same Tudor exteriors and lovely landscaping and the feeling–the glow–of warmth.

Oct 9, 1975
Helpful + Hopeful = Healing

> I'm walking down a long hill. The road is very smooth and ends at bubbling water–light green and frothy, beautiful but scary. I want to turn around but can't. I must go over a narrow footpath with a sheer drop-off to eternity on my right. I cling to a wall, which has thick cloth, wool I think, and grab it for support. After about 10 steps, someone takes my arm, and soon I'm okay and across the abyss.
>
> Now I'm to be tested by a young doctor. He says I don't respond normally to lights in my eyes, but he doesn't make a diagnosis. He says, "You're not one to go under hypnosis." I laugh, "Oh, I can do that on my own. Why didn't you ask me?"

REFLECTION:
I wonder about the significance of my "seeing the light" or not seeing it.

Oct 1975
My Childhood Illnesses Written Up

> I learn something about my childhood illnesses. They were written up in a medical journal at the time. There were some metal contraptions to keep my arms and legs aligned, and a hood-like appliance for over my head and shoulders. I see these in illustrations [in the journal] and then in a hospital display case. I want to know more about the diseases that prompted such treatment. It involved partial paralysis, but I can't discover for how long.
>
> Some of the print on the report has blurred, and no one will give me answers, far less details. I think, Mother must have been terrified. No wonder she didn't come near me!

Sep 30, 1976
The Threat of Death

> In a hospital, my urine is too thick. A doctor gravely announces, "You have 48 parts in addition to a predominating fungus. A person in good condition might have as few as two parts. This is what make urinalysis so difficult and why I must charge you extra."
>
> I'm outside the hospital, "getting a breath of fresh air" [before surgery]. A reporter asks me, "Are you going home now?" Obviously not! Still in a hospital gown, I say, "They've found strange symptoms." The reporter says, "Don't go giving me a long story about your ordeal, like that series a few years ago. I can't stand that much." I think, "YOU can't stand it?"
>
> I say, "I've been happy with my progress. See, here are my wrist bones, and I've been able to see ankle bones for the first time in months."
>
> Now we go indoors. I guess he wants to verify what I've been telling him. Now is when the facial anesthesia and oral surgery begin. Feeling pain and pressure, I think, I've been trapped into surgery against my will! I hear the doctor calling, "Needle" . . .

FEELINGS:
The unknowing is awful. The disbelieving of doctors and the taunts of the reporter unnerve me. I wakened trembling.

Nov 21, 1979
Put Under

> I'm on a gurney, being wheeled to the operating room. Now someone clamps a mask on my face to give me anesthesia. I take a great gulp, now try to cooperate and steady my breathing–it's rhythmic, but shallow. Just as I'm sliding to Unconsciousness, I'm thrust forward [as I once fell forward in a dentist's chair, fainting] and I somersault. This is upsetting–literally–and the nurses are angry. They stand me up, prop me, and administer something highly perfumed. I guess it's magnolia gas.

> [Later] I'm standing by a window in a rather high building. A jet plane goes by, perilously close, and I wish I were on it, that it would deliver me somehow. Now a large plane with propellers that look like spirals of a notebook when they turn, comes more slowly into view. It is very close! I think, If it hits this building, it will get me because I'm on a corner. Now I think, It will hit or it won't hit, and I'll have nothing to say about it either way, so I may as well accept this flight pattern.

REFLECTION:
The scene at the high level focuses on acceptance of whatever is in my future—flying or not, crashing or not—on the mental level as well as the physical level.

Jul 26, 1981
A Huge Needle Used to Control

> A man has a huge needle—about the size of a caulking gun—filled with a pink serum. He's going to inject this in a woman or possibly one of my daughters! I grab it and wrench it away. In the fracas he injects me. I fight off whatever this drug is—whether anesthetic, psychedelic, or aphrodisiac. I need to be a free agent, not just someone lying still and taking it.

FEELINGS:
The sense is of being victimized—either myself, daughters, or women of my acquaintance.

REFLECTION:
Even beyond the sexual assault is something total, including medical, intellectual, and possibly spiritual aspects.

In 1981 I made an inference about a different type of surgery dream, one not accompanied by physical pain and therefore metaphorical. "It indicates one of two things: I am cut off from a part of myself; or I need to cut away from, remove myself from, a painful situation." Yet early in 1982, the following nightmare proceeded from a physical situation to a surrealistic one, and how was I to account for that?

Jan 21, 1982
Drawn into Drama, Therapy, Examination, almost to Surgery!

> [In my poetry therapy internship] I'm observing a group of alcoholics in treatment. Gradually I participate in the therapy session. It's drama today, I guess. This may be better for all of us than my merely observing. The result is disastrous, though. A doctor comes in, strips me to panties, and displays me in front of the group, running his hands all over me. When I finally get a hospital gown, my clothes and shoes are gone, also my I.D. I conclude that this isn't a drama class or a play, but I'm in a hospital, and the staff here are all boldface liars. The doctor ridicules me, makes disparaging remarks about my medical history, and taunts me about symptoms and medications.
>
> Another doctor runs an instrument over my head and shoulders and down my sides. This is a vibrating instrument, which I don't feel at the higher levels, due to willpower, but which causes me to collapse at my knees and ankles.
>
> A nurse injects me and says, "Now tell me how much education you've had!" I say, "I have had a LONG education" [in hospitals]. Now the doctors and nurses are taking me down a hall, toward surgery I think. They're dragging me on my feet, so they may be able to claim I've gone of my own volition. But I'm fighting the whole time. I keep one of their machines away from me, again by willpower, and I refuse to let anyone put an anesthesia cup over my face. I tell someone at a desk, "There will be hell to pay . . . This isn't legal or ethical. If you perform surgery, there will be terrible consequences for this whole place."

FEELINGS:
Betrayal and entrapment; ashamed and angry about the examination; furious at being drawn in and then dragged toward an unethical, illegal surgery; assertive with my willpower, and assertive about my rights.

REFLECTIONS:
1. The vibratory instrument reminds me of the laser battles in "Star Wars," a battle of wits and actually a spiritual battle.
2. Even in waking life, I feel damned if I do, damned if I don't in many poetry therapy situations.

In the summer of 1982, around my 50th birthday, I was hospitalized for six days due to blood clots in my right leg. My Unconscious served up images of *terminals*, to the extent that I had to reassure myself, "The blood-clotting problem isn't a terminal matter. Maybe the message is that I've waited and been detoured a long time and need to terminate the current approach?" (Jul 16, 1982). Further, "It does seem that for every stretch forward or uphill, I slide backward, regress, have an episode of illness, or gain weight."

In September I was in the hospital again, with shingles so severe that spinal nerve blocks were administered. When the nerve blocks wore off within days, I was in such pain that I wanted to die. No wonder that the next scribbled notes on my dream tablet were, "Time is running out . . . chill factor . . . need for study and illumination" (Sep 23, 1982).

Following that were several dreams of surgery that I understood as related to the impending divorce. Also, I was at that time working in unusual situations under arbitrary decisions in the Poets-in-the-Schools Program ("in the pits"). Those two factors prompted what I called a "life history dream," a lengthy, convoluted nightmare. In it Big Nurse was sadistic, "dragging me into a control booth, where I scream, 'I have a right to a lawyer! to a witness! to know who you are! to know what this operation is about!' In the booth a man says, 'We will plug into some pattern in your dark depths that will be your undoing. You will eat your own quark.' I jam whatever they are sending me and focus on The Most Holy One, who is more powerful than all these alien and diabolical persons" (Sep 9, 1983). The struggle was, for the first time, on the mental level more than the physical level, and in this dream I was apprehensive about mind control.

In the next few weeks, in free-writing for greater understanding, I covered 29 half-sheets concerning this struggle and five full sheets of a dialogue with Big Nurse. A growing awareness of my own power accounted for the following dream:

Feb 23, 1984
I Am Delivering Myself

> Some doctors are denouncing me as crazy, out of touch with reality. Nurses, too. Others are explaining the phenomenon of my false pregnancy and my going through labor and delivery for a phantom child or concept or notion. There's a dispute whether I've been "out" via anesthesia? or amnesia? or just "out of my head"? I've reduced many pounds in a few hours—25 to 35 pounds that quickly. My belly belongs to me now, even though the flesh sags.
>
> One doctor says that I screamed. I don't believe him and I ask if he made a tape recording? This is a dispute not only of a patient against a doctor, but more specifically of one person's word against another's and of a woman's word against a man's. More: it's the word of the person who endured the action against the word of an observer.

Four months later, there was a similar dream of delivering myself (Jun 15, 1984). It was prompted by statements of my husband concerning alimony and his unhelpful suggestion that I apply for work at the Bureau of Motor Vehicles. I did not apply because standing all day was impossible for me.

The last dream of that decade of recording (1975–1984) was not a nightmare about hospitals but a concise message about healing:

Nov 18, 1984
Prophecy on a Scroll

> An image similar to freeform paintings I've done, with about 60% taken by one scroll. The message: "The greater portion belongs to music, not to medicine."

REFLECTION:
Here is reassurance that much of my life is not dependent on doctors, treatments, or medications but on my involvement with what I love most—art, music, writing, all creative endeavors.

In 1984 there was a reference in my dream notes to Arthur Janov's *Primal Man and the New Consciousness,* in which the author discussed nightmares as the re-creating of life/death situations, their images representing the original terror. After questioning myself, What is the original terror here? I concluded: It's in my body, not in the dream images. It's the clogged nasal passages, the gagging that wakens me, the threat of asphyxiation, the arbitrariness of sieges, and the feeling of helplessness.

Whatever the original terror was, Big Nurse still appeared occasionally, and my fear of being "put under" did not disappear. Regarding that continuing fear, some explanation about the next dream is called for: I have survived three incidents of carbon monoxide poisoning. The first was in 1955 when some bricks in the chimney of the small house we rented fell inward during a freak storm. The second was in 1985 in an apartment I rented during my year of separation, when wires that someone had jury-rigged in the furnace burned through, allowing only partial combustion of the gas. Those two times I stirred enough, or a Guardian Angel stirred me, to wonder why I was lying on the floor in the middle of the day, and to move out of danger. The third incident was in 1986 in the house that EJ provided with only nominal rent. In that instance, I smelled something wrong and called the Gas Company right away. But their technician told me, "There's nothing detectable and, if you're wondering about carbon monoxide, it doesn't have an odor." It was only after my preparing for a house-warming dinner, serving it, and clearing away the china, that I became sick and went to the emergency room. The next day, men in hazmat suits, utilizing more sensitive detectors, found that my new stove had not been connected properly.

A nightmare within a month of that incident did not address the *issue* of asphyxiation, but did illustrate it with "a foggy night" and with "intruders breaking and entering while I am sleeping" (Nov 3, 1986). My notes the next morning concerned "complete vulnerability" and stated, "I do feel foggy since the carbon monoxide incident, and I am afraid of being overcome in my sleep."

Around that time, there was a shift from the flash-backs to what might be called flash-forwards, in which I was adopting new ideas and new remedies. In the summer of 1987, a dream suggested having a massage, a healing modality that I had long delayed while considering its cost:

Jun 6, 1987
Cross-Connections

> In an underground area, very large, with many corridors and cross-connections, I wait in one line after another, hoping for a massage, sauna or hot tub, or other relaxing techniques. While waiting, I offer to give a slim woman a massage. She agrees, though begrudgingly.
>
> I wander into several other areas, some on the men's side, I infer. No one seems embarrassed although I'm topless, wearing only a white towel around my middle. There's one dangerous area where someone shouts, "Recede!" At length I find some ointment and begin massaging my neck and shoulders. I see another woman doing this, too, and I say, "It's lonely, isn't it?"

REFLECTIONS:
1. The underground location suggests my Unconscious and its many cross-connections.
2. It reminds me of the Roman baths in France and the fact that a church was built over the bath in Aix. So there's something spiritual within this dream.
3. Likely, massage = message. Having a massage on a regular basis might get the message of LOVE to all parts of my body.

Later that summer was a dream of a single sentence that made a deep impression on me:

Aug 24, 1987
A Healer's Hands

> A woman shows me that a healer's hands are palms up, slightly cupped, not with fingers outstretched.

REFLECTION:
This morning I can't help wondering if the dream is trying to tell me that I am a healer.

I had, for about a year, participated in a healing circle of women who met two weekends a month. There I was teased about my "hot hands." In retrospect, I know that I was actually practicing for the healing work I would engage in following a near-death experience three years later. This 1987 nugget of dream was a rehearsal for my next career.

– *Three* –

Death a Fact of Life

When I was little, we lived a block away from St. Francis Xavier Church. My mother, who had converted to Catholicism in order to be married in the church, was attracted to the Devotions to Our Lady of Perpetual Help more than to liturgical events. For a couple of years, she took me to the devotions held on Tuesday evenings, likely out of gratitude to the congregation for their prayers and certainly out of pride in me as a survivor.

In those years, holding a wake in one's home was common practice. When my godfather died, I was taken to his home, which was crowded with people I didn't know. I remember stepping up on a red velvet kneeler and standing on tiptoe to see him in the coffin and say goodbye.

From the first grade through the tenth at St. Francis Xavier School, students attended Mass at 7:50 a.m. before filing to the school building for classes, and we became well acquainted with the concept of death. Our daily Mass was sung in Latin and was invariably the Requiem, because many parishioners gave stipends for a memorial of their loved ones–annually or even monthly. At an actual funeral tall candles on gold-plated stands lined both sides of the bier; at memorials a bier was wheeled down the main aisle, covered in a black shroud.

In the third grade, students were taught from a Gregorian Chant book; we followed the slips and slides of neums on a four-line staff. The melodies themselves were already familiar because we'd heard them hundreds of times; eventually our singing made us officially a part of the congregation. The section of the Requiem that I loved was seldom sung, however, and then by the choir, not the congregation: *In Paradisum deducant te angeli,* May the angels lead you into Paradise. I once had a dream featuring the Gregorian chant book; in it a Voice from on high declared, "The meaning of life is a neum." Baffled, I wrote pages of response before concluding that the meaning of life is death and resurrection.

Three tragic occurrences in my childhood struck me deeply. First, the only other girl in our neighborhood, Marie Therese O'Neil, was hit by a car and almost died when she was four years old. I saw her mother run out the front door, race around the back of the house screaming, and run out the front door again–several times before the medics arrived. I could never play with Marie Therese again because she was like a baby; she had to learn all over how to sit up, feed herself, and talk.

The second event occurred after our family moved away from that sad milieu. A boy across the street, an Eagle Scout, was climbing a tree in his own back yard and fell. He broke his neck and died on the spot.

The third tragic event happened a few years later. Some high-schoolers, out celebrating their graduation, crashed their car in our front yard. Two of those young people died there. I did not see them because my parents covered their bodies with quilts.

These were more than cautionary tales for me; I was even then an empath, *feeling* what others were feeling, a blessing that often seemed a curse.

Now I veer from the exact order in which the dreams arrived, for my personal death-in-life story to be more accessible.

May 29, 1985
After the First Death, There Is No Other

> The first death was my own near-death when I was trying to be born. [In this dream] All I see is a dark blue object–a heavy, oblong box near the floor. It's 3 or 4 feet long and maybe 1 foot in width and height. And I hear those words of Dylan Thomas, "After the first death, there is no other."

FEELINGS:
The night was terrifying. Once I shook the bed in a startle reflex of my entire body.

REFLECTIONS:
1. The box suggests a casket. It also reminds me of the obelisk in *2001: A Space Odyssey*, though lying on its side.

2. The dark blue resonates to the catechism book and to school uniforms; by extension to Catholic indoctrination or to religion itself.
3. There's no one I can talk to about the struggle that continues in me—*a struggle against what I have already survived!*
4. A trigger for the dream is my anxiety about Hiroko's and Maggie's pregnancies and deliveries, knowing that huge babies are possible because of Honton genes.

Another dream presented "A mystery. Investigating the near-death and disappearance of an infant whose shoulder has been crushed. The detective keeps on asking absurd questions, as if there would be a cumulative effect to what one woman is calling a ridiculary procedure" (Aug 9, 1982).

More clues about my birth trauma were given in a dream a year later:

Dec 15, 1983
Delivery by Forceps

> I'm in utter darkness. I've made a turn, or more than one, and this corridor or passageway is short. Worse—it's tight. I have to move my shoulders and arms because something metal is clamping me in on both sides—like Erector Set plates pushing against me, tight. I can't understand how this is. How can my hips be narrower than my shoulders? What's going to happen next? Will my neck and head be walled in next? Even while I'm screaming for help, I wonder who can help me. Only the person who got me into this fix?
>
> Mother is involved. I hear her voice. She's telling someone loudly, almost shouting, "I WILL have strong black coffee, I WILL NOT have weak tea! I WILL have my cigarettes!" This is a big issue, not just a complaint.
>
> Everything is out of proportion. Can't she hear me screaming for help?

REFLECTION:
This is a big dream. I told a therapist, "I'm going to let whatever is crying or shouting for attention come through. I want to deal with

it, heavy or not, Christmas or New Year's or whenever, soon! I want to be open to it, and I hope my willingness will help ease it and the nightmares."

MORE PROCESSING:
1. I've had a verbal dream 24 hours later, the words simply Transition At Risk. Like a caution sign at a railroad crossing and with the feeling: Stop, Look, and Listen (Dec 16, 1983).
2. Working with yesterday's dream, I'm still questioning. Say I can forgive Mother for her weaknesses (I thought I'd done that years ago), what can come of resurrecting a birth trauma? Is there someone here in Columbus who could accompany me through a birth ritual? Even if so, what help would ritual be? I'm already a survivor several times over.
3. But the patterning of death-in-life is very deep. And what I'm undergoing presently is not just metaphor or symbol; it feels like a re-enactment. I have a sense of urgency. I need to debrief, need to process the realizations and the feelings. I'd like to do it through dream work.

POSTSCRIPT 1:
My mother died two days later (Dec 18, 1983) while talking on the telephone with her favored son. I'm glad I didn't terminate her harangue on Thanksgiving, the last time we talked.

POSTSCRIPT 2:
A dream almost three years later prompted me to write this poem for closure:

Figures of Death

> The long-distance line crackles Mother's call,
> distorts her last words, "I'm so tired."
> In her limp hand the telephone
> disconnects with loud bleeps.
> The nursing home robs her of dignity,
> calls her a corpse
> even before the doctor can certify
> or her priest son perform the last rites.

She's left uncovered, her door ajar
like a mausoleum inviting marauders.
Someone removes her jade earrings.
(How many times she'd said to nurses,
"I am naked without earrings.")
Someone unpins from her robe the cameo,
leaves only her wristwatch with its stiff black band.
Someone snatches unopened gifts–
nighties with Velcro fasteners, a bottle of tequila.

This time there are no cigarettes to filch.
Mother kicked the habit a few weeks ago,
a habit begun at age 14 with corn silks.
Though she loosed one hold on a lifetime of neglect,
of hating her body and bodily functions,
at my last visit she repeated, "I hate this body."
Moved from bed to wheelchair by hydraulic hoist,
lowered into a pool for her weekly bath,
she cried again, "I hate this body."
And my body shriveled.

Three years and many nightmares pass
before our final farewell.
Comfortable in my own warm bed,
I feel Mother slide in next to me.
She's never done this before. I'm so glad.
She's cold and doesn't know how to snuggle,
so I move close to warm her.
She can't seem to relax,
so I turn and hug all that remains of her,
a corpse.

The following lengthy dream, even with its bizarre elements, displayed other concerns about death, especially my need to forgive:

Oct 8, 1983
Resurrecting Skeletons

> Like a vision except so physical. In a park that was a cemetery, though no one presently is aware of that. Someone says, "Did you see that right hand?" and another, "A head! an arm!" It looks like a human skeleton imbedded in the earth, facing the sky.
>
> Now two persons are raised–from the dead? or a frozen state? They act as if just wakened from a nap, so we don't tell them the circumstances, afraid the shock would stop their heartbeat finally. I venture into complete darkness and awful cold, step onto thin ice and into slush, carrying one of the re-vivified but not yet warm manifestations.
>
> Now I kneel to embrace a skeleton figure that is stirring and trying to rise to a sitting position. I'm holding her completely against myself, and it's as if she's imbedded in me now. There's tremendous joy for me, though only a sleepy awareness for her.
>
> Now I'm lying flat and carried on the shoulders of six persons, up a wide staircase of maybe 20 steps. I'm carried not as a sacrifice but as a symbol of resurrection.

REFLECTION:
What I embrace is the power of the Life Force. When I feel the warming, joy overcomes both my surprise and my tendency to be judgmental.

In my advanced years, in this 21st century, I have prepared for my death with the necessary legal papers, conversations with my children, exercises in conscious living and dying, and investigation of hospice care. Even though I have a long medical history, I foresee that my transition will be smooth because of my children's loving attentiveness.

– *Four* –

Genesis of My Creative Child

This theme involves several periods of my waking life: my birth; the 12 years during which I delivered eight children; times when my writing and the editing of others' manuscripts generated new life; and occasions of the spontaneous birth of ideas.

For this section, I have separated examples of my Female aspect from those of my Male aspect because I recognized the extraordinary baby girl as my Creative Child many years before I had to deal with the distorted and often tortured baby boy and could imagine any creativity emerging from him. Here is an early example of my Creative Child:

Aug 25, 1975
A Most Unusual Baby

> A baby whom I diaper and whose head gets bumped a little as I lay her down. People look at me accusingly, but the baby, who now has developed to about two or three years old, smiles lovingly and gleefully. She gets up and shows the onlookers an intricate dance step. Nothing's wrong with that child! I'm terribly relieved, very happy, enjoying the performance.

In a dream a few months later, I was baby-sitting a little girl. "After her parents leave, I discover what is in the sack of goodies she's not supposed to touch. It's a baby boy, very lightweight, about the size of a hand puppet. I feel I've been tricked into added responsibility" (Dec 1, 1975).

At Christmastime there was a highly emotional scene about mothering: "I'm being prepped to deliver a baby. Have a terrible pain in right side and low back. The woman in the bed next to me says, "My water broke," and boasts, "I would rather die in labor than not labor." I think, You haven't got much choice in the matter. On that same date there was also an inference that "difficult deliveries = manuscripts submitted" (Dec 26, 1975).

The next variant had my youngest son, Even-Stephen, "pointing to something astonishing–a newborn baby! Who could have done such a thing? Who was physically capable of bearing and delivering a baby? Who looks empty now? I wrap the baby in a pink shawl of mine and look for a blanket to wrap myself because I, too, am naked" (Jan 28, 1976). This dream was about creation and creativity; it also concerned how bereft I felt when a writing project was completed.

In the only account of an androgynous child, "She feels her genitals and is aroused. I see an erect penis, which is when I notice the problem of identification" (Mar 29, 1977). Three months after that, came the following dream:

Jul 13, 1977
A Baby with Super Powers

> I see a small child fall into loose dirt. There's no trace of him immediately after. I ask someone to investigate. Finally I reach my hands down through dirt and garbagey stuff and find a hand of the child. I'm amazed that he's alive. Will he breathe? He needs mucous passages cleaned out. I want a doctor to do it, but he sprawls on a chair, asking questions but not helping me or the baby.
>
> The baby's recovery is amazing to watch. After a bath, he's more like a three-month-old. Soon he's six-month size but acts like a two-year-old, walking, running, talking. He may be a genius, but I don't let his super-powers intimidate me. I'm awed by the propensity for growth and I think, This is what is meant by "survival of the fittest."

REFLECTIONS:
1. My use of the male pronoun *he* is not meant to be limiting. I didn't want to say *it* when referring to humanness.
2. While in the dream, I have no sense of this being a dream, rather a surety that this is a miracle, saying, "At my age! Imagine welcoming a child at my age!"

3. Assuming that this baby is my Creative Child, it's I who care about it from the beginning and who, in effect, love it into life and watch it grow.
4. I do not question this delivery or the whys and wherefores of it. I do not question my worthiness or ability.

Dec 7, 1981
My Bouncing Baby

> Here's the beautiful, bouncing baby, almost newborn, ball-shaped and rolling or bouncing off the edge of a pool. I intended to bring her into the water—it's very warm, inviting, relaxing—but she's come in of her own sweet will. I'm afraid she'll drown, but no, she dunks her head in and comes up laughing. She doesn't swim. I don't see her arms as separate from her ball-shape.
>
> She's a ball of joy and delight, mostly just skimming on the water but also spinning, so every surface of her ball-shape is touched. There's no struggling, just enjoyment.

REFLECTIONS:
1. This is how I picture myself as a baby—fresh and playful before my illnesses, never a troublesome youngster like those occurring in recent nightmares.
2. Regarding the times I was "saved" in childhood, my own efforts—like those of this baby's "own sweet will"—may have saved me as much as my parents' faith did. Is it possible that a three-year-old has the will to live? has the belief that life is worth living?

Another version of the bouncing baby occurred three years later in "Rescuing a Black Baby" (May 3, 1984). In that instance, "the baby does a backward dive or somersault, flinging itself from a height of eight or ten feet. I catch it, like a heavy football, and clutch the baby to my chest as if to run for a touchdown."

Years later there was an additional inference: "The presence of the Creative Child is like an invitation to play. My inclination, though, is to unclutter my desk first" (Dec 18, 1988). A month after that statement, there was a discussion in Dreamtalk about birthing in dreams—how it is not always one's own child arriving. Especially when labor is protracted or fierce, it is a metaphor for transition, a rite of passage that is in progress but has not presented itself yet (Jan 20, 1989).

The concept of transition would account for the following dream images at a time when I was stuck on the Mental Level with writer's block, and felt weighted down on the Physical Level: "A baby girl about six inches tall climbs up the end of a crib and is almost strangled between the top bar and the wall. After I've dislodged her, the mother arrives and says, 'She's forever getting into tight spots, but nothing stops her' " (Jan 26, 1989).

Another dream was more specific about *writing* being one's baby. "I'm feeling pregnant, full-term and overdue, yet I have a choice whether to deliver a baby or produce something on paper. Either will release me. But how awful to carry this for over nine months and not give birth to a child. Yet, considering my age, would it be fair to a child?" (Jan 15, 1999).

The twisted, tortured baby boy is an unsolved mystery to this day. At first I inferred that he represented my childhood and the distorted thoughts I had in my earliest years. There was so much that I repressed regarding pain, hospitalizations, and what I felt were betrayals, that the tortured images did not seem exaggerated.

Later I thought that he was an antagonist to my Positive Female aspect; consequently, a Negative Male aspect. Here is an early example: "A baby boy is turned backside to, and his penis is like a tassel on his head. When I get him folded back, partially restored, his testicles have been severed—cut off on a flat plane the way wood or marble is. There's no bleeding, just a cross-sectional design, and someone holds the testicles in the palm of his hand" (Aug 19, 1983). Another example: "A little boy, a baby, has caught his head between the bars of his crib. He twists and forces the bars apart with his head, and comes out crying" (Feb 24, 1984). This is suggestive (or reminiscent?) of the birth process, also of my hospital confinement at an early age.

Some years later, speculation about the tortured boy went along these lines: "I want to write about the possibility of my having thought, at a tender age (maybe when I was in the hospital and my parents weren't around?) that my genitals had been cut off. Also, when I had pain and burning with urination as nephrosis was developing, I must have wondered, Why am I hurting so? What did I do wrong? My big brother and my baby brother don't hurt so. Well, that's one way of accounting for the dreams of castration and other mutilation of the tortured boy. If there's another way, I don't yet know what it is" (May 11, 1993).

A powerful nightmare four years later suggested that even empathizing with the tortured child caused me pain:

Sep 7, 1997
A Toddler Risks His Life

> He's holding onto a chain-link fence. Now lets loose deliberately: one hand . . . pause . . . then the other . . . and falls about 12 feet.
>
> I see it happen and rush to the spot where I think he landed in a field, but can't find a trace of him. I call out wildly. My chest hurts. I'm thinking, If this is grief, then I've never before experienced grief. How can anyone live through such pain?
>
> I expect to find a crushed body and am afraid to touch the remains, yet I need to. My mind races. I'm cold and terrified of what I may find. But not finding is even worse, as if a denial of reality itself.
>
> [Much later, in another scene] I imagine a miraculous rebound for the child, as in some children's story books. The infant is sitting up, smiling. I'm overjoyed. I want to touch him, hold him, assure myself this isn't a mirage.

REFLECTION:
Most important is that the boy child–whatever aspect he represents–survives, whole and smiling. He isn't bleeding, twisted, or grotesque, as in many other dreams.

Here I need to interject a reference to a recently published book that might have been tremendously helpful in the years when I was dealing with this theme: *Dreamworking* by Christopher Sowton, ND. He has produced a "Table of Rebirth Stages and Corresponding

Dream Imagery" that is nothing short of astounding and certainly helpful to anyone interested in construing problematic dreams. Here is an example from the 23 stages–pre-conception through bonding and attachment–that would have helped me understand many of my dreams:

Stage of process	Corresponding perinatal stage	Corresponding dream motifs
Difficulties in the last phase of transition	Hard contractions with no movement into the birth canal	Dreams of being pushed, crushed, squeezed, caught, wedged, buried, suffocated

My hopefulness for the distorted boy continued in a short dream a few weeks after that nightmare. "My male infant is perfectly formed but minuscule. There is precociousness and sweetness in this infant, such as I've witnessed in my Creative Child. Though not speaking in a foreign language, he is talking. He can develop and speak for himself" (Oct 20, 1997). But less than a year later, I viewed him as not having his needs met.

The next time a dream focused on this mysterious boy was sixteen years later:

Aug 8, 2013
Defiant and Determined Boy

> The boy advances from infant to two years to kindergarten age in the time it takes me to find clothes that fit him. I'm trying to coordinate his clothes, but find him defiantly choosing a plaid shirt with awful shades of brown, yellow, and green that does not go with his burgundy pants. He's determined to dress himself, to wear motley colors, and to go in his own sweet time, not a moment sooner. I say, "All right then, I'll write a note to Miss McDonald and tell her you're NEVER going to kindergarten!" This is a threat, but he doesn't respond.

REFLECTIONS:
1. Though in the dream the boy's defiance vexed me, as I write it

seems infinitely better than his abject helplessness on previous occasions. I admire his spunk in taking his time and in skipping kindergarten.
2. Relative to *my* showing spunk, I have written a full-page letter to the surgeon and the anesthesiologist scheduled to work on my knee, with a final paragraph in red ink for the attending nurse: "If you can't get my vein for the I-V setup in the first try, call in a phlebotomist right away. I will not be the good patient while feeling like a sacrificial victim, ever again."

My Subconscious may have been dealing with problems that were not all mine, notably those of my husband, who refused to look at *any* problems. As early as 1978, in a dream entitled "Little Boy a Responsibility that Should Not Be Mine," I had difficulty identifying him: "Not a brother, not a son, not a bastard. Oh, am I married? Yes! and there's little chance that I'll ever have a fresh start on adulthood, career, or marriage" (Jan 27, 1978).

My husband refused psychotherapy, saying, "I don't have any problems, this is just the way I am." Yet his early childhood was as troubled as mine. His mother died a few days after he was born, and he was kept in the hospital nursery, where he was the center of attention, until age one. Then he was entrusted to his step-sister and her part-time housekeeper. His sister was 22 years older than he and handicapped, eventually needing a wheelchair. Moreover, his step-brothers were grown and gone away, which left him with no role models.

Throughout his life, Ed rarely saw his father, JP, who spent long days and evenings as manager of a restaurant or else was gone fishing with friends on one of the Great Lakes. JP projected guilt on Ed for many years before he said explicitly, when his son was a teenager, "You know, you killed her, the only woman I ever loved." That would have been hard to hear at any age!

In the year of separation from my husband prior to the divorce, I wondered how often, and to what extent, my dreams about the tortured boy were based on *his* behaviors and feelings. At length, it seemed that *I was having to feel his feelings for him.* Though I gradually refused to "mother" my husband and confirm his neediness, I remained empathetic in most instances.

The most recent variant of giving birth and nurturing prompted several questions, yet carried a feeling of optimism:

Jan 8, 2017
Precocious Male Infant

> I check on him, a newborn. He's sleeping I suppose, but no. He's awake, sitting up in the crib, and has somehow pulled down the guardrail. He's smiling, a triumphant expression.
>
> One safety pin is off his diaper. Did he do that, too? The diaper isn't wet, so I take the boy to the bathroom. Actually, he walks there! I stand him in place to urinate. He does, but because he's looking around, he sprays everywhere. I don't scold him, I'm so proud of his accomplishments.
>
> I'd like to show him off to family and friends, but decide they can observe and comment in their own time.
>
> The infant is talking from the get-go. Short words at first, and within days he's speaking in full sentences and making sense. I think about making a list of his words for a baby book, but he keeps ahead of me.

FEELINGS:
Surprised, proud, amazed at his vocabulary.

REFLECTIONS:
1. This dream resonates to a story from the New Testament, when Jesus tells a man who has suffered for 38 years with an infirmity, "Take up your pallet and walk." I myself can't do this physically–walk in frigid weather and snowdrifts–but I can be more faithful to my indoor exercises and increase the number of repetitions.
2. Why would I consciously do away with anything that promises safety? I ask for guidance: Is this dream mostly reassurance that I don't need the underpinnings of my parents' religious beliefs or other safeguards that caged me in? <u>Yes.</u>
3. I've been dealing with my adult Male aspect, positive and negative, for some years, so why the infant now? Is this a hint of a newborn spirituality? <u>Yes.</u>
4. Do I need to incorporate an additional spiritual exercise this year? <u>Yes</u>, incorporate joy in whatever you write.

– Five –

The Dreamer as Artist

Every person is a dreamer and every dreamer is an artist. Too simplistic? *These are facts.* Yet a friend asks, "Well then, how account for one dreamer elaborating on adventures, a second recounting fine details, and a third speaking blandly of plain-old-vanilla dreams?" The differences lie in each person's attention to dreams in general and responsiveness to their own dreams in particular.

The Artistry of Dreams

The Unconscious is a supreme artist and combines images in ingenious ways, ranging from bizarre clips to soap operas to documentaries, and can dish out comic relief as well. The Unconscious has a wonderful cross-referencing system and can call up images, lived experiences, and vicarious experiences, not only by major categories–subject, place, time, situation, actor, and action–but also by coincidences, flashes of color or sound, and tone of voice.

Above my desk is a statement about artistic passion: It's How You Craft a Flawless Definition of Yourself From Everything You Touch. All right, my expression of artistry is making poems from dreams. Very likely your expression of artistry is something quite different. Your vocabulary, motifs, and themes are unique, your experiences having provided abundant materials for dream work and dream play.

Space does not allow me to convey the meanings of the colors in my dream palette, but I will allude to the *textures* of colors. When flowing colors are noticeable, as in garments or fabrics, they are a cue that I am engaged on an emotional level. Highly polished silver and steel are cues that I am engaged on the intellectual level. Whenever I deal directly with light–colored or white–I am aware that this is the spiritual level. For me gold, especially molten gold, relates to the Divine. Gold is expressive, too, of the Life Force throughout my entire body and aura, as in a dream titled "Experiencing Gold." In it "gold makes its way into and through grooves, rather like the leading of a stained-glass window, the gold lines outshining the translucent areas. All very slow, graceful, seemingly purposeful, quiet, and lovely" (Jun 4, 1982). Soon after that dream, during magnetic resonance imaging (MRI) with radioactive dyes coursing through my veins and spinal fluid, I was able to re-imagine that experience of gold. And later, during a prolonged period of recovery, I directed healing energy along the same pathways.

The Artist's Milieu

The artists I have known generally lived in a meager space in order to rent a studio with adequate space and good light. Some of my dreams show concern about the *apart*ness of an artist, creating tension with words such as *apartment, departing,* and *compartment.* Feelings vary from freedom to lonesomeness, as if there is a place for everything but everything is not in its place.

Dec 12, 1977
Displaying Art in a Department Store

> In a large department store, crowds are ushered into an upper hall where there are displays and where orders will be taken at long tables. Some displays hold works of art–statues, blown glass, freeform ornaments 18" to 24" across. They have no purpose other than to feature color and shape.
>
> People sit docilely at tables, like kids in a lunchroom when silence has been commanded. The floor walker (or sales manager or whoever), very haughty, talks to women at the first two tables.
>
> After looking at the scandalously high prices, I walk out, hitching up my sagging knee socks as I go.

REFLECTION:
If only I were a painter, this dream would be valuable for its brilliant images.

Two years later I found myself in more gracious settings. In a cathedral of my dreams, "my surroundings could be used as a course in art history" (Jun 3, 1979). Also, "in a well-lighted chapel that I didn't know existed, some statues look like caricatures of old Romans, some very fleshy, and all look as if in conversation with the others ... maybe about me!" (Jun 6, 1979).

Mar 1, 1980
Art and Architecture

> An image of apartments in two dreams. I don't know if this refers to artists apart in solitude or to artists in the schools, but it has something to do with my career. In the first, my Creative Child is given an opportunity to become an architect. In the second, plans are carried through and apartments are built. But the works are threatened by vandals, and a sensationalist newspaper publicizes the damage.

REFLECTIONS:
1. I appreciate that my Creative Child takes an opportunity and carries through on her plans.
2. These dreams resonate with statements made at a symposium on art and science that I was reading last night. George Segal, a sculptor, declared, "An artist has to put his whole life into art; the immoral behavior is in being taken away from that discipline." And Alex Katz, a painter, insisted, "You put all your energy into your art and anything else becomes immoral behavior."

The title of the next dream showed my devotion to art:

Jan 17, 1983
Artistry Above and Beyond Assignments

> This concerns a son of mine, maybe Chas, maybe Stephen, who refuses to do assigned homework. He makes glorious paintings on canvas, on cardboard, on toilet paper, and pages of a coloring book. But he will not write his spelling words three times. So I ask him to write the names of objects in his paintings three times. He does—in script, then printing, then calligraphy, all with brush strokes.

> Somehow I feel responsible that he complete his assignments [unlike me to prevail on the children this way]. I stand near him, mentally willing him to perform, but finally sit on a bench near him and watch. The conflict seems to be in me. He's not being obstinate, just engrossed and self-directed.

FEELINGS:
Frustrated, concerned, incomplete; admiring, adaptable, conflicted.

REFLECTIONS:
1. I can't force creativity and, no matter how strong my discipline, I can't impose logical thinking on glorious creations.
2. The artist will be an artist, no matter how meager the opportunities or tools available.
3. I am a poet, come what may. I am an artist.

The next year a black-and-white dream placed me in a final exam situation. "The monitor asks, 'What degree did you hope to earn?' as if I'd flunked even before taking the final. Everyone knows the degree I've been pursuing. [In waking life it's jobs I'm pursuing.] Yet I hesitate . . . a long pause before answering, Art . . . Art Education" (Aug 17, 1984).

Six months later, when the bulk of my work was in editing, I had a compensation dream:

Feb 2, 1985
Delight in Artistry

> I waken with a start, hearing, "The world will delight in your life and performance." I know this refers to Charlie Chaplin. Yet I think, It applies to all artists–including the choreographer Carol Anderson and myself. It applies to all loving humans, this emphasis on life and performance, not on products and achievements.

FEELINGS:
Startled, thoughtful.

REFLECTIONS:
1. In Chaplin's "Limelight," he tells a ballerina he's saved from suicide, "Life is desire–the desire of a rose to unfold itself as

a rose, the desire of a stone to be utterly stone." Of course he was lecturing her about the desire of an artist—to fulfill the artist within.
2. I do not abandon that desire when I am editing.

A month later came a dream that I marked at the time in capital letters: Very Important.

Mar 23, 1985
Laying One Light Strand over Another

> I'm matching small segments of written or spoken words, in the method that I've used for paste-up of the anthology. These words appear to me as strips or strands of light. I lay one strand of light on top of another strand of light, to get perfect alignment of the first line, and all the following lines fall into place.
>
> There are two dominant colors: light blue that's almost white and light yellow that's almost white.
>
> [In this process] My hands are out in front of me—in the air, in the middle of the group, in the middle of the room—and the light strands appear there for everyone to see.

FEELINGS:
Illuminated, effortless, magical.

REFLECTIONS:
1. These "almost white" colors in dreams, I associate with illumination. In this particular dream, I associate them with manuscripts.
2. The words, via light strands, that are written by my hands, again relate to manuscripts.
3. The underlay and overlay suggest several of my works:
   - poems already written + revisions
   - mss. already in the works + new approaches to them
   - *Opening Night,* + the marketing of it
   - Poets-in-the-Schools experiences + poetry therapy
   - dream notes + poems derived from them.

I conclude these dreams about the artist's milieu with one that showed practical challenges to the artist in me:

Oct 26, 1996
Working at a Disadvantage

> I'm in a swanky hotel, at a banquet. There are many speeches, some awards, lots of politicking. Now most people have left and I clear a place—pull back a tablecloth—and work on a wood surface. I paint about a dozen pictures. When I spread them to dry, I'm pleased even though I see some of the same motifs and similar colors in a few of them.
>
> I want to give them titles and include a hallmark or logo with my signature. But I'm stuck! There are so many distractions now—the power plays about grants and other ways of funding. So like the Ohio Arts Council affairs—some people yakking and maneuvering to great advantage, others self-congratulatory, simply expecting to be winners.
>
> Here I am, blissfully productive—prolific!—yet at a loss for words, even words for the titles of my work.

FEELINGS:
Disadvantaged; distracted, frustrated; integrating, dedicated; prolific, pleased; blissful.

REFLECTIONS:
1. I was thinking about Abiqui, New Mexico where Georgia O'Keeffe lived and worked for so many years. DR [my massage therapist] knows a woman who has property near O'Keeffe's Ghost Ranch, which I will check out on my next trip.
2. Last night I spent almost three hours gluing the final collage of my "Fire And Ice" series. Unhappy with the result, I covered it with kraft paper, telling myself, "Maybe tomorrow . . . " Yet how many poems have I put to bed in the same way and been glad for them the next day.

Four Motifs Related to Artistry

Because my focus has been on dream *themes* rather than on *motifs*, I probably threw away many other examples of art in my dreams. Here I include four motifs, each of which led to an understanding of the theme Making Art.

Art Glass

The first instance of art glass in a dream was in the 1970s. That image, too, referred to my writing. Here are the final lines of a poem transposed from that dream:

> Do you hear my thought-wings beating?
> Now folding inward like origami birds,
> now outward like geometric petals
> –centers and borders greeting–
> they expand into a great rose window.
> Does it touch . . . the stained-glass glow?

Another instance of that glow occurred in a dream with three perspectives. An explanation is warranted here: During workshops I often ask writers to *get into* a landscape or a situation in one of the dozens of pictures I have provided and to proceed from there. That is what occurred in the following dream.

Jan 1, 1989
Getting into or through Windows

> The first window has dots like the "snow" in crystal balls at Christmas time. There's not much for me to see in my surroundings, yet a sense of beauty and awe.
> The second window has checks of various widths, strands, and weaves. I feel barred or hemmed in (by social customs?) and wish for stripes and plaids.
> The third window is stained-glass. This is multi-dimensional, and its blues and greens suggest open vistas. I sense a questing, though at this time no decisions have to be made.

REFLECTIONS:
1. I'd love to have a crystal-ball window that reveals important clues for living!
2. Stained-glass windows offer congregants an invitation to meditate on Scriptural stories, and in my dreams they signal revelations of the Holy Spirit.

3. I'm reminded of Chagall's glorious windows that almost shout *Hosanna!* Through them Divine Light shines.

Aug 21, 1983
Shimmering Projects

> I find in the bottom drawer of my desk some outlines for stained-glass projects, also a few finished pieces made of cellophane papers. Lots of angels–mostly a shimmering blue with silver or gold highlights. Not sparkling, not something in the cellophane, but a quality of shimmering.

FEELINGS:
Too many tidbits. Yet there's a new dimension of feeling when light shines through!

REFLECTIONS:
1. If angels here = inspirations, the dream hints at the numerous projects in my desk drawers, which just lie there shimmering in the dark.
2. If angels = messengers from the Divine, they needn't be honored solely during the Christmas season.

A special art glass is cranberry glass, rarely made since the early 1900s because gold is required to produce the unique color. In my dreams gold related to the spiritual level, so I was eager to learn what cranberry glass might portend in my waking life. My first written entry on the subject included the question, "What do I hold up in the light and admire?" (Jun 30, 1986). At that time it was artistry generally, though there was a hint about spiritual development: "It also resonates to healing meditations." One year later there was an additional resonance–the ringing tone of the glass–that was related to life changes I was making and the stretching of boundaries:

Jul 13, 1987
An Extraordinary Piece of Cranberry Glass

> There are several pieces of cranberry glass, but none the shape and size I want. Now there's an extraordinary piece that changes shape and, in the stretching, the glass becomes very fine, delicate. There's a new tone each time

> this occurs, depending on the thickness of the glass. I'm
> more interested now in the tone than in the size or shape.

FEELINGS:
I'm not questioning or wondering, as in most dreams of the past several months. Nor am I awestruck, yet pleased, intrigued, drawn.

QUESTIONS:
Where and when will cranberry glass materialize in my waking life? If it is only a metaphor, how will its meaning manifest in my days?

I managed to locate one cranberry glass pitcher at an antique store during a Poets-in-the-Schools residency, and then another pitcher at another site, without knowing its significance. Dreams with that motif continued.

Nov 27, 1988
More Cranberry Glass

> I find many small pieces of cranberry glass on top
> shelves of cabinets in antique shops. There's always a
> problem, though—wrong size or shape or weight, not
> tagged for sale, or chipped, or pressed glass, not blown.
> I fear I might knock over or pull down several pieces
> while reaching for the one pitcher that I want.

FEELINGS:
Glad for the abundance; hopeful that I'll find what I want; concerned that I might become acquisitive and greedy; pleased seeing the glass with light passing through it.

REFLECTIONS:
1. The cranberry glass may be a self-image in the sense that I don't generate the Light but that Light does emanate, stream, and occasionally sparkle when passing through me.
2. Another idea that's been suggested to me (more than once) is that I don't have to *do*, only *be*. I don't have to learn hands-on techniques for healing, and I don't even have to focus the Light (cranberry glass does not), only *be*. Sparkle when the Light shines and simply *be* when it does not.

There were numerous dream scenarios in which I found cranberry pitchers and a few in which I purchased them. It was the artist Sandra Shuman who revealed, in *Source Imagery*, that pitchers are similar to chalices and signify a tool or an ability to dip into one's Unconscious. If so, I have an abundance of tools and abilities, in a whole spectrum of color vibrations. And I don't need to put them on display, just appreciate that they will be part of my children's inheritance.

Dreams with that motif continued regularly for five years and occasionally after that.

Mandalas

One of the ways that I responded to dreams was by making a mandala when images showed four-foldedness. (By that I mean four persons or elements well-balanced in a dream.) It is possible that the first mandala I recognized in dreams was in 1986. I had prayed for "images that will help me enjoy my birthday and become genuinely optimistic about my future." Forthcoming was "an image of near-wholeness that I see through opened windows, not through glass. It's a mandala, with a circle in the center and four equal 'arms' touching it at right angles, suggesting intersections. There's a singular star, very bright, to the east of it" (Jul 19, 1986).

Another mandala also appeared in the 1980s. That dream began with my taking a ring and a loose diamond to a jeweler to have a four-petaled brooch made, with the diamond in the center and four rubies balanced around it. The four-foldedness became clear as the dream developed, showing me as: (1) a cleaning lady, (2) the wife of an elected official, (3) a teenage girl, and (4) a personal maid. A question remained for all these self-images: "Why is loving so easy in dream situations and so difficult in everyday life?"

A few years later, four-foldedness was illustrated by white flowers appearing at regular intervals. Though I did not know their significance then, I am sure from my present vantage, decades later, that they represented four eras of my life: gardenias, my wedding flowers; daisies, the "loves-me-loves-me-not" feelings in marriage;

crocus, my revival following serious illness; and fragrant mock-orange, my Self as a late bloomer.

The next mandala was geometric. "It's a diagram and more–a dynamic at work. This is a rose-window that's continually expanding and contracting, unfolding and infolding, with a quality of intensity in the center and ease on the periphery" (Jan 3, 1992).

I advanced from observing four-foldedness to participating in its design. "I'm supervising the creation of an intricate, formal garden beyond french doors. The garden has hedges in geometric patterns, also herbs in contained areas, and there's to be a bush with gorgeous white flowers at the center of all this" (Nov 13, 1992).

A more personal mandala, with accompanying sketch, showed me "lying in bed with four emblems surrounding me" (Aug 21, 1995). As in the Native American medicine wheel, my head was oriented North and the sides of the bed honored the four directions. To East was a stuffed polar bear associated with true love; South, a clown associated with Reiki demonstrations; West, a pillow sometimes employed when I do distance healing; North, a doll representing my Child Self. Between the directional images were books, jewelry, and clothing.

Wood-Working

I was pleased to learn, when making a concordance of my dream images, that

wood-working = word-working = writing,

which is how my acknowledged artist expresses herself. Wood, whether rough-hewn or finished, from window frames to parquet floors, from reliefs to retablos to carved statues, is a cue in my dreams to a conscious aspect of writing. A couple of the earliest references to wood-working (*i.e.*, my writing) were "as opposed to abstraction" (March 1975) and "as opposed to concrete" (May 1975). A clue regarding the conflict between the abstract and the concrete was my submitting poems in competition at the university and manuscripts elsewhere, as well as my judging some state contests. Evidence of the conflict between abstract and concrete appeared on my dream tablet on New Year's morning 1976 in the following lines, to which I added only the final line to round it out:

> All evening I have puzzled over
> 500 pieces of a painting by Dali.
> After the midnight ballyhoo
> I will burrow under cover
> until a welcome thawing when
> correspondence can come through—
> scribbles, post-its, poetry
> of eagerly awaited vigor.

A year later, the relation between wood-working and word-working was explicit. "A little girl wants to go to the Wordsmiths who are working on a slanted gray roof of a house. I tell her to go talk with Smith if she wants. She does, and there's a romantic spark in her. But he is sent on an assignment—about matching wood for the gables of another house. The girl is forlorn. She writes him a note and tells me, "He knows words, and he will know what I mean" (May 16, 1977).

In another dream about wood-working, the focus was on the workshop itself and a courtyard surrounding it:

Aug 30, 1980
Restoration Projects

> In a mansion I'm visiting, a huge room is a workshop where the owner restores wood carvings, cabinets, and altars.
> The mansion is spread out in several low wings, like a motel except the rooms are connected.
> Now I'm physically unable to walk forward, yet able to push myself backward around the grounds and to propel myself fairly accurately without seeing behind me.

REFLECTIONS:
1. The restoring of wood carvings, cabinets, and altars resonates with the anthology I've been working on, *I Name Myself Daughter and It Is Good: Poems of the Spirit by Feminists*.

2. It also resonates with my ardent wish to restore a relationship with a loving God.
3. The "spreading out in low wings" resonates with my poem, "You Have Set My Feet in a Spacious Place."
4. Propelling myself backward to go forward refers to my desire to have the *Take Fire* book published this year. Those poems deal with the past three decades, and now I desire to go forward.

In this new century, a dream relating to wood-working, and thus to my writing, was congratulatory:

Aug 24, 2016
Three Images of Wood

> [First] Brush trimmings shredded for mulch. I commend someone for this recycling.
>
> [Second] A mural in royal blue and white swirls, in a large room. Brush strokes are from right to left, making overlapping waves. Yet there's a suggestion of a woman, of three women, in a position like the final swoop of a romantic dance.
>
> [Third] A wood sculpture hung vertically, off-center to the right, on a long wall of a "great room." Heartwarming. The wood has no knots in it but many swirls, likely heart-wood. It has a smooth finish and high gloss, with a glow like honey. I can imagine this as a totem because some of the swirls suggest faces.

REFLECTIONS:
1. What I'm recycling are dream notes for *Dream Encounters,* and this is commendable. Even if I'm brushing through themes in a backward way, the result is like a flowing dance. This memoir brushes past an infinite number of details to achieve that flow.
2. The descriptors "heart-warming, heart-wood, smooth finish" represent my life's work from my present perspective.
3. That the final piece (this memoir) has no knots indicates a selective process that does not deny the existence of knots in my life but chooses to highlight other features.
4. That the 3-D sculpture is hung vertically suggests another dimension, one related to Time.

Appreciating the Artist Within

The examples I've given of artistic *motifs* proceed to the *theme* that they engender: Appreciating. I was introduced to making art in a roundabout way. During my internship in Poetry Therapy, one site was a psychiatric wing of a university hospital, where art therapy was a healing modality for adults as well as adolescents. There the art therapist proclaimed, "Whoever comes into my sessions does art." I enjoyed splashing tempera paints on 18" by 24" paper and loved mixing colors on a small metal palette. Because I was given the task of cleaning up after the patients left, I asked if I might play with their unused paint. The therapist said, "Whatever you like," so I often covered five sheets of paper before going to the sink with the remaining drops of paint. Such fun! During that internship, there came the following dream:

circa 1975
The Artist in Me

> I'm painting–in oil!–a picture of an ocean, the beach, and a man embracing a woman. The figures are dressed in sarongs of red with gold flowers. I think there should be purple in the color scheme.
> Now I take a board with pegs or nails and scrape it across the huge palette affair. I'm going to paint waves or else wavy fields in the foreground. I'm torn between doing a Gauguin or a Van Gogh kind of painting.

At that time there was another allusion to painting, of which only one sentence remains, "Time drips from the artist's brush" (1975). A note written the next morning claimed, "That was not a metaphor, but a reference to the multitude of actions in my waking life."

The art therapist's insistence, and my experience in her lab, convinced me that every person has an artist within. Even though I could not draw other than the stick figures of a kindergartner, I appreciated that my inner artist worked actively in dreams.

In a dream a few months later I was "judging the authenticity of paintings hung sideways or upside down" and I chose "Whistler's

Baby" (Feb 2, 1976). Later in that year was a written exclamation, "Aha! Another painter dream!" There was also mention of paintings and other art objects in galleries and on the porches of a circular house, after which I was "subjected to an art quiz on actual objects, including abstract paintings, a carving that highlights the wood itself, and a Madonna" (Oct 29, 1976).

Paintings in my dreams often referred to a particular artist, but sometimes to an era. For example, I had a series of dreams that progressively revealed social and religious customs at the turn of the 20th century. In one of those dreams, "Portraits come to life, though I don't remember any of them making speeches. I am the one giving a speech to an afternoon group of ladies. It's about a magnificent reproduction of a flower. The flower is carved wood, possibly oak, and enormous–easily three feet in diameter. Petal by petal is laid one on the other, yet assembled loosely enough that it looks delicate" (Oct 27, 1976).

Nearly all my dreams are in vivid color. The rare black-and-white dream concerns decision-making and prompts me to ask myself, Is this an absolute? Or am I exaggerating differences? Or is this someone else's Stuff? Even more rare is a dream in sepia; it occurs relative to an etching, a daguerreotype, or other work of art that I've seen but can scarcely remember; hence, to an event in my life that is hazy.

The following dream (Oct 5, 1996), to which I added a few rhyming words, dealt with the colors that, in the Oriental Five Elements paradigm, are ascribed to personal energy fields.

Dreaming Elemental Colors

This time as if light could be thrown
on a potter's wheel,
and this time a ritual–
to each element an invocation.

For Fire/red I intone,
"Passionate love, friendship, loyalty,"
almost as edifying as for Metal/silver,
"Love of the universe, oh great shining one."

I proceed to Earth/yellow, Water/blue
but I've missed a cue . . .
dear goodness, Wood/the greening!
Wood, the welcome to every beginning.

– *Six* –

Challenges from Childhood

In early childhood I developed techniques to release taboo feelings; for example, whirling on the lawn, also retorting to my brother with nonsense syllables. And I liked to whistle when walking the five blocks to a bus stop, even though a neighbor warned me, "Whistling girls and cackling hens come to no good ends." A more approved outlet in childhood and adolescence was daily piano practice, which was seldom intruded upon. But as an adult I felt less resourceful, until I began studying my dreams.

Considering catharsis as "a therapy that encourages or permits the discharge of pent-up, socially unacceptable affects," I knew, within one year of writing dream notes, that a great number of my dreams had that result. At night my dreams portrayed feelings that I could not let myself express aloud. The following morning, my naming the feelings and commenting on elements of the dreams brought reassurance and a sense of self-worth.

Repetitive dreams revealed not only the sources of my discontent but also the release I experienced within or following them. Three themes are included in this section: Cleansing or Purging; Cleaning up Messes; Shouting.

Theme: Cleansing or Purging

Though I have not lauded bodily fluids in my poems, as some contemporary poets do, I certainly have acknowledged them in my dreams. Here is an example from early dream notes:

Jun 5, 1978
I'm Cleaning up Shit

> It's my own. I'm in school and have found a toilet
> stall without trouble, but seemingly have an endless

> amount to get rid of. There are even turds on
> the floor! I pick them up with toilet paper.

REFLECTIONS:
1. This shows that I'm eliminating some unnecessary Stuff from my life, but the dream doesn't specify what.
2. Right now my most obvious challenge is to revise my concept of religion and to entertain new ideas about God.

Less than a year later, as I was questioning my marriage, I lamented that "I've had everlasting dreams when I'm cleaning up shit, hoping no one else will come down with this (whatever this is). Now, hauling trash and garbage, checking garbage pails and washing them out, I'm tired and depressed. No anger or a sense of martyrdom, just compliance and the sense that this is never-ending"(Mar 24, 1979).

A dream with a much later date, indicates I was concerned about how other people might regard my shit [my Stuff] or my attempts to be rid of it:

Jan 12, 1993
Passing Black Shit, Hard as a Brick and That Large

> It hurts. It seems endless. Now I know what evacuating means. Can the toilet flush away all that I'm passing?
> I see draped everywhere [in the bathroom] hand washing, sheets, towels, underwear, more. I'm indignant and carry these things to the utility room. This is a large, heavy load.
> All this time I'm aware that I haven't passed all the shit. There's pressure still and rawness. I need some oil to get rid of the crap and ointment to help heal the area. Every step I take hurts. People must notice that I'm walking in a peculiar way.

REFLECTIONS:
1. The tough shit and bricks = passing a major crisis. When will I ever get a break?
2. Releasing so much black is, according to a friend, "releasing all the old laws I have ever owned".

Enough of this theme! The root word of *catharsis* means *pure* and, by extension, cleansing. This leads to the next theme, which may seem less intense than Purging, yet it continued over years with numerous variants.

Theme: Cleaning Up Messes

Because, as eldest daughter, I had cleaned up many messes in my childhood (soiled diapers, soiled sheets from bed-wetters, a brother's vomit, junk in the basement, attic, and garage), those incidents haunted me in dreams. When I had children of my own, there were similar challenges, but I had a different attitude: I cared.

There were also messes of my own making, especially when I returned to classes and endeavors at the university. This theme was at its peak in 1975 and 1976, with 17 occurrences in each of those years, after which its frequency dropped abruptly to almost nil.

Sep 21, 1975
Forced to Scrub Walls and More

> I'm baby-sitting two horribly naughty children. Their mother throws heaps of clothes on the bathroom floor and forces me to clean walls, toilet, linen closet, windows, everything.
> Now I'm in a kindergarten, where Nora Jean and I have enrolled our last children. She looks immaculate, of course.
> Mending old stuff, especially patching old things, is non-productive and frustrating. No one is satisfied, much less appreciative, so I should go out and start everything fresh. I join several groups for Civic Betterment, but can't attend meetings because I'm still too busy cleaning up at home.

During my last two years at the university, when I did poetry readings fairly regularly, I did not appreciate other poets' expounding on blood and guts, piss and shit, and some reviewers calling it "strong poetry." My dream notes were calling such images "same old, same old," as in the following:

Nov 25, 1975

> A small child messes up plans and house. He drinks Windex from the bottle, then vomits. Black dirt accumulates—as black

as printers' ink on upholstery and curtains. Monica promises to
clean one room, but every time I look, she's studying for finals.

Feb 28, 1976

A child finally gets a clean outfit, then wets himself and his
high-top shoes. The puddle runs over the floor and under
a dresser. "About wet towels left on the hardwood floor,
I spell out the meaning for my children: Total ruination
and a black mark for the occupants of this house".

Aug 1, 1976

"I've given him the best years of my life!" I cry [about my
brother], even though it sounds melodramatic. He putters
around after I have him ready for school, messes his clothes
while tinkering, loses track of time if he has any sense of
it at all, doesn't give a rap for anything I'm trying to do.

Yet occasionally there were signs of greater awareness and/or progress, such as these:

Mar 5, 1976

A son cleans up the bathroom! Uses a light blue bath towel,
and I don't even stop him—that's how desperate I am for help.

Dec 27, 1977

I'm rearranging, ordering, composing the house the way
I would a poem or an essay. I paint some furniture in
aqua and turquoise, and some cupboards in royal blue.

Jul 6, 1985

I'm wondering if the old china cabinet can be
restored. Its wobbly legs are a threat to its contents.
My solution is to cut off the legs and have a
balanced cabinet for daughters to play house.

Four years later, dream notes indicated a turnaround concerning my cleaning up messes:

Aug 22, 1989
In a Large Airplane, I'm Scrubbing Carpet

> I'm scrubbing one area that's had traffic or spills. Now the other areas look dingy. Only one other passenger, a woman, is scrubbing. We paid our way, too, so why are we doing this menial work? Because we have low, low self-esteem.
>
> Now I'm scrubbing a large wing-chair. It looks like printed vinyl to begin with, but may actually be light brown or gold-tone leather under all the dirt. The results are so noticeable to everyone, that I don't even consider again about my being a paying passenger.
>
> When I get back to my seat, I do wonder what kind of maintenance there is on a plane's interior.

FEELINGS:
Humiliation when first scrubbing; satisfaction later; ease when I get to my seat.

REFLECTIONS:
1. I thought I had dismissed the scrub-woman image; this weekend, after most of the family had left on a trip, I didn't even dust furniture.
2. This dream indicates that my ingrained habits and values—cleanliness high on my list—can prevent me from enjoying loftier beauty. And my automatically being of service to others can deny me pleasure, delight, comfort, and restfulness.
3. This dream implies that I can travel comfortably on the physical plane while carried by an unseen Pilot on the spiritual plane.

Even after I had practiced Reiki daily for over a year, and had achieved relative calmness, I had a crowd dream that focused on messes:

Feb 6, 1992
Unending Projects

> I've just told Mary Lou that I have probably 30 projects underway, certainly 15 projects that I've never carried through.
>
> At a lakeshore campsite, classes of young children on vacation mess up property, even pull apart a dock.

> Babies get into hazards because the area isn't baby-proofed. I've been delegated to cook meals, in two shifts. But there's not enough food for children and adults. Sopping wet clothes lie on counters and on floors.
>
> There's no privacy, even when I'm dressing. People from my past arrive, one at a time. I recognize some by their voices, but can't guess why they're here.

FEELINGS:
Pleasure in seeing Mary Lou after so many years; from annoyance to resentment to anger at the destructiveness of children; curiosity about unannounced guests.

REFLECTION:
It's odd that I don't tell Mary Lou about Reiki. She's a nurse, after all, and she belongs to a group of Catholics who "speak in tongues." Yet I sense that she's ultra-conservative and would be skeptical about hands-on healing.

In a dream seven months later, I am assertive, insisting that one child after another clean up one mess after another. "I'm willing to help for a while, but not to be a rescuer or a Cinderella. I try to clean up an old typewriter—an inky job and a thankless one that the children could not appreciate. But I want words to come out clear" (Sep 15, 1992). This dream in its entirety has "many examples of powder spilled in heaps and trails. Talcum powder resonates to the heat rash I'm treating on thighs and underarms. Tooth powder relates to disciplines in early childhood. Cornstarch recalls the treating of childhood diseases. Scouring powder applies to messes generally."

The next variant of Cleaning Up Messes was 12 years later. I include it because of the intensity of feelings.

Apr 26, 2005
No Lids on Bubbling Pots

> I'm fixing dinner for the family, who have been away on a trip. Ed comes in and goes to the basement [his office]. The children file through, all of them their present adult age.

I move to a very large kettle and use a large spoon to stir. Oh, there are clothes in the kettle! I ladle out jerseys and blouses of Monica's or Maggie's, and I'm even more troubled seeing that there are jewelry pins on them in the bubbling water. There's a small gold filigree pin of mine [to save] during this rescue process.

Now I'm stirring something in my largest skillet, the grease splattering. I've already looked in cupboard, storage room, and refrigerator for the lid. I'm almost sobbing to Angelyn about not having a lid to put on. She says, "I have the same problem, I can't find my lid anywhere."

FEELINGS:
Fearful; astonished about the clothes and jewelry, and near despair about their condition; baffled that something valuable of mine is also in this mess. I wakened crying.

REFLECTIONS:
1. Most obvious is my trying to put a lid on feelings.
2. I'm doing fine until there's all the interference–other people dumping things and leaving them for me to extricate.
3. Angelyn was to see her dad [who is dying] last evening and today; she will drive back to North Carolina tomorrow.
4. Cathy has reminded me that a lid is for closure and that, in our family gatherings, each of us is striving for closure.
5. Whatever I'm stirring up in appointments with the therapist, I'm afraid of a splattering effect.
6. Looking for a lid, even in therapy, isn't all a defensive action; the lid may preserve what's worth savoring.

The most recent dreams show conscious organizing that precludes cleaning up messes. There is also gratification in doing my work. Their titles are sufficient: "Cleaning out a House in Advance of a New Tenant" (May 27, 2016), "Organizing My Milieu" (Nov 1, 2016), and "Helping a Woman at a Retreat Center Clean up Her Past" (Nov 20, 2016).

Theme: Shouting

When I was very little, I pledged that I would not grow up to be a shouter. As a teenager I broke my rule only at football games. As an adult I made efforts to have a well-modulated voice. But I may have carried my pledge not to shout to an extreme. For example, once when I was angry at a teenage daughter, I lowered my voice an octave and said very slowly, "Your Name Is Mud." Forty years later, Magdalene told me, "I never forgot that day."

Stephen remembers an incident when I did shout. It occurred in public, after our repeated trips to the Bureau Of Motor Vehicles for his beginner's license. When a clerk demanded yet more paperwork, I, standing nearby, blasted, "Not again!" (That caused a ripple around the room.)

And there was one occasion that my family has not heard about. As a substitute teacher for two weeks in a classroom of unruly seventh graders, I was tested beyond my limits. One day I left the students, closed the door behind me, stood in the hallway, and let out a *Yeow!* that caused other teachers to look out their doors. Then I re-entered the classroom without a comment. Surprisingly, I was not reprimanded by the principal.

I recall a happier day in my own kitchen, a day of revelation when, instead of exclaiming like Charlie Brown, "Augh! I can't stand this!" I said, very simply, "I will not have this."

Yet, circa 1975, I had many dreams from which I wakened crying for help. My voice was so loud that I was embarrassed; other tenants in the apartment could surely have heard my cries.

When I began shouting in dreams, instead of crying for help, that showed increasing assertiveness on my part. In the 14 dreams that featured my father—all of them 8 to 15 years after his death—I shout at him only once. The title, "I Oust Daddy as an Authority Figure," carries the meaning, though not the intensity of emotion: "I'm in a king-size bed with a young man embracing me. We're all tangled up in the sheets and coverlet when Daddy comes in the bedroom. He criticizes me about the lover I've chosen, and accuses me of being unfaithful. I say loudly and firmly, 'I've been thinking about this a long time and I've decided I'll make my own decisions!' I sink back into the bed, luxuriously" (Jan 10, 1979).

In my dream notes, my mother was featured in 50 dreams in the six years prior to her death; in the eight years following her death, she was featured in 23 dreams. In the earliest example of my attempting to shout at my mother, "the dream setting is a Thanksgiving get-together. Too many foods, too huge portions, too much noise, too many manipulations by Mother. At one point I'm going to scream at her, but Daddy sees my face and advises, 'Say a prayer to St. Teresa.' I say, 'Ha to Saint T! I do not like Saint T! I do not like Mary, I do not like praying! Leave me alone!' " (May 23, 1976).

In a similar setting a year later, "Mother accuses me of never finishing anything and says, 'You won't amount to anything in life.' I'm so angry, I snap back, 'The only time the attic ever gets cleaned is when I do it. The only time the basement ever looks decent is when I've cleaned it. This house would fall down around your ears if I weren't here to keep it in shape.' She pulls that *Mah-gah-ret!* affronted attitude, but doesn't intimidate me" (Mar 14, 1977).

Later that year, the scene was less realistic, more metaphorical:

Dec 24, 1977
Someone Is Dragging Me Down

> I'm hurrying to class at the U of M. I need to propel/ pull myself by using the cracks in the sidewalk for a frog-like maneuver that I sometimes resort to when I can't slog along. (Whatever happened to flying?)
> Someone–Mother probably–is dragging me down, and I have to shrug her off my shoulders, even though she protests.

REFLECTION:
Mother has been here only one day, and I'm letting her get to me. She's already said, "Don't talk to me as if I were one of your children!" She gives me quizzical looks, and she's probably registering me now on her black list as one of those "sharp-tongued people." Sharp because they can actually cut through *her* barrage of words? I'm not trying to cut at all, just trying to be myself.

With the passing of years, there were fewer actual visits with Mother (our going from Ohio to Michigan or, rarely, her coming from Michigan to Ohio). Yet each year as Mother's rheumatoid arthritis advanced, both Maureen and I made conscious efforts to understand her and her upbringing.

In a dream three months after Mother's death, I noted, "Good feelings! I hear Mother speaking in a young, lilting voice. It's as if she's reviewing her life and finding things to be happy about. She even understands that some actions of Daddy's that she'd called unforgivable were the best that he, or anyone, could do at the time. There's relief–to her and to me" (Mar 8, 1984).

– Seven –

Coping Strategies

Upon rising some mornings, I enjoy a sense of total well-being–not euphoria exactly, and not hoopla, yet a centeredness that speaks well of self. I credit some dreams with accomplishing this integration of body-mind-spirit, particularly those with the theme of Swimming and Diving, also the theme of Singing. Typical of these themes is an introductory scene that illustrates a problem, followed by scenes that develop strategies for dealing with the problem.

Theme: Swimming and Diving

Two of the earliest entries for this theme focused on competition, with these implications: "A husband and wife can't both be winners, even in separate events" (Apr 18, 1975) and "such competition preferably turns into love play" (Jun 15, 1975).

When diving into a basement pool (my Unconscious) and then into a sub-basement pool (possibly the Collective Unconscious), I faced other hazards, as indicated here: "I'm going to swim in a women's gym, like Pomerene Hall. I'm elated at the prospect and dive into the water while a woman and two men are still asking questions and having reservations. Now I'm in the deep basement of 1908. It's full of dangers: piled furniture, a rocker sticking out, the central furnace, the possibility of electric wires and nails. But I swim happily anyway" (Feb 18, 1976).

A few months later, while still comparing myself to others, I had to accept that "I'm an amateur in swimming, surrounded by Olympic caliber women" (Apr 13, 1976). When the pool was drained, "This indicates that my energy is low and that I need rest" (May 14, 1976). There was usually a quick recovery, and I gradually developed strength and stamina, as in the following:

Sep 18, 1976
Successful Diving

> I'm diving, first in a small area, now in a huge pool marked into squares, with many different depths of water. I dive 1st from a side of the pool, almost a straight falling-down, 2nd thrusting myself down, 3rd using a springboard. I touch bottom with the palms of my hands and push myself up again, though this phase is too slow for comfort, and I'm worried if I can hold my breath. There are cheers from spectators.

FEELINGS:
Successful, trusting, daring, worried, reassured.

REFLECTIONS:
1. The buoyed-up feeling is a rich one, something like flying.
2. Diving relates to experimental plunges of all kinds. Presently I'm interviewing for jobs in clinics and in school systems.

There were signs of progress in my dreams; for example, "swimming in an Olympic-size pool, many laps, and I don't get winded. There's a wonderful rhythm to my breathing and all my movements. Non-competitive and good" (Feb 15, 1977).

There were also setbacks: "I'm in a city pool like Hunter, with walks around and high ceilings. It gets over-crowded, first with great gray rafts and other floating devices that I remove, next with too many people going in all directions, as if at a beach. I tell them, 'This is my pool,' and a threat is implicit, 'I can send you away' " (Sep 20, 1978).

Images developed into metaphors at an emotional time when I had asked my husband to participate in marriage counseling, and he was unwilling. "I'm testing the water. It isn't right yet, maybe too early, but I try it. The sense is darkness, yet not scary and not cold. Muddy water. Murkiness. I get on the dock to rest, and now see a large turtle emerging from underneath or out of the reeds. It's a snapping turtle–does a snapping turtle bite? I take my chances and dive from the other side of the dock" (Mar 14, 1979).

During another crisis, one of a physical nature, "a physical therapist gives me a bright fuchsia swimsuit that fits comfortably. I go down some walkways, like the boardwalks in the Everglades. I can't find the therapy pools, but am determined to swim, go down a gangplank, and dive in. The water is slick, entangled, with slimy vegetation (water lilies?) going down very deep. I can't keep my eyes open or mouth open, and my arms flail about. Now there's something grabbing my wrist. Is it an alligator? Now something is grabbing my shoulder" (Aug 31, 1979).

My dreams so clearly illustrated a need for swimming regularly that I was compelled to purchase a pool membership (which I maintained for 40 years). Within a few months, there was a new development regarding swimming and diving, the inclusion of several aspects of Self: adult, child, mother, lifeguard. "I've found my swimsuit and get myself together. I'm going to dive into a very deep pool of clear water, no green or blue tiles giving illusions. I think, This isn't a dream, I've been here before, it's a continuum, even if I don't know where I'm going! High above me a little girl (three or four years old) stands on a balcony railing, ready to jump into the water. There's a woman below (mother? lifeguard?) with outstretched arms shaping a basket to catch her or bounce her, somehow to reassure her. Time stands still. I'm not scared, neither is the child or the woman, yet it's a moment of breath-taking" (Jan 26, 1980).

The next development involved self-assurance: "I design a pool of my own. Surprisingly, I know the right dimensions and proportions, though I only begin to realize, This is going to take a lot of water! Someone buys the idea and blueprints from me. Construction is underway quickly. I see the billboard I've painted–with a bolder message now and with wide, colorful, vertical stripes between the letters: ROLL AROUND PLEASURE CENTER. The idea is to use it as a skating pond when it isn't a swimming pool, so there'll be year-around pleasure" (May 30, 1981).

Though I remained faithful to swimming for therapy, I faced other challenges, too; for example, respiratory infections that prohibited swimming and left me feeling deprived. Occasionally a dream of wish fulfillment helped me through such a difficult time. Here is an example:

Oct 1, 1984
Energy Pickup and Letdown

> I'm swimming in a large indoor pool that has foliage all around and diffused lighting–like the Sheraton Spa except much larger. I'm mostly floating on my belly, and my straps are down, breasts partly exposed. Now I pick up some energy and begin doing laps, feeling good that I can do this, I can!
> Even underwater I hear a clear, rich music–a tenor voice. There's a man on a chaise in the middle of the water. He reminds me of a gondolier except he hasn't an oar in his hand but a small guitar, almost a mandolin. He's singing Italian, arias I think, surely love songs. Talk about liquid sound! The pool resonates, not an actual echo but a tremolo effect.
> I swim by him a few times and now notice the pool is draining, one lane at a time. Lifeguards are unrolling plastic to cover the remaining lanes. This is so ducks and geese won't come in.
> Marshy plants begin to grow, the way they are in an open pond nearby. I consider swimming in that pond, even if it is muddy. On my way there, I hear some glorious birdsong. It's coming from a little red bird, a scarlet tanager?

FEELINGS:
Warm, delighted, awed; disappointed; adaptable.

REFLECTION:
This dream is like a reprieve–my shoulders are easing while I'm reviewing it. There is a sense of hope, even though I foolishly didn't take the antibiotic at 5 a.m.

The next variant suggested an intra-uterine relationship with my Positive Male aspect:

Jan 5, 1986
Infant Swimmer at My Left Side

> In a large lake with no unusual landmarks as guides, I'm swimming in the dark, in warm water. There's an infant at my left, maybe eight months old, gliding and swimming effortlessly, smoothly as a duck. The

> child (a boy I surmise) doesn't speak, just glides along, and I manage to keep abreast of him. Does he know where he's headed? Am I supposed to care for him on dry land? I wonder who's responsible for whom.

FEELINGS:
Comfortable, comforting; slight confusion about roles.

Three months later there was a climactic dream of diving, with both positive and negative valences:

Mar 17, 1986
Diving into an Enormous, Bright Pool

> The dominant color is sunshine yellow. The pool itself isn't painted to suggest blue water, the water is wonderfully clear. For some reason I have a jug of Clorox with me and I set it at the side of the pool. Also I'm wearing reading glasses and set them by the jug.
>
> Many people are splashing around, like at a beach. In a dozen or more lanes, people are swimming laps. Yet there's always room for me, even if I must fly over the center of the pool to dive in. There's so much fluctuation of water and people that each dive is a challenge. A wonderful thing is, I break the water cleanly and don't upset any swimmer with a big splash or commotion. I swim fast and effortlessly, with long, effective strokes.
>
> After a long period of exhilaration, I notice some hazards. There's an orange contraption, something like a crane, in the shallow end, very dangerous. It's for obstacle-course training and requires that swimmers keep eyes open at all times.
>
> The other threat is what finally makes me get out of the pool. A dozen men have formed a square with their bodies, about 12 feet on each side. They are holding back the water so there's an almost bare place in the pool where there are insects—not many, but huge, like bull ants. I have a feeling that the men are gambling on the speed (or strength?) of the insects they have tagged. I hear one lifeguard telling another, "These insects are egg-layers, and we'll have to scrub every inch of the pool."

FEELINGS:

Spaciousness, exhilaration, freedom, grace; dismay, disgust.

REFLECTIONS:
1. The Clorox suggests my need to be free of germs; I fear eye infection as well as the ear infection.
2. As with other construction/demolition images, the orange crane resonates with my ex-husband. In this instance, the crane is an obstacle and dangerous.
3. In other dreams, insects usually encrypt pain, especially the fibromyalgia.

One dream in a foreign setting gave much-needed reassurance:

Jul 15, 1986
Swimming in a Foreign, Exotic Country

> It may be in the USSR, anyhow in a cold country. The hotel I'm staying in is luxurious in a Medieval or Renaissance way. Each story I go up, it's more opulent: velvet draperies, gold-framed pictures, ornate lamps, overall lavishness.
> My room is #609, and I forget the key the first morning, so eager to be out looking at the sights/sites, and locating a place to swim. In a group of people near an observation window, there's a tall man in a rich fur-trimmed coat, who answers my questions. He's not a native, but he's visited here numerous times. He says, "Swim? Don't you know the lakes here are hell frozen over? Even the stream doesn't stream for tourists this time of year."
> He urges me to enjoy some indoor diversions, perhaps films of the area in warmer seasons. This man is garrulous, yet I rather enjoy his talk. Somehow everything he says conveys warmth and good humor. Also there's a feeling of intimacy. He stands very close to me and, because I'm wearing only a dress and not heavy outerwear, I feel snuggled in his great-coat.
> I'm surprised now to see that he has a wife, a young woman very slim and blonde, wearing a spotted-fur coat (leopard?) and a trifle too much makeup for this early in the morning. She says something that suggests that

her husband is not much more than a teddy bear to
her and that I am nothing, not even in the picture.
    Now I go my separate way, still hoping
to enjoy the great outdoors.

FEELINGS:
Awe, eagerness; attracted, intimate; snubbed, invisible; hopeful, optimistic.

REFLECTIONS:
1. The forgotten key may be the *number* 609, which is the same when upside-down and reversed. That is the way I feel in waking life when venturing into unfamiliar territory–upside down and backward.
2. Such a contrast between exterior coldness and interior warmth!
3. My sense of isolation yields to an ability to continue alone on my separate way.

I found no additional variants after this. I learned that, instead of focusing exclusively on the problems encountered when diving into emotional depths, I could use some of the frightening images in a collage, to discover what was positive. After that I was able to transpose those images into the following poem:

Into the Teeming Matrix She Plunges

The water, self-healing, folds together
without a scar.
Down, down the diver hurtles–
past drowned sphinxes and sunken columns,
beyond breathing, beyond reason.
She streaks by stingrays and sharks,
avoids the underside of things–
icebergs, whales, humongous turtles humping.
One sideways glance
and she's caught by tentacles.
She shudders, feels how it is to fear
every new thing as alien–
blanching, then reaching out to crush.

At a great depth she realizes:
Fear does not have me,
I have merged with it and can release.
Now she knows fluidity, and whirls
past battleships and schooners,
past remnants of luxury liners,
beyond robotic arms
that grope for unclaimed treasure,
beyond the murk.
She arrives at the deepest place
unharmed, upright on patterned sand.
Here within the centrifuge
she finds three figures in the round:
an encrusted thinker pondering
a marble goddess musing on
a gold dolphin poised in welcome.
The diver springs to greet them.

Theme: Singing

For most of my life, one outlet for unexpressed feelings was singing. In high school and at the university, I enjoyed singing in glee club and choir. After Monica (my fourth child) was born, I auditioned for Symphony Chorus and reserved every Tuesday evening as "Mom's night to howl."

I was never a soloist but I could sing any soprano, mezzo, or alto part and, when necessary, could fill in for a tenor.

In the first dream I found relative to singing, "I waken myself singing a moving alto part from the Mozart "Te Deum" that we've been rehearsing" (Jan 19, 1976). Two months later there was a longer dream about singing in church, with layers of feeling:

Mar 21, 1976
Not Physically Fit or Nicely Outfitted to Sing

> I'm wanting to sing in choir at St. Francis [church of my childhood], but the platform and risers are crowded, and no one will make a place for me. I have no music,

and no one will share. They know I can sight-read
but not ad-lib, and they may want to shame me.

    They wear nice Sunday clothes, I wear an ugly green
dress. I'm doubly angry because I could be wearing my
black sheath or my black concert gown. I decide to go
to Tim's church, where I may fit and be appreciated.

REFLECTIONS:
1. This hearkens to my having to leave the Music School after my junior year and to finish with a degree in Education. When will I ever get over this?
2. I am grateful to Professor Weatherford in the English Department, who said, when I was accepted into a master's program there, "Do your singing in poetry."

Following the dream of being snubbed, "I am called on to replace a spoiled boy for singing at a concert. My voice soars, ripples, does incredible things, and I'm caught up in sound, soaring with it, surprised at the beauty but never doubting my ability" (Jan 10, 1979). Yet I still felt ostracized by chorus members until one day when "I'm called to tune the altos to A, and I give it on perfect pitch!" (Jul 26, 1979).

    My abilities were tested again in a dream (as they were in a waking-life Poets-in-the-Schools residency), when "women and girls and babies in high-chairs are to sing for a PTO or somesuch evening event. I've rehearsed them, both singing and accompanying them on the piano. At the last moment, the whole setup is moved from one room to another. I go there and [as if for the first time] see and hear the motley group. Most obvious is a chocolate-brown baby girl, about nine months old, in her high-chair, waving her arms like a windmill and crowing in delight" (May 12, 1983).

    The happy response of that baby was matched by adults in a very different place and time:

Jul 14, 1986
From Signing to Singing

> In a natural arena, around a very small lake, there's a
> finale to some activities, perhaps a spiritual retreat. A

> big woman like Meg Tucker sings a couple of lines,
> then motions for everyone to follow her. I'm about 10
> yards behind her and begin singing. She turns to me,
> hearing my voice match hers and then harmonize with
> hers. She smiles broadly—a welcome, a blessing.
>
> Soon the arena is echoing with song. Now this develops
> into a call-and-response. Wonderful, freeing. The message
> is carried throughout the audience and over the little
> lake, all about freedom of expression and innovation.

FEELINGS:
Natural, relaxed, harmonious, responsive.

REFLECTIONS:
1. Meg, the signer for the deaf at Poetry in the Park, actualizes transformation when she changes a poet's words and a poem's meaning back into images for the hearing impaired. In the dream she transforms signing to singing.
2. Meg is a model in another way. She's a large woman and very attractive. She looks comfortable and graceful in her body.

In the following year, registering another peak for me, "Maestro Whallon takes an E from me and has the whole orchestra tune to it!" (Apr 13, 1987). In contrast to that dream, fast-forward to another rehearsal:

Jan 12, 1995
An Embarrassing Moment in Chorus

> Some of the Chorus have already rehearsed, or at least
> sight-read, this piece with Maestro Evan Whallon. The
> notes I have are just that—mostly words scribbled in pencil
> on looseleaf paper. When Evan raises his baton, I sing
> loudly and clearly. It's an easy refrain to begin with.
>
> He stops and looks directly at me. Half the Chorus looks
> in my direction. The person on my right nudges me. Okay, I
> see it now: For Men Only in the opening section. Someone
> starts to explain pedantically, and I say, "I understand,
> I get it, don't take more time away from rehearsal."

FEELINGS:
Confident; embarrassed; businesslike.

REFLECTIONS:
1. On waking I think, My subconscious was playing a trick, wasn't it? I consciously knew the part was For Men Only; I had written notes on the score to remind myself. Yet subconsciously I wanted to know if my voice would even be heard among the voices of many men.
2. That Evan heard me doesn't surprise me; we've always been attuned, in waking life as well as in dreams. In most dreams he functions as a Guide, leading me toward more self-discovery.
3. Great reassurance here: My voice is clear, on key, and heard, not muffled or stifled among men.

The refrain of Singing recurred often and I transposed the images in the following poem:

Sometime Sonata

12 a.m.   Main Theme
I'm __ singing in the rain __
like Gene Kelly at his best,
totally in love with love until
a conscientious cop appears,
questioning my sanity.

1:30 a.m.   Inversion
Roses are red as my heart
that reveals itself in counterpart—
ruby opposed to burgundy.
Violets are electric blue
growing into hybrid trees.
Yet I wander left and right,
longing for pure white:
daisies singing *I love you.*

3 a.m.   Exposition
I run naked in a meteor shower,
singing to the sky—
something between a dirge and a lullaby,
a keening that carries from one hill to the other
through fields of alfalfa and clover
up stems of night-blooming cacti,
a song every mother's daughter knows
about passion: more heat than light.

4:30 a.m.   Secondary Dominant
Tonight, singing in light opera,
I wear a costume of white brocade
with rose and gold embroidery.
Standing behind me is my tenor
dressed in flamboyant frippery.
When I raise my arms for drama,
he starts tickling me,
but I don't miss a beat until he
runs his fingers down my spine.
He gooses me and I shriek a high C,
upon which he reaches from behind
and grabs my breasts.
I'd call a policeman to arrest him,
but the tenor says, "Don't make a scene."
I ad lib, in Italian coloratura,
"None of this is in the script,
and I've no truck with the obscene."
So I deck him and, with my foot on his neck,
command him to apologize.
The audience rises, showering hurrahs:
"Brava, Bravissima!"

6 a.m. Resolution
At the San Francisco Opera I see
a full chorus rehearsing with the symphony.
It's a major work, but I don't know the score.
The stage manager dares reprimand me,
"You're the one we've been waiting for?"
I'm the head-liner, but I don't know:
Am I here to I sing? or to play the piano?
The maestro acknowledges me
and I sing as never before–
my voice a stunning vibrato,
my self jubilant–a virtuoso
in shimmering white,
emanating light.

7:15 a.m. Finale
da capo al fine . . .
It's sonata form, ABA,
and now I sing the theme this way:
 __ O what a beautiful dream-time,
O what a beautiful day,
I've got the loveliest feeling
Everything's going my way __

There was only one variant on the theme of Singing dated after my move to Pueblo, Colorado. It was very lengthy and ended with questions. Here are some excerpts:

Dec 4, 2000
A Choral Work I've Written Is Being Premiered

> In a large cathedral, I go down the main aisle and sit in the fifth row, next to a woman in a royal blue suit. But she crowds me, even when I squeeze myself over to the edge of the pew.
> Now both of us are in a corridor that leads to a sacristy. We watch as some dancers and a large chorus come in procession. I can't tell if the clergy

are actors or if they belong to the cathedral. Their robes are of finer material than most costumes.

Now I realize that the woman in blue is a critic. She's written some pages even before the music begins in our dress rehearsal. She asks a man nearby, and then me, if we have any paper she can write on. He says an emphatic NO. I look at my program, thinking there may be white space on the reverse of it. But it's not a program, it's the score that I've written, and I won't part with it, not even to have a favorable review published. Actually I've written only a section of this, to insert in a more operatic work. I'm not relying on the score now, just following along to appreciate the performance.

The man mutters to me, "The critic just wants to copy some words . . . words. She needs to listen to the music and get the words." I'm more sympathetic and wonder how many words will come through to her and to the general audience.

FEELINGS:

Honored, pleased; the prospect of fulfillment, no matter what the critic thinks or writes; the sense of rounding out an earlier work with this contemporary section.

REFLECTIONS:
1. This time I'm sympathetic to my Inner Critic, though not yielding to her.
2. The man is my Positive Male aspect, who dismisses my Critic and thus reassures my Artist.
3. That I'm holding the full score shows me as an authority figure in my own right. I anticipate fulfillment, and without anxiety!
4. There's no *ex cathedra* proclamation from the church to prohibit or inhibit the procession and performance.

CHALLENGES:

How does this dream reflect, or comment on, my present situation? How can it help me in decisions about promoting Reiki and Resonance Repatterning in this conservative community? How can I "listen to the music and get the words" of folks in a place so different from any I've lived in before?

When I was working on this theme of Singing, I took a break one Saturday for a nap (Jan 14, 2017). When I woke, I had no images, only a sense of singing that, when I reached for a pen, came out this way:

Vocalises

>my mind drops words onto my tongue
>my tongue tastes and caresses them
>my hands are busy sending Reiki
>and cannot pause to write them
>my voice projects an aria

– Eight –
Wayfaring

While there's no denying that prenatal and early childhood experiences are crucial to the way a person views self, others, and the environment, I'll keep the synopsis of the first half of my life as brief as possible. In today's jargon it might be called the "back story" to the dream stories.

That my mother was over-anesthetized and I was nearly asphyxiated while nurses awaited the arrival of the obstetrician, has had lasting effects on how I have viewed life itself. Also, that my right shoulder was dislocated during the delivery, and I was finally brought forth with forceps, very likely programmed me for passiveness and acquiescence through childhood and beyond. Certainly they were the template for nightmares during my life.

At age three I was sent to the University of Michigan Hospital, the largest hospital in the United States at that time. After numerous tests there, I was diagnosed with tubular nephrosis, for which there was no cure. The doctors thought the kindest thing for me and my parents was to send me home to die. Our parish priest brought some water from Lourdes, and my mother measured a few drops into my drinking water each day. By slow increments (I was bedridden for almost a year) I returned to the land of the living. "A miracle," so the story goes, and with it my parents' belief that I was *saved to do something important*. More programming of my psyche! And more cause for guilt feelings! I labored under that yoke for too many years before deciding that any miracle that may have occurred was due to my parents' faith and constant ministrations, and that I myself was not required to do something important in my life.

Before age five I had another brush with death, when surgery was required on my right ear, affecting the mastoid bone. At that time there were no antibiotics, and if a child developed a severe infection, there was only a 50/50 chance of survival–she lived or she died. I lived.

For a more complete picture of my childhood, add a mother who played people as if they were a game of bridge: bidding and overbidding, trumping, making little slams and grand slams. Then subtract an absentee father, who was away on government contracts during World War II. Next multiply by the number of cruelties inflicted by a brother. The product was a girl with fearful loyalties, a girl on the defensive to the extent of acquiescence.

Fast-forward to my graduating from a Catholic high school, receiving a Regents Alumni Scholarship to the University of Michigan in Ann Arbor, and being accepted in the School of Music. After three semesters, I married and became pregnant almost immediately—lucky for my husband, because he got a deferment from the draft. Within months I was in the emergency room at the U of M Hospital, where a request was made for my previous records. They were so voluminous that they could not be sent through the pneumatic tube system but had to be trundled in on a cart! My pain, so uncharacteristic of pregnancy, was eventually diagnosed as gallbladder attacks and, immediately after the delivery of my first child, I underwent surgery. While recovering from that, I lay in a ward of a dozen or more beds—a ward shockingly similar to the one where I was interred at age three—and that setting added to postpartum depression and the lingering effects of anesthesia.

Coincidentally, the first dream for which I made written notes was an ether dream. It occurred in 1952. After prolonged labor with my first child and the wearing off of a spinal anesthesia, I was given ether. (Never again!) Here are the notes, unedited except for the deletion of two lines at the end concerning the newborn Angelyn:

>Past ether's fiery discs
>>Nebulae
>>The milky stars
>Heaven: a white delivery room
>>Mercy angel answering
>>>A telephone's white ring
>>A girl it is

> Routine scans for signs of life
> >On distant planets nothing
> >Unusual to report
>
> This is your life
> >Closed circuit
>
> Admitted: Yes, all girl
> >Come right
> >This way
>
> Beyond: White
> >Flaming
> >>Discs

When I married so young, and was a mother so soon, my husband and I made a pact that I would complete my education. So I pursued a few courses by correspondence and skipped a few courses by acing an oral or written exam. Then, after my youngest, Stephen, was born, I applied to The Ohio State University and attended during summers; when he went to kindergarten, I attended OSU as a full-time student. I received my master's degree in British and American Literature 25 years after graduating from high school. My education included challenges on all levels–physical, emotional, mental, and spiritual. There were marital difficulties, too, including my differing with political stances of my husband when he was an elected official. All these factors announced themselves in dreams.

Most significantly, what led me to study my dreams was a highly emotional situation while I was at the university: In 1971 I had to leave the School of Music. There was no getting around the fact that, although I was talented, I was not gifted. Moreover, the professor who admitted me without an audition (in the midst of campus riots) later accused me, at a full-faculty meeting, of having deceived him! That brought on a mid-life crisis and nightmares regarding the very idea of a career.

By 1975 I had shaped that series of dreams into a poem of 16 parts entitled "The Pilgrim's Piano." Its theme is Journeying and its major motif is a piano that transmutes to a harpsichord, an organ, a vehicle for flying to great heights. The parts excerpted below are in various styles because I stayed close to the wording and nuances of the dreams. Though the early encounters with renowned musicians are invitational, each offers a challenge:

The Pilgrim's Piano

Neither flat nor sharp,
with lots of accidentals,
I'm on Cloud Nine in Carnegie Hall,
accompanying Gabriel Satchmo.
He tells me, "Sister, discipline!
Not too much noise from that grand piano
when the Saints go marching in!"
I cry in anguished Mixolydian,
"This is no concert grand, Satchmo,
it hasn't a big enough harp."

In the deepest darkest . . .
Dr. Livingstone, I presume?
No, it is Dr. Schweitzer.
He stands by my side as I presume to play,
woodenly, on a dummy keyboard,
a little prelude and fugue,
and he hears every note that falls false.
I stand by his side as he plays,
impeccably, on a dummy organ,
a magnificent double fugue,
and I hear the heavenly harp.
Now we agree on a chorale, and sing
in perfect silence, resting in rests:
Komm, süßer Tod, komm selge Ruh,
in the deepest brightest . . .

Riding another jet stream,
I discover Antonia Brico
conducting her orchestra in Colorado.
She seats me at a Concorde piano
with dual controls; teaches me to fly.

And now I solo–
part the clouds, swirl through the sky,
streak supersonically
through concert-pitched air,
propelled by the dynamic force
of Maestra Antonia Brico.
Her final cue as she waves to me:
Do not be deflected. Do not be
deflected from your course.

The dreamer begins to realize that she is a Pilgrim seeking to develop qualities represented by her beautiful Wegman piano–uprightness, a sound mind in a sound body, harmonious vibrations–and she appreciates Helpers along the way:

Seeking the house of many mansions,
I climb the holy mountain–
groping, scrabbling, falling in the dark.
Alone I try again,
aided by spotlights in the village below
(Hollywood producers doing *Oberammergau*)
and by maps etched on my raw hands and knees.

Now I have a companion.
I the novice, she the guide, we ascend
–neither leading nor led, both drawn–
to the monastery at the summit.
Waiting for the porter's salutation,
I see through the grille a piano
grander than eye has seen or ear heard.

In a cabinet of cedar and teak,
one hundred forty-four keys–
a range to scale, a range to glissade.
All mountain climbers
are not mountain climbers:
I must try that piano,
play by heart, listen fluently.

> In the entry I see a *player* piano
> sans rolls, sans pedals. I try the keys . . .
> the struck tones are unpredictable.
> Next, a prepared piano
> with tissue and bamboo across the strings.
> These are not for me!
> In the house of many mansions, I search
> for the elusive harp of perfect pitch.

Ultimately there is a test on all levels: physical, emotional, mental, and spiritual:

> Echoing through the celestial domain
> is the summons of my name.
> The spirit of my dear teacher of piano,
> Louise Longfield de Zeeuw,
> beckons, and I follow.
> She escorts me to a great assembly
> and announces my musical genealogy.
> Tracing my heritage back to J. S. Bach,
> she traces his lineage forward to me!
>
> She arranges a final audition—
> the full faculty jury
> my entire musical family.
> Bowing to sacred tradition,
> I approach the Harpsichord of Destiny
> praying, "An untroubled spirit renew in me,
> and direct the works of my hands for me."
>
> The name of the tune is Transcendence.
> I lift the lid of the piano, peer into the coffin,
> am terrified by what is going on inside.
> Dry bones, my bones, hammer
> on triply taut, overstrung wires—
> nerves resonating every pang of my life.
> A far from perfect performance . . .
> It might merit more purgatory,
> but torment?   No!

> I try to stop the hammers . . . they splinter.
> From the dry bones' hollow,
> where once was such sweet marrow,
> erupts the primal howl:
> Why, oh why? Why me?

Though she does not achieve perfection, the Pilgrim finds solace in her foremothers. And they inspire her to continue her adventuring:

> Now I feel the firm touch
> of Maria Anna Mozart.
> Now Clara Schumann
> confirms that I am attuned.
> Now Gertrude Kuehfuhs,
> stroking, loving the keys,
> draws my attention to a higher truth—
> the cabinetmaker's signature
> above the centering c.

> That golden scroll
> on the piano of my youth
> burns incandescently:
> *WEGMAN*
>   Wayman
>   Woman
> Wayfarer and Way!
> I hear the pure soprano
> of Anna Magdalena Bach:
> *It is so. Well done,*
> *Pilgrim and Pianoforte.*

It was only in retrospect, almost 50 years after the music school fiasco and those dream visits by renowned musicians, when I noticed that many of the subsidiary *motifs* preserved in "The Pilgrim's Piano" continued for several or many years. Some examples are: suspensions that never get resolved, dancing light, successful and unsuccessful performances, overstrung nerves, task masters, attunement, helpers and guides. I was further surprised that some of my major dream *themes* had presented themselves in that series: Journeying, Searching, Ascending, Changing Course, Flying, Being Tested.

That series of dreams was both a review and a preview. It made clear that I was a pilgrim, and that music–as represented by the piano/harpsichord/harp–was what had been leading me on my journey. Yet I had to learn that there was no mapped trail for me to find and follow, that I had to blaze one for myself through unknown territory.

I often wished for a sign that would make my journey easier, but only rarely did a literal sign appear in a dream; for example, a red light or a STOP sign. In one reassuring dream, a sign said ADVANCE; in another situation the words were YOU'RE IN THE WRONG BALL PARK. Less kindly was the warning YOU'RE OUT OF YOUR GOURD! At a time when I was fretting over what I thought was betrayal by a friend, there was a billboard with the image of Ann Landers and the advice KISS AND MAKE UP.

Over the years, dreams were replete with crossroads and intersections. Some were signed accurately, such as High and Broad in Columbus, Ohio; others metaphorically, such as High and Handsome. There were no AAA TripTiks or their dream equivalent (far less a GPS guide). And there were interruptions along the way, some of them bright and cheerful, as when I was caught up in a parade one time, and when I detoured to a sideshow another time:

Aug 21, 1976
A Carnival with Sideshow Dancers

> A young woman, billed as Holly, stands on a platform and needs encouragement to go ahead. There's a receptive audience. Now she breaks into an exuberant dance. She's wearing a red, short-skirted outfit like a cheerleader's drill uniform.
>
> Now her sisters come onstage behind her, wearing long dresses of chiffon. The dresses are sewn or maybe woven in wide bands of light green, pink, yellow, and blue. The sisters mostly sway, a Greek chorus kind of body movement that contrasts with Holly's hard-rock style. They do not steal the show from Holly.

FEELINGS:

Encouraged, delighted by the colors and the dancing, reassured.

REFLECTION:

I understand Holly as wholly involved. She is (I am) capable when the audience is receptive. Also, I have backup–supporters who do not detract from my performance.

– Nine –

A Rude Awakening

The dream dog stalked me again last night. Why now? Why add night-time assault to daytime injury? I'm trembling. Like when I was seven–shaking inside my invisible armor, hurrying past Hugo's Wholesale Beer & Wine, where a guard dog paced. I tried to charm it with an incantation: Back, ye beast! Die, creature deprived of joy! Could that charm work on night terrors now? On the dog that's growing more vicious each time? He's slashed my left arm–wrist to elbow–mauled my left leg, mangled my right leg.

That was my lament in early Spring of 1975 when, in my persona of "mature student" at age 42, I was completing my last courses and a thesis for the master's program, submitting poems to literary magazines, and readying a book-length manuscript of poetry for a national competition. Meanwhile, in my persona of "dutiful wife and mother of eight children," I was engaged with school projects, honors assemblies, and class plays, as well as the mundane chores of managing our home.

Nevertheless, the dream dog was a recurring beast that I could no longer keep at bay. I vowed to challenge it in any forthcoming appearance. When that strategy proved successful in my sleep, I decided to utilize the dream information in waking life, too, by transposing it into a poem.

Attack Dog on Premises

On Wednesday, in my electric wheelchair,
I corner him at dusk on a dead-end street.
Who are you? I shout, ready to club him.
What do you want from me?
The attack dog snarls, "I am Competition,
and I am going to eat you up!"
He lunges, I clobber him.

> The next time, though wary, he comes
> out of the shadows in daylight.
> Cursing, I crack down and muzzle him.
> Within a week he's under control—
>   collared and coming to heel.
> This beast may not have to die.

Today I'm in physical therapy,
resting from labored swimming, when
the attack dog plunges for my right arm.
Back! I command. *Back off, do you hear?*
He executes a reverse jackknife—
up to the springboard, dripping and trembling.

> The threatening dog turns blue
> and melts into a Skye terrier
> that pleads to be caressed.
> Frolicking in the water, I cry,
> Why should I care?
> You stroke your own strokes.

I climb from the pool unaided, calling,
Come here. What can you do for me?
Competition shows me his pedigree,
blue ribbons, loving cups, contracts.
He offers me his leash, and now
—both of us with full faculties—
we venture the future in tandem.

Competition as an issue was not completely resolved, however. In May of that year I had a dream whose immediate prompt was a statement by Robert Frost, to the effect that writing poetry without rhymes was like playing tennis without a net. Because in the dream I recognized James, a fellow graduate student, as my competitor (we had both submitted poems for the annual spring contests), I did not make demands on him the way I did on the vicious dream dog. Our interaction shaped up as a tennis match.

After the judging was completed, and James and I had each won a contest, I breathed more freely. Yet I decided to transpose the dream about competition into a poem, with the intention of releasing pent-up energy. Here is an excerpt:

The Incredible Tennis Match

On the rolled lawn you appeared,
my competition with a beard,
    dressed in white, impeccable.
I looked down at my tennis clothes–
    marvelous–a perfect match!

You served, I served, we volleyed, tied,
    and might have gone home satisfied
    but that our playoff had a catch.
I knew (did you?) how tennis goes,
the challenge undebatable:
    a tie is not the way it's scored,
    only one player gets the award.

        Rematch
     Serve   Return
     Point   Recover
Thonk Twang Thonk   Twang
Drive Smash   Slash   Sweat

What a relief when I wakened to judgment
on a promising green lawn day,
convinced that you and I could play
      the game
      our game
      competitively
    –with or without a net–
not letting verbal volley threaten
      point   game   set.

Because problem-solving is a function of the majority of my dreams, I include numerous examples in this memoir. It is not my purpose now to expand on the problems that triggered dreams and nightmares, or to delve into particular solutions to any of those problems; I simply state that there was no end to challenges. Some were solved successfully, either in dream life or in waking life, but others were not. Here I include three problem-solving dreams, one each from three periods: my earliest records (1975), 13 years later (1988), and my advanced years (2008).

While at the university, a second soul-searching incident occurred in the final quarter of my master's program: the professor of Seventeenth Century Poetry threatened to flunk six of her nine seminar students, myself included. She demanded that each of us choose a second topic for a term paper and develop it to her satisfaction, all in one month's time. If she were to flunk me, I would not gain my master's degree until another quarter; further, the printing of my thesis would be on hold, and opportunities for employment would be in abeyance. Nightmares carrying my fear and anger, which amounted to hatred during that springtime, assailed me for many years after that, and are still instructional.

The first dream about that benighted professor concerned attempted murder (May 14, 1975). Cues that it concerned her were: "a process of elimination, knives sharpened, cyanide," all of which related to her cynicism. In the dream I was active, "kicking out triple-pane [pain] windows, letting in fresh air, and leading other persons to safety." But in waking life I was not active in my opposition to her; on the contrary, I was trying to appease her.

In a dream the next night (May 15, 1975), while preparing the guest-room bed for that professor, "I make it up with fresh sheets [fresh pages of composition], even though I feel that she is putting us out." Below is a longer excerpt from that dream. I include it because it marked the first time that I solved a major problem during sleep: how to write a thesis acceptable to that professor.

May 15, 1975
Trying Out for a Leading Role, I Am Warned

> I'll have to share the stage with a professional, who not only has good lines but knows how to deliver them and has a following. That doesn't bother me, I will wow the audience.
> The play has several murders by stabbing in the back, some of them spurting raw blood! The leading lady wants to call attention to herself, and uses this method.

FEELINGS:
Warned; competitive, self-confident; upstaged, shocked.

REFLECTIONS:
1. Somehow this dream segued from knowing my lines to deciding how to proceed with the term paper. "Lines Written In Lemon Juice," a poem by Abraham Cowley, was my starting place.
2. In the morning I saw, scribbled on my dream tablet, an outline for a whole "theory of poesy":
   - The reader becomes co-author of a poem.
   - A poem has little value unless there is a reader for it and a flame of interest–of love–to bring the letters and words off the page.
   - There is a matter of sacrifice to the gods in the whole business of writing.
   - The destruction of a poem–whether unread or consumed in flames–does not involve the destruction of the poet.
3. I am awed by the breadth of this problem-solving. Such a gift!

I would like to say that from then on "all systems were go." But being gifted in dream life is one thing, carrying through in waking life is another. I did not have the support I needed from my family. Here is one example: While I was carrying a full course-load and working in the English Department Library, I was still managing the household. My husband added to the tension with uncalled-for criticism. So, the morning after my dream, "Trying Out for a Leading Role," I loaded the car with typewriter, textbooks and notes, some food and a few clothes, and left for an unspecified motel to write my paper in peace. My husband did not realize that I was gone until he came home from an all-day bicycle tour and found no supper on the table.

To an outsider, that leave-taking might seem a small action, but to me it was huge–allowing dream notes, rather than my husband's criticism, to be my guide. Thereafter, my taking actions based on dreams–especially those with authority figures who made arbitrary commands, unnecessary demands, or unseemly criticisms–continued, and eventually gave me the courage to leave the marriage of 31 years.

Within three years of my systematically writing dream notes, I recognized similarities between creative dreaming and creative writing, and on a dream tablet I outlined my inferences: "Images or words occur and, not knowing what to do with them, I try other images and words to see if they are a better fit. Very often odd juxtapositions or actions are explained by what ensues. If I miss a cue, there may be a leap, causing a sense of incongruity, or even a replay of a scene with elaboration, until there is a sense of wholeness and sometimes of completeness" (Jan 22, 1978).

My first gainful employment after commencement was in the Poets-in-the-Schools Program (PITS) through the Ohio Arts Council. Therein I faced numerous problems, among them geographical, administrative, competitive, literary, and adversarial. Most challenging was working with teachers whose idea of a "poetry unit' was throwing together words according to a pattern they had come across, usually based on counting syllables. A solution to this problem came from my dreams: Read to the classes a few of my dream poems, explain the privilege of persona, and then ask the students to engage the super-powers they experience in their dreams. When students realized that they could be anyone–man, woman, boy, girl, animal, thing–and go anywhere without reprisal, that resulted in some genuinely creative writing.

Another problem around that time arose in a dream called "A Federal Case" (Mar 21, 1978). It challenged my integrity and caused me to wonder whether I was competing against my Self!

REFLECTIONS:
1. A federal case is something huge, like kidnaping someone and carrying him across State lines. I don't want to drag a reader [of my poems and essays] across lines; I want to invite him or her to coast along with me.
2. Like a detective working on a case, I'm suspicious of anything that comes too easily. I expect a poem to operate on more than one level, and this requires *making* it, not just letting it come. But maybe that's exactly what I need—letting what wants to come through, come through.
3. Is my problem that I question my integrity? I must not become a mere compiler of others' images or a repository of others' metaphors, or even a copier of my own.

I did not realize at the time that my struggle was with integrating qualities that were considered masculine—such as competing and dominating in one's milieu—with my accepted feminine qualities—such as staying power.

I was 15 years into making dream notes when the idea of looking for levels of awareness in a dream "rang a bell" and resonated as clearly as a carillon. That occurred during a retreat, in an extraordinary group session based on Jean Houston's *The Possible Human*. Participants were given four exercises in imagination, to address four levels of awareness. For the first exercise, we were given one minute of clock time and were reassured that it was "all the time you need." For the second exercise, two minutes; the third, three minutes; the fourth, four minutes. It took more time to tell the story than to imagine it, and much information came forward in those short periods. That is eminently true of dreams also.

That very night the imaginative process continued with a complex dream of nine scenes. In four scenes, there appeared two wrestlers (physical level), a younger woman and myself (emotional level), two professors (mental level), and myself naked, baring my soul but getting no response from all those people (spiritual level). The next morning the four levels of awareness helped me sort through the density of images and arrive at a basic problem: being pressed for time and "blamed for everything—all the losses and thefts, past memories, present frustrations, invasions of privacy—all my fault."

REFLECTIONS:
1. Life allows all the time I need for living it. I hope to get rid of any anxiety about not having enough time, especially about not achieving a personal goal within a specified time and not meeting arbitrary deadlines imposed at work.
2. I wrestle too much with blame that's thrown at me. I must not internalize it.
3. My affirmation this week will be, "I am enough and I have enough time."

On the dreaming-waking continuum, another problem for most of my life was dealing with physical pain. Dreams have often alerted me to a concern about my health, thus serving as a preventive of a more serious condition. One example: In March 2008 I had an infection of an eye tooth and was in suspense concerning whether it would have to be extracted. As if in sympathetic vibration, my Unconscious provided a dream that illustrated too much pressure and pain:

Apr 18, 2008
Sight-Reading a Very Difficult Composition

> It starts in two # and modulates to three #. There are many accidentals, too, which make it difficult to ascertain what is the tonic. So many ledger lines below the bass clef that I only guess what a note is, and one time I think my left hand will go below the keys! My right hand ranges widely/wildly, too. This will take lots of practice to master.
>
>   When I get to the third section, I expect repetition [as in sonata form], but there's only a hint of former themes. I should have guessed that an atonal piece would abide by its own rules, not adhere to a set form.

FEELINGS:
Exploratory (both curious and anxious); pleased that I can carry through; diligent; aggrieved that there's difficulty upon difficulty with no let-up; yet a sense of mastery.

REFLECTIONS:
1. This is about pain and its going from two # (too sharp) to three # (even more sharp).
2. There's a pun about accidentals in life, and this includes dentals.
3. The difficulty of this atonal music = my difficulty in an atypical situation. Doctors haven't been able to "ascertain what is the tonic" for me.
4. The wide ranges of right hand and left hand represent my left brain and right brain in seeming opposition. I need to utilize both intuition and logic to master the situation.

COMMENT THREE WEEKS LATER:
This eye-tooth trauma is one I cannot master. It requires extraction of the tooth by an endodontist, administration of wide-spectrum antibiotics for several weeks, and a dental implant six months from now. Thank heaven, the infection did not go to my knee replacement. My orthopedic surgeon has spoken of dire complications if that were to happen. Some pressures and pains are not just metaphorical or symbolic messages, in waking life or in dreams. This eye-tooth drama is based in the reality that no one on Planet Earth goes through a lifetime unscathed by pain.

What felt like "two steps backward for one forward" continued, as evidenced by a dream six months later, "A Safety Patrol and Judgment Calls." In it "two colors predominate: a yellow slicker of a Safety Patrol outside, and black garb of another person at my front door, maybe already inside the entrance" (Nov 18, 2008). "Underneath all this is the feeling that they can't help me, that I can't be helped, that I'll have to pull myself up by my bootstraps. At one point I'm down on a gray terrazzo floor, on hands and knees. But I realize I can't do this with my knee replacement. So now I'm prone, trying to slither my way toward help." This dream made it clear that I needed to return to physical therapy. I did, pronto.

My Unconscious sometimes works overtime to get a message through. Evidence of this were verses scribbled on my dream tablet. I was mystified, having no memory of writing them during the night... how could that have happened? It was several years before I came across an explanation, a statement by the psychotherapist Wilson Van Dusen concerning the autonomic processes involved:

> If one lingers in the state between sleep and waking, the hypnogagic state, one can focus on a thought or experience and suddenly have very clear imagery and sometimes hear voices. It is a delicate phenomenon. If you try to grab the image or to awaken too much, the phenomenon vanishes. If one is reflecting on a problem, it can suddenly be seen in a new light and solved.

Grateful to Van Dusen, I now honor the "delicate hypnogagic phenomenon" that produced verses welcoming readers to participate in my dreams:

Conjugating Dreams

dreaming scenes that might have been
    or never ever could have been
dreaming love that might well be
    or has been stillborn, suffocated
dreaming witty repartee
    and action beyond my imagination
I hold to hope—however slippery—
    because *I am, you are, we be*

– Ten –

The Give-and-Take of Dream Notes

When I began exploring dreams, I followed two premises that were stated or implied in various dream books available in the 1970s. First, every dream image–person, animal, or object–conveys an emotion and can be regarded as referring to oneself. Second, every word describing a person, animal, object, situation, or relationship is a carrier of emotion. Gradually I became aware of mercurial aspects of dreams; for example, an abstraction may turn into an animal, and a motif may turn into a theme.

From the start I uncovered a great deal of punning, also *double entendre*, that provided clues to understanding a dream; also I recognized that homonyms (such as right/write and pane/pain) are often clues. Nouns may revert to verbs, and persons may carry through the actions from which their names were derived. All forms of my name, even my initials, indicated personal involvement. In addition, names of persons I have known in the past suggested other times and places; for example, the name Robach told me to row back to an earlier event. Spielmaker reminded me to avoid exaggerated speech. Hartman and Newman had positive connotations, whereas Falter, Lynch, and Schaaf had negative ones. McPhilamy could be positive or negative, depending on what filled me at the time. Elderkin I have yet to embrace.

Sometimes a dream image is a recognizable portrait or a mirror image; other times a caricature of a trait that I would like to enhance or to erase; a snapshot of a prevailing mood; an etching of the impression I make on others; or a sketch of an activity that is questionable.

Each person in my rogues gallery of dream adversaries, as well as in my portrait gallery of family and friends, illustrates a quality, or even a philosophy, that I need to explore. For example, when I first encountered violence in dreams, I was reluctant to claim it as my own. Yet I had to admit that, even when violence seemed to emanate from Other, I had internalized it to some degree in Self. Similarly, even when a person in a dream was recognizable as Other, I still needed to deal with my part in the relationship. Dreams alerted me to what I was projecting onto others and what others were projecting onto me, and that required a great deal of sorting!

Images in the Context of a Dream

Occasionally there was only a single image that I recalled, due to highly-charged emotions. An instance of that was when I wakened myself shouting, "Not an ice chest, Jay!" Later, in a dialogue with the image of a Styrofoam ice chest, I better understood my concern. Its response was, "I keep the hot and cold in," which was a problem in our relationship at the time.

Even a single feature of an image can call attention to a greater whole. In literature this feature is called synecdoche; in cinematography it involves zooming in on a facial expression, a hand holding a revolver, a medallion, a stamp, or anything emblematic of the plot. Here is an excerpt from a dream, "Yippie Yi Yay" (Jul 15, 1977) wherein clothing and a voice convey the scene:

> In town, dungarees sit erect, mad for the rodeo,
> and bright neckerchiefs salute one another
> before the competitions begin.
> A silver-spangled announcer challenges,
> his voice compelling as an auctioneer's:
> *Come if you dare! I'm here when you dare!*

A very brief dream that carried a powerful message for me was composed of only two images and one word: construction sand; fine, white play sand; and *combine* (Feb 21, 1996). From them I understood a need for balance when working on a book–a need to include playfulness along with the serious business of construction. That became my practice in the succeeding 20 years.

Dreams without Images

For me a verbal dream, one without images, is rare. An example is a two-word dream, "Oh, Govern!" that led to the realization that "the governing of one's Self comes from within" (Mar 4, 1978).

A verbal dream carries intense feelings, often reassurance, and sometimes a realization about a problem or situation. One such realization came to me fully formed: "Lumps of anxiety and knots in muscles can be available as energy. Energy in suspension can be called on when I need it. There doesn't have to be heat-conversion each time from energy to action" (Jun 30, 1979).

In the following verbal dream, which still astonishes me, I speak on many subjects and hear a response from a feminist critic:

Sep 14, 1986
Performing Extemporaneously

> I'm performing extemporaneously a poem that goes on at considerable length. Every phrase has energy and pushes toward a climax. I realize how eloquent this is and wish a tape-recorder were capturing it. I wonder if I can possibly reconstruct the piece in writing.
>
> Some of the closing lines incorporate or else paraphrase a penitential psalm that begins, "Out of the depths I cry." My whole performance poem is about depths, hollows, cylinders, spools of film, darkness, blankness, the registering of images, the clarity of images, fullness, ripeness.
>
> The poem conveys something about the positive forms of technology that enhance natural forms and flows of energy. So many abstractions followed by a twist, "How sweet it is!" [a la Jackie Gleason].
>
> There's a woman in the audience or class or seminar who picks up on an oral cue, "I cry to you aloud." She notes, "The male aspect of divinity is not stressed. Also there's a pun, aloud/allowed. Crying is allowed, protesting is allowed; these are actions as well as sounds and may take us out of the depths."

When I have a verbal dream, it often leads me to more verbalizing, either by journaling or by drafting a poem.

Doubling or Repetition of Images

Images when doubled or repeated, and themes when repeated in close succession, demand my full attention. Some are like instant replays of a televised sporting event, showing a close-up view or a detail that might not have been noticeable the first time around. Repetitive dreams ask, sometimes command, me to stand at attention, salute, and carry through with appropriate action. Repetitive dreams come in several ways: in a *cluster* on one night, in a *constellation* covering several consecutive nights, or in a *series* occurring over a long period– sometimes years between them, yet picturing such strong emotions that they are memorable.

My Steps in Recording Dreams

My practice has been to write dream notes during the night, without turning on a light, and while resuming the same bodily position as when I wakened from the dream. (A Fisher Space Pen® allows me to write in any position.) As I scribble the notes, I often leave a bracketed space [ ], which keeps me in the dream and allows me to fill in a fact or a relevant association in the morning when I write my Reflections. When I pose a question within the dream itself, I also utilize brackets so I will not be distracted from the immediate dream experience.

With the Reflections in the morning, I focus on the exact words and images written during the night. I have found it does not profit me to veer into free-association or to spiral into analytical interpretation, yet I sometimes note an immediate prompt for the dream such as a book, movie, or conversation.

For presenting my dreams in dream groups, I use a font that resembles handwriting for the notes made during the night and a book-face font for the Reflections made in the morning. The following is a dream that speaks to the efficacy of handwritten notes:

Jul 24, 2010
Composing while Writing Longhand

> This may be in a test situation. At any rate, there is a deadline involved. I'm writing fluently and serenely, breathing deeply. I never write this well when under duress! I stop momentarily to admire the penmanship. My grade-school teachers would be proud of this penmanship—legible and lovely, even though not as prescribed in class.
>
> I'm delighted that my composition is moving so well. But now I'm distracted by someone who asks me a question. When I look up to answer, I realize that no professor or publisher will accept handwritten pages. Manuscript has lost its original meaning.
>
> I leave off in the middle of a sentence and move to my computer, filled with doubts of how to proceed. The joy has dissolved. I'm afraid the inspiration has, too.

FEELINGS:

I can't recall another dream that has so many feeling words within the story! In the morning I add these: unacceptable, afraid, confused.

REFLECTIONS:

1. Happily, there is no deadline for my poetry book, *Suspending Disbelief*. The "legible and lovely" refer to these poems. This dream's questions and distractions resonate with my book about dreams, *Dream Encounters*, which is underway but not a source of stress.
2. Relative to "manuscript," my misgivings are most likely about the dream notes themselves because many are still in scribbles, never typed.
3. The distractions, questioning, and doubts resonate with my Inner Critic, who still insists on prescribing and classifying.

CHALLENGE:

How can I achieve greater cooperation between my Critic and my Creative Child?

My Steps in Processing Dreams

For the processing of my dreams, I allow up to one hour each morning to list feelings and reflections, assign each dream a title, and enter any new motif or theme in my concordance. I stay with the dream and its puns as my primary source. Some of the themes I have explored through decades are universally known, such as flying dreams and sexual dreams. Others themes are highly personal, such as catharsis dreams and my versions of death and dying.

My next step is taking a dream that still puzzles me to a dream group. I was a member of Dreamtalk in Columbus, Ohio from its inception in 1981, until I moved to Colorado in 1997. We met weekly and followed the guidelines in *Appreciating Dreams: A Group Approach* by Montague Ullman, M.D., who is often referred to as "the grand-daddy of dream group work."

Sometimes another step is necessary for me to achieve closure on a dream. If so, I add that to the original notes under a side-heading, either Challenge or Action.

When I am completely stumped about meaning, I honor the dream not by analysis but by action. Sometimes the action has been allegorical. For example, I honored a dream about a little girl who, like her counterpart in a Mother Goose rhyme, "when she was good she was very, very good, but when she was bad, she was horrid." For her I pasted a gold star on my forehead each morning for a week. Most often the action has been practical, such as following a dream suggestion about the state of my health, the safety of my car, or the fragility of a friendship. Other actions range from wearing a gemstone of the dream's main color, to applying an essential oil that resonates with the dream; from vocalizing while holding a single dream image in mind, to transposing the entire dream into a poem; from sketching a mandala based on a dream's images, to incorporating them in a large collage.

Determined never to impose meaning on a dream, I look for meaning to emerge from the seeming chaos. If it does not emerge in timely fashion, I recite the mantra, "Be at peace with your soul. The universe is unfolding as it should."

Distinguishing Motifs and Themes

Regarding people, places, and things in dreams, I do not call them symbols; I refer to them simply as images. A *symbol* is a representation that is recognized universally and through generations or eras. Examples are flags of countries, the Red Cross, some international logos, the Christian crucifix, mathematical symbols, computer icons, and most punctuation marks. Carl Jung's predecessors gave a convincing argument that archetypes are symbols, having been recognized over centuries and around the world. Jung went a step further, asserting that archetypes are not only recognizable signs but have a life of their own. (More about this appears in the section "Me and My Shadow.")

An *image* is more discrete than a symbol; even when it develops into a personal symbol, I would never claim that a dream image of mine has the same meaning for another person, far less for a group of people. Therefore, when I write poems derived from dreams, I strive to give readers enough clues for them to recognize meanings that are personal to me, whether or not they might be construed as archetypal.

In the dream concordance that I developed, and in this present book, I also make a distinction between motif and theme. A *motif* is a figure whose characteristics can change in various contexts while still maintaining its essence. A motif is not always consistent; the context of each dream allows for emphasis on different features. For example, in my dreams a canary is aesthetically pleasing as a songbird; it also can be a warning about my shallow breathing, a carrier of a bright idea, or a messenger on the spiritual level. Another example of a motif is from a single lengthy dream (Aug 25, 1975), in which a spotlight occurs in six scenes:

- on a Coca-Cola truck, more a warning than publicity,
- on the invisible wall of an elevator,
- overhead, probing, as in old police interrogation movies,
- ahead of me and a patient, like a flashlight,
- over a doctor and his patient, their auras,
- on a dancer.

When a motif appears repeatedly, it may lead to the discovery of a theme. For example, my notes on the *motifs* "staircases and ladders" led me to recognize the *theme* of Ascending. Another example, my notes on the motifs "crossroads and intersections" led me to recognize the *theme* of Making Decisions.

A *theme* is developed at greater length than a motif, is usually an action (or several actions), and maintains its characteristics in a variety of contexts. In the variants of a theme traced over several years, the situations, images, and motifs may differ considerably.

Characteristics of Dream Cycles

I was slow to realize that different dream periods have different characteristics. I learned this gradually from my own dreams and from similar observations by other members of Dreamtalk:

- The falling-asleep dream is short and its images reflect the activities or concerns of recent days.
- The middle-of-night dreams are longer and they process feelings on a deep level.
- The dawn dream, which anticipates the new day, is vivid when the dreamer is wakened by an alarm clock; therefore, it is easiest to recall. The dawn dream, literally cut off by the alarm, rarely has a conclusion, thus leaving the dreamer puzzled and exclaiming, "That was weird!"

If a dawn dream of mine is not interrupted, it may reveal strange bedfellows: characters from books, film stars, political figures, my kindergarten teacher or my dentist, any person of my extended family, and any animal from a pet to Adam's off ox. There follows a poem derived from a constellation of dreams that occurred over consecutive nights, at the times noted. It exemplifies dream cycles; the variety of verse forms conveys the variety of presentations within those cycles.

Royal Flush

12 a.m.   King
A king dubs me Venerable.
Next, offers a sliver of his pie chart,
expecting reciprocity:
You owe me.

1:30 a.m.   Queen
My home is a castle inviting the tourist.
In the great hall, on a table of ebony,
is draped a medieval tapestry
whose theme is hunt-to-feast.
Its warp and woof are weighted down
by bowls and tankards, pewter and silver.
I would yank it out from under
all that unaccommodating treasure,
wrap one end around my shoulders,
covering myself with embroidered flowers
stitched by radiant handmaidens
who now dance in a heyday circle,
allowing the hounds and the hunters
to bark their way at the end of my train.
Queen of all I survey, I reign.

3 a.m.   Knave
Someone has left wet towels
and large black circles
on my golden oak floor.
I, who am left to restore
the wood, tell everyone in sight,
"Move the furniture away.
I need to sand and varnish, too."
They do.

But no sooner than I say, "Okay,"
Two Men and a Truck take over,
move every piece back,
and frustrate my putting things right.

4:30 a.m.   Tenterhooks
You, the gentlest of men, make magic—
pull poems from behind my ears,
produce gems as large as metaphors,
intertwine scarves with such brilliance
I can never forget.
You place your hands above my shoulders
and gift me with a deep flush
of loving benediction.
Your final gift: a rabbit
to keep our memories warm.
I cherish it as long as life allows—
snug in my caring until
someone with a wet blanket
comes and smothers it.

6 a.m.   Joker
I, garbed in a royal-blue blanket
that slips provocatively over my breasts,
the men in the seminar bare-chested or nude,
none of us a prude, one of us joking:
Are we sufficiently mature
to be explicating
the bawdy lyrics of Chaucer?

In the dream that I transposed into the poem "Royal Flush," there are several *motifs*: home as castle; tapestry, scarves, and towels; animals predator and prey; men of varying dispositions. The one constant is the Queen facing challenges. What is the *theme*? Gambling for high stakes, to cancel the IOU held by the King.

Respecting the Complexity of Dreams

Starry-eyed at the beginning of this endeavor, I supposed that I could trace progress year by year. Ha! Whatever progress I have made as an adult has gone through several patterns. For the first pattern, a line drawing can suffice: a steep learning curve. For the second, the pattern is two-dimensional: a labyrinth. The third pattern is three-dimensional: a spiral, its every upward arc followed by a downward arc, rising slightly higher with each turn.

Only after five years of writing dream notes did I begin studying books on the subject, because I had vowed "not to be led into temptation" (*i.e.*, analytical interpretation) by eminent authors. After that I read widely for information, guidance, and sustenance, and within 10 years, I acquired over 75 books devoted to dream studies in all their complexity.

Unfailingly helpful to me over the years has been Jill Mellick's *The Natural Artistry of Dreams: Creative Ways to Bring the Wisdom of Dreams to Waking Life*. I love her motto, "Delighting in Diversity," and have been guided by her philosophy, as set forth here:

> Dreams, creative expression, and soul are inseparable. They operate in an endless cycle. Each plays a crucial role in your inner life. Each needs, nourishes, and leads into the other. Treat each with the quiet, curious, and loving respect it deserves.

In the 20 years since the publication of Mellick's book, the book of dream studies that I value most is *Integral Dreaming* by Fariba Bogzaran and Daniel Deslauriers. Here is a capsule report on their scientific and cultural studies of dreaming:

> From an integral perspective, *dream awareness* is the practice of being present to one's inner life in its full integrity. The simple but powerful act of being present to one's dreams helps dreamers perceive aspects of their selves that are perhaps the growing tip of their own

being. Often this perception reinforces the dreamer's wish to know him- or herself better, thus helping to overcome self limitations. Dreams become a potent vehicle for creative insight, connecting seemingly divided or unfamiliar parts, or even discarded ones, into a more complex, interconnected whole.

My focus has always been on the appreciation of dreams' complexity and power, not on the dissecting or dismantling of them. I have found Jung's discussion of *meandering* very helpful. In *Man and His Symbols*, he states that meandering goes on continuously in our Unconscious and manifests in our dreams, often with highly personal images. Some figures, landscapes, or situations recur until we realize a series and can readily see changes that have gone unnoticed. Further:

> If one watches the meandering pattern, in which individual strands or tendencies become visible, then vanish, then return again, over a long period of time, one can observe a sort of hidden regulating or directing tendency at work, creating a slow, imperceptible process of psychic growth–the process of individuation.

In processing my dreams for more than four decades, I have become increasingly aware of Jung's qualifiers: "a long period of time" and "a slow, imperceptible process of psychic growth."

– *Eleven* –

In Awe of Dream Animals

Dreams featuring animals were so prevalent and so intense when I started making notes, that I immediately transposed many into poems (and threw away the notes). Those poems I gathered into a chapbook, *Horse of Another Stripe* (1987). In that collection, equines were featured in diverse ways: from Mobil Oil's Flying Red Horse to Pegasus, from the horse of Chinese astrology to a mythical horse 30 to 40 feet tall. Back then it was the zebra who appealed most strongly as a model, discounting a black-and-white dichotomy and emphasizing inclusiveness: "not only but also."

For *Dream Encounters* I considered separating the animals into two camps: protagonists and antagonists. But my dreams do not set themselves up that way; to the contrary, they alternate stories having positive and negative valences. Consequently, what I present in this section are dream notes in sequential order. In the first decade of my note-keeping, there were 30 dreams featuring animals; in the second decade, 34; in the third decade, 11; in the fourth decade, only one.

That animals are featured in so many dreams, and that they have persisted in coming to me all my life, is due to several factors. Each animal may represent one or more of the following:

- a visual or verbal pun ("on his high horse" or "my dogs are killing me");
- a role (the lion as "king of the jungle" or my tigress as "queen of all she surveys");
- a person I know, masquerading ("wolf in sheep's clothing");
- a quality I need to integrate or to release;
- a lesson from a fairy tale or fable;
- a spiritual messenger.

This partial list explains why a dreamer must avoid all set definitions, such as, "A horse means driving power." That might be true for one person or society, but decidedly not for another person or society. The dreamer must consider the context of any given dream and its dominant feelings. Here I need to re-state my priority of appreciation of dream images over the analysis of them. In *The Dream and the Underworld*, James Hillman focuses not only on the dream animal's presence but also its actions, considering how they contribute to the richness of the dream. Hillman has persuaded me that spirits, embodied as animals, speak to us in this manner:

> First, they [animals] are not ours, or us; second, they are not images of animals, but images as animals. The least we can do for them is to pay them that primordial respect of the cave man drawing in the dark, face to the wall, that respect of Adam, so closely considering them that he could find for each one its name. We need large caves and loving attention. Then they may come and tell us about themselves.

Having engaged in energy work for almost 30 years, I would paraphrase Hillman this way: The energy is not that of animals, but energy as animals, who may come and tell us about themselves.

For years I worked with two animal dreams that I considered sacred, until I was able to shape them into poems that expressed, to a slight degree, those experiences. In both dreams, the energy of a numinous being presented as an animal, possibly that the brilliance would not overwhelm me. (Below is the first instance; the second is included in the section "Epiphanies.")

The Flight of the Chaste Peahen

She didn't sweep through a cotillion,
a socialite in shimmering white,
or promenade as a beauty queen
in footlights or spotlights.
She didn't survey public opinion,
or proselytize on television.
In darkness and silence she came to me,
and I wondered what this could mean.

No mistaking her brilliant white aura
for a Communion dress or bridal veil.
It was more than a halo,
she was more than an angel.
She was light–
composed of filaments of light–
regal and serene,
her body of white-gold cilia,
her crest of yellow-gold filigree
that dipped in a whisper of air.
A rare bird, I said to myself,
but I don't know what to make of her.
And so said others–among them thieves–
when she materialized in feathers,
wearing a crown of diamonds and sapphires.

Three men stole her away.
They stripped the crown of the chaste peahen
and dumped her in a shed at the edge of town.
Shadows against their campfire, the thieves
wagered and grappled all night,
each one claiming the crown.
By daylight they lay paralyzed,
jewels embedded in their flesh like thorns
poisoning the bloodstream.

A tale of the Brothers Grimm, I thought,
or a yarn of Scheherazade, except
she came to me.
Sacred to Juno and to the Hindus,
revered throughout India and Java, yet
she came to me.
To what avail? What could I have done?
What can I say or do? What can anyone?

> From within the shed came a raucous call.
> The white peahen stepped forth—
> inviolable, more brilliant than before.
> She flew to the top of a 30-foot tree,
> embellished as in ancient myth—
> feathers of an angel,
> voice of a devil,
> and innards to match any thief.

What I was left with was a feeling of awe, a recollection of brilliance, and a sense of being caught up into an expanse beyond my ken. William James used the word ineffable regarding such an experience.

When I re-read this dream poem 40 years later, the scenes struck me as rape and recovery from it; then I knew what it referred to. When I was about five, some older boys in the neighborhood molested me. Saying, "You want a tail? We'll give you a tail," they got me face-down on the ground and rammed what I thought were sticks in me.

The dream of the inviolate peahen came at a time when I was open to forgiveness of them and of myself. It had taken me half a lifetime to realize that those "big boys" had been only seven or eight years old and may not have known the deeper significance of what they were doing. Yet, in this 21st century, considering the revelations of #MeToo, I am convinced that the "boys will be boys and girls will be quiet" attitude concerning abuse of any kind during childhood is what has allowed it to continue in adulthood.

For those boys it may have been only a power play; for me it was a total rejection of myself as a girl and as a person. Also it reinforced the fear I had when, every night at bedtime, I was obliged to recite with the rest of the family the Confiteor, saying: "I have sinned exceedingly in thought, word, and deed. Through my fault, through my fault, through my most grievous fault." Though my only fault was having been a tag-a-long, I took on the guilt that the boys were able to shrug off. The dream of the white peahen, coming at a time when I was open to its grace, accomplished a genuine healing.

Thus far I have not come across an explanation for the prevalence of *white* animals in my dreams. I knew that Bear is revered as Teacher by Native American tribes, and I felt the polar bear to be of unique importance. In my dreams the polar bear was whiter than is natural and came so many times that I honored it as my totem animal by placing four fetishes of it on my Reiki grid.

I kept watch for information about the polar bear and, twenty years after that ceremony, I came across *Animal Spirits* by Nicholas Saunders, in which he notes the association of polar bears with shamans:

> When a Canadian Inuit shaman wants to fly, he transforms himself into a polar bear because, when seen swimming through clear water, a polar bear's movements make it look like it is flying. . . . Among the Labrador Inuit the polar bear was seen as a form of Tuurngasuk, the Great Spirit.

Later, in James Hillman's *Dream Animals*, I found corroboration of that mystical awareness:

> Let us then suppose these great white bears to be dream images of divinity, displaying something elsewhere and distant . . . and presenting to the dreamers the dilemmas, agonies, isolation, quiet patience and redemptive qualities of what Jung called the "religious instinct."

> Of course, a bear is something other than a religious instinct. . . . Beyond all interiorizing of the bear—bringing it "inside" and taking its image as representing a potential within our own personal selves—is the bear itself. Beyond "instinct," beyond "theophany," is the utterly free-moving spirit of the great white bear.

Nightmarish Animals

The first nightmare that I remember came at around age five. It portrayed tigers about to eat me, and I wakened screaming. My mother tried to calm me by saying, "It's only a dream." But I cried, "I'm like Little Black Sambo, with tigers all around me." Her answer was, "But he tricked them, didn't he." If only she had asked, "Is there something you're afraid of?", I might have been brave enough to break through the boys' threat, "Don't you ever tell."

When I was compiling *Dream Encounters* and discovered that a female tiger had appeared frequently during my child-bearing years, that seemed remarkable. And that I'd welcomed her completely, addressing her as "old tigress, ancestress," astounded me.

A common misconception about the word *nightmare* is that it was adapted because of the ferocity of horses in many dreams. Actually the word comes from *mara* (Anglo-Saxon and Old Norse), meaning a demon, one that might possess a dreamer unless spells or prayers were said at bedtime to prevent that outcome.

Realizing that my menagerie of dream animals—wild and domesticated, zoological and mythological—would daunt readers, I have chosen to highlight only four. Because encounters with Dog, Bear, Tiger, and Bird best represent my personal development over the years, I focus on them and their transformations in each of four decades.

Dream Animals in the First Decade: 1975–1984

Dream dogs challenged me in several areas. A pathetic little dog left untended or abandoned was a reminder that indecision is itself a decision and can lead to regrets. Another small dog, which often grew large, revealed itself as my Underdog, and was more demanding. Here is an example:

Mid-1976
Two Dogs Yipping and Nipping

> A little one nips at my feet and arms. I toss it aside several times, but it thinks this is good play. I am serious. When a big dog lumbers into view, the little one goes hiding someplace.
>
> The big dog is ugly, heavy, and slow, and it growls at me. When it starts biting me, I hit it with the lid of the pressure cooker. Now a really strange split—as if the

> dog sees its body being punished and dying. The head
> reacts powerfully, and now I'm whamming the heavy lid
> at the head, too. The pointed part [where the pressure
> gauge fits] goes deep into the dog's head and kills it.

QUESTIONS:
1. Are these watch-dogs, and I'm ignoring their warnings?
2. Can they be preparing me for the appointment at the Ohio Arts Council this morning? There's a split in the Top Dog between its physical body and mental body.
3. Does the ugly, heavy, slow dog represent my weight problem? Maybe the big dog represents what happens to the little, playful me when I've given up on my diet and exercise program.

In dreams my courage increased to the extent that, when a very large dog closes his jaw on my wrist. I say, "That's taking playfulness too far, and command him: Down! " (Sep 3, 1976).

Another issue at that time was my *pro bono* editing of an anthology of poems for the Women's Poetry Workshop. When I presented the first draft with editorial marks and, in one case, a request to delete four lines of a poem, there was begrudging compliance by several persons and outright antagonism by one, who demanded a showdown. The tension persisted for months, and dreams featuring animals replayed my feelings, as in the following.

Dec 10, 1976
Tiny Lapdog Tangled in a Chain

> A tiny lap dog, maybe a Chihuahua, is not getting the
> attention it needs. It gets tangled in a chain, almost choking
> until someone rescues it. Even unchained, it yips and
> squeaks for attention. I'm supposed to walk the dogs, this
> one and a dachshund that's turned into a Great Dane. I
> feel put-upon, assigned to walk the dogs. But I get ready
> anyway. Everywhere I go, there are piles of dog shit. One
> pile is the size and shape of the dachshund, as if it had
> eliminated–in a pattern of its body–everything but its head!

FEELINGS:
Distress, futility, betrayal.

REFLECTION:
For the first time in dreams, I recognize others' problems as not being caused by me.

I was not free of resentment, though. When, two years later, a manuscript of mine was rejected, my Underdog developed worse characteristics:

Jul 11, 1978
Emaciated, Muzzled Dog

> The dog bends over backward, and I see its ribs. It's all bones, not much fur, and I pity it, truly. When I take it outdoors to get some food, I don't get the leash clamped onto the collar. No, the collar and the muzzle slip off its skinny neck. Immediately, the dog turns on me and lunges for my left breast.

REFLECTION:
This pictures my dismay when I realized that *Take Fire* [a collection of poems responsive to the Wife of Bath] has been rejected nine times, not four or five times, as I'd thought.

With only rare exceptions, birds in dreams have brought me solace. Here is an example:

Dec 4, 1976
Bird in the Sanctuary

> A small black-and-white bird is here, learning to fly. Very hesitant, yet enjoying itself. Each movement brings more pleasure to it, and to a little boy watching, and to me watching them both. Someone says, "So it's returned!" I point out that it's obviously a baby bird. "No, it was here before, playing with the boy. See how they love one another."

FEELINGS:
The bird stirs in me (oh, now I sound like G.M. Hopkins) feelings of playfulness, as when I saw water ouzels dipping repeatedly in a mountain stream.

REFLECTIONS:
The boy and the bird resonate with apocryphal stories about Jesus, and the statement, "See how they love one another," resonates with the New Testament. Yet, even if a bird presents itself as a spiritual messenger, it may not be free from harm:

Mar 17, 1980
PT Bird Is Threatened

> His cage is knocked over, the tray falls out, so do the dowels, and he has no place to perch. Now he's suffocating because someone has placed insulation all around him. I rush to rescue him—stiff and brown—and he does survive. I'm glad that he warms to my touch. Now he fluffs up his feathers, his own down jacket!

FEELINGS:
Threatened, suffocating; resourceful, glad.

REFLECTIONS:
1. PT is Monica's canary, in my care for awhile. I value him most for his astounding versatility in singing. Do I feel that my ability to sing is threatened?
2. PT has come to represent home to me, the way I have for years represented home to Ed. Here the canary is—alive and glad to be alive—beautiful and undemanding.
3. Even if I do feel caged or suffocating when at home, the dream shows the removal of the cage as threatening. If I were to leave home, where would I perch?

Next, what began as real turned surreal, when "our gerbils are playing with a toy that's like a catnip mouse. Now it's more like a live praying mantis, and the gerbils are tearing it apart. Now it's a big cat menacing the gerbils. A cat-and-mouse game, but how does it reflect on my life?" (Feb 1, 1978).

That scene is one example of a great many in which animals transformed from one size to another or one species to another. In a subsequent dream, "A kitten turns into a cat, a large dog into a wolf, and one wolf into two that I'm fighting off" (May 21, 1978).

Soon, when a bear meanders through my house and goes to my basement [Subconscious] "I ponder whether the message concerns something I have to bear? or the bare facts? or baring my soul?" (Jun 10, 1978).

Dream animals have portrayed several of my daytime challenges. For example, "Looking out a plate-glass window, I see huge animals, black-and-white, galloping. They aren't horses, or gigantic skunks either. Oh, panda bears!" (Jun 6, 1980). I ask myself, Who is pandering to whom?

Similarly, "Looking out a window, I see a flicker? a partridge? a pheasant? what? A cheetah! (Nov 10, 1980). I ask myself, Does my feeling cheated of PITS residencies account for the case of hives, their itching, my scratching?

Happily, in a spiritual encounter, "I'm surrounded by birdsong. Is it a nightingale? or a skylark? that I hear in daylight" (Feb 23, 1981).

When another dream featured three birds—a mother bird, a baby oriole, and "a tiny bird that's mostly flowing lines and colors," I understood them to represent the Holy Spirit (Dec 17, 1981).

Not surprisingly, when I was applying for fellowships, Competition dogged me again, in triplicate! I was "accosted by three terriers that yap fiercely. What surprises as much as hurts me is, they not only bark but also bite—deeply, into my ankles" (Jan 17, 1983).

Dream Animals in the Second Decade: 1985-1994

I was greeted in the new year by "20 miniature parrots, green, about two inches high. They are able to fly in all directions, like hummingbirds" (Jan 6, 1985). Next to visit was "a baby eagle, an eaglet. Its feathers are divided and wrapped, the effect similar to a groomed poodle or a horse whose tail has been wrapped. The same material has been pleated around its head and looks like a baby bonnet or else the headdress of a nun in the Middle Ages" (Jan 16, 1985).

In the second decade of writing dream notes, I was familiar with many dream animals and their messages, to the extent of my greeting some offhandedly, "Oh, you again." But there was one breath-taking dream, "from which I wakened with my upper torso heaving and my breath wheezing":

Jun 11, 1985
Three Snakes Entwine and Bite Me

> I see three snakes—a black, a bright red, and a bright green—about three inches in diameter and four or five feet long. They are near the foundation of a school, near the kitchen. I avoid them successfully, though terrified, and get into the school kitchen where I think I'll be safe. I sit on a chair and draw my legs up off the floor and talk to the cook who's in an alcove. How can she be sure a snake won't get in and wrap itself around her leg or arm?
>
> Suddenly the black one is around my left arm and has both fangs in me. I squeeze the necks of the other two, and wonder how long before paralysis from the venom will force me to release them, and they'll eventually strangle me.
>
> I shout for help. A youngster about six years old comes in, and I'm afraid will also get bit. No sound [of warning] comes from my lips.

FEELINGS:
Terrified, attacked, struggling, unsuccessful.

REFLECTIONS:
1. I've never dreamed of snakes before. I was so scared that I got up and turned on lights to be sure there were no snakes in this basement apartment.
2. I haven't got the message, not even with three snakes calling for my attention.
3. The three = simultaneity of issues, not a cause-and-effect relationship. Possibly related to the three books I've just finished editing? and the politics involved in getting them published?
4. I thought about the caduceus and physicians' oath "to do no harm." Was surprised to find that the caduceus is the staff of the god Hermes, who escorts souls to the underworld in death. Not the staff of the healer Aesculapius. Anyway it has two snakes entwined, not three.

5. When I checked Aesculapius, I found an icon of him with one serpent entwined on his right arm, also a reference to his sending to the people of Italy his healing powers in the form of a great serpent.
6. I'd like to think of this as an initiation into hands-on healing, but it seemed too fierce.

Around my 53rd birthday there were notes about animals transforming. In one title, I used an exclamation point, as if I had never before seen this process occurring in dreams (an indication of how fleeting the memories of dreams can be).

Jul 6, 1985
Animals Transforming!

> A huge black squirrel opens its jaws as if to smile, and out of its mouth bounds a black bear. After a few steps, the bear opens its jaws, and out leaps a wolf. The fourth black animal is a panther. As each is left behind, there's an empty fur pelt, like a bearskin rug. The animating spirit/life force continues in each succeeding creature.
> Now I see a paper-wing moth, very large, its wingspan about four feet. The moth looks as delicate as a paper doily. I touch it and find it's very strong, like parchment. More remarkable is that it changes shapes! From stylized shapes like origami to delicate sculptures, very graceful. Now a unicorn, now a heron, now a prancing white steed. Someone is trying to keep it in captivity. I feel it's wrong to pin down such a creature, like a butterfly on a cork-board.

FEELINGS:
pro for freedom, *con* for captivity.

REFLECTIONS:
1. Here the animals open their jaws to smile, not to snarl or otherwise threaten me.
2. All this evolving suggests reincarnation.
3. I'm reminded of a conversation with son EJ a few days ago. He declared, "Plants are to provide oxygen, and animals (including humans) are to provide carbon for the world's eco-system." He

couldn't even consider reincarnation; I couldn't, either, when I was 30 years young.

Here I include a poem–generated in dreams in the 1980s–to honor the energy inherent in dream animals.

The Animal that Leaps in Me

when married–a cottontail rabbit
fertile and reproductive,
hopping when Peter says hop,
a soft bundle panicked at twilight
in the middle of a thoroughfare.

when separated–a kangaroo,
pouch empty, light and springy,
able to leap over barbs,
recognizing what freedom's about:
thousands of acres unfenced.

when divorced–a gazelle
altering her course in mid-flight,
eager as lightning that splits the horizon,
luminous as a rainbow that arcs
over a stream of flamingos.

While Bear has shown many aspects, here is a dramatically different feeling response to it:

Mar 17, 1986
Almost Domesticated Bear Has Left My Cabin

> I try to find it before neighbors are alarmed. I see
> it standing full-length and reaching high, as if to
> touch the moon. Now it's yawning and stretching,
> after a busy day and night of adventuring.
>
> Now it's gone into the woods. Someone has alerted
> the sheriff, and wardens are stalking the bear, carrying
> big guns. When they sight it, I plead for its life. But

> they kill it. Why didn't they let me take it to a zoo?
> Why didn't they pacify it with a dart of medicine?
>
> I'm left with the bearskin. I make it into a coat–not a fashionable coat but something a shaman might wear, emblematic of the bear's great spirit and strength.

FEELINGS:

Affection, respect; anxiety over what the bear might do to strangers; anger at the guns and at the one-track mind some people exhibit.

REFLECTIONS:

I feel sure this bear is related to the mythic creature that presented itself in a dream a month or so ago, even though that was huge and prehistoric and this bear is contemporary and almost domesticated.

A few months after the "almost domesticated bear," when family members had returned to their various States after attending their dad's wedding to Melodee, I was still emotionally unsettled. "Some wild animals are crawling the walls, throwing vases and books and anything not bolted down" (Aug 26, 1986).

And a few weeks later, when I was applying for financing of a car, there were images of "gorillas and men in gorilla suits, also a nasty black camel, at a car dealer's lot" (Sep 2, 1986).

When I calmed down, I was granted a vision of "hundreds of butterflies darting toward my windows. They come in clouds: pink-and-blue, blue-and-yellow, yellow-and pale green. All pastels and a shimmering effect. These glorious creatures seem angelic" (Sep 8, 1986).

Early in 1990, which developed as a fateful year for me, I was awed and soothed by a series of birds:

Jan 19, 1990
Extraordinary, Brilliant, Delicate Birds

> The scene is rustic, like a retreat center in a secluded area. There are woods about 50 yards away. I move out onto the deck and look below. I see a brilliant creature, like a dragonfly except larger, mostly blue but iridescent when its wings move. I wonder, a hummingbird? But I never know because it transforms into another brilliant blue bird. This is exotic.

> [It reminds me of feathered ornaments, circa 1925, that only Mother was allowed to place on the Christmas tree.]
>
> This live bird is about 6 inches tall. There are several here now, miniature kingfishers? One does look kingly, its crown more noticeable than the others'.
>
> Without turning away from this sight, I say to a man and woman behind me, "If you want to see some gorgeous birds, come here!" By the time they get here, the brilliant blue birds have gone. There's now a gathering of finches—yellow, green, purple, rose, and other colors.
>
> I say, "Such a variety!" But that's not right, it would be more accurate to say, "Such a rarity!" I feel warm and connected to the sky, the earth, and humans.

FEELINGS:
Awe, delight; curiosity, connectedness; serenity.

REFLECTIONS:
1. What might a painter do with this?! "Gorgeous" is an understatement.
2. On the physical level, the elongated form of the first bird and the long legs of the kingfishers resonate with exercises I'm doing daily, stretching my right leg to match the left.
3. On the spiritual level, this is a reminder that my everyday activities can be imbued with lightness and color.

Two weeks later was the car crash that changed my life. Three weeks after the crash, when Chas came from Cleveland to keep watch over me, he said that I talked a lot during my sleep, and "carried on two parts of a dialogue for quite awhile." That was probably the night when I had the following dream:

Mar 18, 1990
Images of Pain

> There are a half-dozen or more insects, each with 8 legs and a snout that has poison. Any time the snout touches my skin or chest, it injects poison and I have immediate pain. I lie very still, hoping the insects will leave me and the pain will subside.

They scatter and become big like rats. They are fewer in number and don't get on my body. Yet I still feel threatened by them in my vicinity.

Now it's one big dog, the kind of ugly attack dog that lives across the street [a Doberman Pinscher]. It snarls and snatches at my right leg and thigh. It doesn't draw blood but does set my muscles into spasms. I fear for my life.

REFLECTION:
With family in the house, I did not process these notes. I knew that the images had come from physiological sources, and wondered to what extent some of the recent nightmares also referred to present pain more than to past experiences of pain—when I'd felt invaded or attacked by injections, invasive tests, and wrong diagnoses.

The following springtime brought some relief, when there appeared "a canary that looks healthier and more colorful than I've seen in years" (Apr 18, 1995); when "a two-year-old girl, dressed in a yellow canary costume, plays with the muppet Big Bird (Apr 24, 1995); and when "brilliant black-and-fuchsia birds build a nest in the topmost branches of a tree" (Apr 24, 1995).

Yet medical issues still weighed heavily on me, and a dream illustrated the fact. "A tiger leaps over me, then plops down beside me and begins licking my neck. The weight against my ribs almost suffocates me. I hear voices and I cry, 'Call 911! Call the zoo!' Someone says, 'We are the zoo. These are our animals'" (May 2, 1995). This was a very long dream and had lengthy notes processing it, so I include here only one note: "The zoo keepers feel like medical personnel or pharmaceutical researchers watching the struggle to see what will develop. They have no regard for pain or for side effects, but insist that the drug is 'declawed' [safe] and that it's only my fear that causes problems."

A year later, when medical issues were still not resolved, I faced a dream attacker again:

Dec 28, 1995
Ferocious Tiger

> A son (8 or 10 years old) has found a small tiger. He builds a wooden cage for it and takes it to a metropolitan park. I am relieved.
> Now a huge, ferocious tiger flings itself at me, full-body, frontal, its paws on my shoulders. I call, "Help! Help, it's so heavy!" Now it changes into a panther–eyes glaring, claws digging into my chest and my legs. I'm still standing upright, though unbalanced.

FEELINGS:
From fear to relief; pride in my son for being so resourceful; caught unaware; burdened, terrified.

REFLECTIONS:
1. When I made the collage of totem animals two years ago, I put an upright tiger at the top. I thought I'd understood it way back then. Why am I still so afraid of using my power?
2. Here my young Male aspect is not a crippled or maimed figure. Here he's unafraid, whole, helpful, resourceful.
3. I've been reading *The Edge Of Tomorrow* by Alan Vaughan, in which he carries the motif of a "dream tiger" through two chapters. He refers to it in a way similar to Patricia Garfield's invoking "dream power." Vaughan's thesis is that we scan the future, especially in dreams, and he concludes that the dream tiger has the function of premonition. "He wakes us so that we can sound the alarm or flee the approaching menace."
4. I accept Vaughan's statement that "the dream tiger can be trained but never tamed." That still leaves me with his challenge to "ask the dream tiger for dreams of promise instead of warning."

Dream Animals in the Third Decade: 1996–2005

There were only two animal dreams in 1996, each of which indicated a turn for the better. In the first dream, "Underdog No More," there was "a little yipping coming from my basement, and I see a darling puppy–black with tight, curly hair. It must be a pure breed, it's that beautiful and perfect. And it's able to communicate with me!" (Jun 8, 1996). In the morning were these inferences: "Maybe this is a comment on my doggedness relative to having my needs met. I can yip lightly to convey needs, relying on the affection of care-givers and the support of my High Self."

In "Gunning for Bear," the scene was a hunting lodge. "I am here for a weekend with several young men. They decide about the bear-hunting—who will take guns and who will carry guitars to soothe the savage beast" (Dec 22, 1996).

One springtime, on consecutive nights, there were dreams of birds, each dream conveying different feeling. In the first, "A canary, drab and bedraggled, is making a nest inside its cage, using tangled yarn that may be a wig from a doll. The bird has a pained expression—not just forlorn but almost desperate. Maybe it's making a burial shroud, not a nest?" (May 19, 1998). In the second, I found "numerous bright blue feathers, almost iridescent. Can they be fake, like the decorative ones used in Easter baskets? I still hope the gorgeous feathers are real—a good omen in my life!" (May 20, 1998).

A year later, a most unusual dog appeared, as if in a children's storybook. "A Chihuahua pulls a large carriage for 10 passengers. In the carriage are a medium-sized dog, a very large dog, and people with lap robes all a-jumble" (May 17, 1999).

A year after that, when Bear appeared again, I had mixed emotions:

Apr 20, 2000
Asking a Vet to End the Misery

> A large brown bear is on the floor, writhing in pain. I say, "We need a veterinarian to end its misery." Son Joe agrees. I visualize, but don't actually witness, that the vet will give one or two lethal injections. I wonder if the bear will claw the vet? No, it's been declawed.
>
> The bear has been around since I was about 10 years old. That's 57 years! And I wonder if that's a full life for a bear. I'm not grieving. Rather, I wish to console

> the bear, reminding it of its long life. I want to say something like, "A long sleep, the best hibernation."

REFLECTIONS FOUR DAYS LATER:
1. I can't find the process notes on this dream!
2. The bear is not a self-image as much as an indication of something I've been bearing since age ten: excess responsibility.
3. The vet is a veteran, someone with considerable life experience; therefore, myself at my present age. Here I am compassionate.

Five months later, another dream with animals also addressed the need for rest and for transformation. Here is an excerpt:

Sep 8, 2000
About-Face on Prospect

> I start walking southward, hoping to find a secluded spot to sleep and then waken in the right city. My disappearance won't scare anyone, and I don't even think about how startling my reappearance might be.
>
> Now animals are involved. A huge dog, larger than a Great Dane, comes directly to me. We roll around on the floor, and I'm so glad he knows me.
>
> The people here, some of them family, also know me, but they take me for granted. Well, this may make my disappearance easier, produce less fuss when I die. I don't even have to say goodbye. I'm grateful that this great dog is to be part of my transition.

REFLECTIONS:
1. This dream shows, on both the Emotional Level and the Spiritual Level, my orientation toward the afterlife.
2. I've done an about-face on volunteering at Hospice, for two reasons. First, the director said that that I could do Reiki there, but then changed her mind. Second, I'm impatient with families who want "heroic measures" taken, which just prolongs the agony.

Birds became instrumental in giving solace not only to me but also to the family. In the following dream they referred to my ex-husband's imminent death:

May 9, 2003
Canaries as a Gift, also a Responsibility

> I hear marvelous birdsongs and go out to see what and where. There's movement in branches, but I can't guess how many songbirds. Oh, canaries!
> Now I'm indoors, looking at a birdcage–not antique but not new, either–with two canaries in it. They are different colors, one male and one female, and both are singers. Glorious!
> The bars of the cage are very wide, and the birds can get out easily, but a cat or other animal can't get in. One bird comes out into the room, and now I see Ed watching me for signs of delight. I'm puzzled because I've promised not to have a pet–too much responsibility.

REFLECTIONS:
1. I once said in a therapy session that I was like a canary to my husband, a stay-at-home in a decorative cage, always ready to give solace through my beauty. And I could be untended for a week at a time, if at night he just put a cover over me. I was kept.
2. I wonder if I met Ed on the dream plane last night? Possibly this dream is his final gift to me.
3. Ed and Melodee have responsibly made preparations for his death, including beneficiary checks for each of the children.

Subsequently, on the main level of my house [my Consciousness], animals raised a question about my being a survivor:

Dec 13, 2005
Who Cares about Freed Animals?

> Two medium-size tigers are a golden yellow, not even tinged with orange. And there's one large brown bear, two armadillos, and another tall, fuzzy creature with a stupid? or malicious? look on its face.
> Zoo-keepers arrive in several vehicles that look like paddy-wagons. Now one keeper holds one of the tigers, and I say, "Isn't she beautiful!" He says, "No," and shows me deep gashes on her face. "I don't know

> if we can even save her." I'm shocked, but of course the animals would fight in such a crowded space.
>
> Now I see the bear laid out on a gurney, and I wonder what has happened to her? What will become of her?

REFLECTIONS:
1. Two months have passed since my ex-husband's death. The golden-yellow tigers represent my original concept of marriage: bright, sunny, compatible, with no fierce conflicts. Well, the marriage wasn't saved, neither my concept nor his, so why this nightmare now?
2. The armadillos = the armoring of both my husband and myself.
3. The creature with the stupid or malicious look on its face = my Inner Critic.
4. Of course these traits would fight in my crowded Unconscious. Why does that shock me now?
5. That both the tigress and the female bear are injured suggests that I have not yet appreciated how valiant and courageous I was in my roles of wife and mother.

Dream Animals in the Fourth Decade: 2006-2015

Here is the final entry portraying dream animals. I regarded it as a death-processing dream:

Jun 27, 2010
Caring for a Black Dog and Her Four Puppies

> I'm in a long line of people in some kind of detention center, to be herded somewhere. We have no luggage, no tickets, no choice in the matter.
>
> A black dog comes to me. It's very restless. I ask a Boy Scout to check its sex. He announces, "She has four pups." I say, "No wonder she's so restless!" She's been curling around my feet, then turning abruptly and pacing. No whining though.
>
> I take the dog to a private corner, where walls make a small cave. Other women in the line pass me two small bottles: one looks like it holds birdseed, the other some

baking seed. I suppose the women mean this as nourishment for the mother dog. One of the guards is clearing away some dishes, even though we've been given no food. I ask him for an ashtray that can hold enough water for the dog. He allows me to get water from an outdoor spigot.

The four puppies come when our backs are turned. I talk to them and give each of them a name based on their dominant features. "You're Porcupine, you're Prickly, you're Roly-Poly." The fourth is so scrawny and withdrawn that I say, "And you're Pathetic." This isn't condemnation but sympathy.

FEELINGS:
Regimented, deprived; concerned about the dogs' welfare; restlessness that gives way to peacefulness; sympathetic; playfulness with the puppies.

REFLECTIONS:
1. The "long line in some kind of detention center" suggests how weary I am of this rehabilitation process. Yet, like the mother dog, I'm not a whiner.
2. The names of all four pups are self-descriptors. I relate most strongly to "Pathetic." That's how I've been viewing myself since a physical flare-up has obliterated the progress of recent weeks.
3. The four puppies represent responsibilities. So I'm glad there are four Helpers willing to support the mother dog: Boy Scout, guard, and two women.
4. The "no choice" is simply that I can't choose when, where, or how my death will occur. That I'm restless is a fact, though I'm not "turning abruptly and pacing." Not quite.
5. If I change my attitude from "herded" to shepherded and from "guard" to guardian, there's a feeling of acceptance that outshines my aversion to added responsibilities.

– Twelve –

My Love of Flying

In one of my early flying dreams there was an image and a sensation that I have never forgotten. In a long, involved sequence of travel, "I fly over India. I laugh to myself and exclaim *In-ja!* It looks just like the globe in geography class—water deep blue, land green, people poor, temperature hot and humid" (Feb 9, 1976). I know, as I transcribe these notes 40 years later, that the descriptors were derivative and childlike, but my feelings were those of an adult, awed and grateful for glimpses of our world from a higher perspective.

Wishful thinking is not my cue for flying; rather, recent daytime activities are the most likely prompts. In one period when in waking life I felt like a failure, then got help, and then could see my way clearly, a flying dream developed this way:

Apr 10, 1979
Three Stages of Flying

> One: I'm trying to fly, being jeered at. I get to the top of furniture for take-offs but always fall. There aren't any thuds or crashes, only the failure to fly. There's a feeling of power when my shoulders touch the ceiling. And false elation when I'm doing a side-stroke until I realize I'm on the floor.
>
> Two: [In a dream within a dream] I see a girl flying. She looks back at her alter ego [me] and is puzzled that I can't fly. We both reach out, in hopes of helping and being helped.
>
> Three: I see a sky with gold stars, individually and in clusters, and a gold Milky Way. I think or say, "That's the way it is—flying is heavenly!"

To convey the uplift and expansiveness I feel in flying dreams, I offer this exclamation from Willa Cather:

> The landscape one longed for when one was far away,
> the thing all about one, the world one actually lived in,
> was the sky, the sky!

Because my flying dreams are so extensive, I have collated them in six categories.

Modes of Flying

The mode of flying that I have most often heard told by other dreamers begins with a falling sensation. My experiences began that way, too, as in this instance: "I'm falling and realize, This is a dream and I want to go places from here. I tumble, arrange for a soft spot to land on, decide I don't have to land, and take off. I fly backward until I get low enough to touch a building and can push off with my feet and get sailing again. No noise, no pollution, no people, no traffic, no busyness, no distractions even from planes or birds" (Jun 3, 1975).

As I developed self-confidence in waking life and dream life, I experimented with many modes of flying. The abbreviated list below conveys both my pleasure in flying and my delight in the humor that bubbles up from the Unconscious:

- I'm suspended on top of a snowball made from freshly fallen snow.
- I take off from a trapeze, and there is a rigger below to catch me.
- I tilt back, without a seat, inhale deeply, prolong the pleasure, and liftoff.
- Floating on a staircase leads to flying.
- Holding onto a rope or cord, learning glider-pilot techniques.
- Springing up with a basketball, touching the balcony, now the ceiling!
- Flying straight up, like a hummingbird or a helicopter.
- Arching one shoulder, I lift myself in a lovely, curving movement.
- Swinging, then Flying from a Maypole.

Vehicles for Flying

My flying vehicles are often colorful and/or strangely shaped, as in this dream: "A huge silver sphere comes overhead. Everyone thinks it's an advertising campaign or a celebration. The sphere bursts like a balloon. People rush to grab a piece, which is purple and as soft as jersey material. More spheres come, now bearing aliens. Every conceivable vehicle comes from the sky–derby racers, tricycles, bicycles, more".

Here are a few more:

- A space ship, gold and silver, and 39 helium balloons drawn to it.
- A dirigible or a luxury hotel that's suspended.
- A balloon, though it's more like a blimp. Not the Goodyear blimp, though.
- A government test-vehicle shaped like an ice-cream cone.

When sorting my flying dreams, I placed them in four heaps labeled according to the goal or destination reached: for adventure, for escape, to orgasmic heights, to spiritual realms.

Flying for Adventure

Jan 27, 1986
Testing Vehicles for NASA
>First: In a small plane, very maneuverable.
>I get close to a skyscraper and the navigator
>estimates, "We're at about the 70th floor now."
>   Second: I'm wondering about the training of a
>pilot. S/he must be concerned with the panel in front
>of him/her, not with the immensity of the sky or the
>hugeness of the ship, or the number of passengers,
>or even the responsibility for so many lives.
>   Third: I'm in a new kind of space vehicle and
>I've succeeded with several experiments or flights. I

tell a young woman, "That's why the government is allowing me on the next space exploration–because I've discovered some scientific principles helpful to them."

I learn from hearsay that there's trouble for me in the space program's school because, allegedly, I've "disrupted the camaraderie, released sexual feelings, and brought forth many deeply repressed feelings in other astronauts."

REFLECTION:
Unrelated to the dream itself, except for the date, is the fact that one day later, Jan 28, 1986, the space shuttle exploded, about 1.5 minutes off the ground. There are seven dead, including the woman teacher from Akron, Ohio. May they rest in peace.

I concede that flying is not always fun and games. Here is a serious example:

Dec 9, 1979
Rocketing Backward

Lying on my back, I'm propelled smoothly enough–not on my own power, but not against my will. I go backward, fast as a rocket, into space. Oh, not hurtling into infinite space but into infinite distance, which is different. The overpowering sensation is speed. I'm being pushed? pulled? to my limit, and weighted down by the force of gravity.

The feeling is that of departing, not of arriving.

My chest is tight, my neck, my head. I wonder how much longer I can breathe. Am I going through a time warp? There's a painful flattening out. I'm drawing in, toward a center perhaps? or imploding like the walls of buildings in a tornado?

All this time I'm aware that if I move very much, I'll put everything out of whack–my trajectory, my dream, and perhaps my body.

REFLECTIONS:
1. I would like to believe that the sense of imploding is an expression of energy directed inward. Also that compression in this situation is as good a modality as expansion is in other situations.

2. My working with dreams and dream notes is likely the source of this time-warp feeling. It may not matter whether I go backward in memory or forward in imagining, as long as the process helps me integrate feelings and ideas.

In dream flying there is often ambivalence of feelings. Consider the following, with its "mixed calls of encouragement and derision" concerning my ability to fly:

Nov 19, 1993
Attempting to Fly a Glider

> Multi-talented Laurel is adept at flying, has quite a reputation, and I trust her when she says I can, too. But she doesn't explain the controls. I don't see a control panel–this must be a glider! It doesn't take off from a high place, either, so I have to propel it up from the ground. I do this several times but no higher than one story.
> Now it's dusk, after a party where all the guests have had their fill of food and drink–except me because I have this tremendous desire to fly under my own power and can't afford to feel queasy. I become acutely aware of guests watching and of the little height I attain. Also I fear wires and tree branches where I might get entangled.
> Someone laughingly says, "Margaret has her own way of flying." Another adds, "Oh yes, haven't you ever seen her?" Some look puzzled, some seem caring, and I'm so on the defensive for not having succeeded with the glider that I admit, "Mine is a sort of levitation, but I don't get very high off the ground." I don't know how to explain that my levitation involves spiritual and sexual uplift for me, and that it's not for anyone else.
> I hear mixed calls of encouragement and derision. Now I feel I'm just a spectacle, something for the evening's entertainment, and I couldn't levitate now even if I wanted to.

FEELINGS:
Desiring; cheated in not having controls; frustrated, disillusioned; very disappointed.

REFLECTIONS:
1. Historically, a laurel crown is given to poets. So I infer that this dream refers to my career. I do not "rest on my laurels," and I do make repeated efforts to propel my work into publication. Yet what little height/success I attain!
2. The entanglements probably refer to the Poets-in-the-Schools Program.
3. I shared this dream with Laurel Richardson (a sociologist with academic books and popular books to her credit). She said, "We've discussed this before—the idea of trust and of gliding without known controls." Then she added, "If guests had challenged me, I'd have been feisty. I'd have shown them a thing or two!" I can't imagine myself as feisty.

In retrospect I find it notable that within 10 years I proceeded from the role of a passenger to that of pilot; from commanding a space craft (Aug 23, 1986) to flying in my own body, without any vehicle. And, continuing to explore, "I land in other realms: China (chi), Japan (ki), and here in my own home, doing Reiki. This three-point landing provides grounding and a solid, triangular base for my healing work" (Nov 8, 1992).

Flying to Escape

In the earliest examples of my flying to escape, two included my worst fears:

Aug 10, 1976
Escaping as a Fugitive

> Escaping, I'm stopped by a block of some clear substance—not ice, maybe Lucite. I'm to unite with a man who is also a fugitive. We are being sought for complicity in a murder or a serious robbery.
>
> Two persons beckon from beyond the barrier. I go through it and now I'm in suspension. Now on my back floating a great way at immense speed, and time stands still. I'm upside down and backwards, like fainting or going under anesthesia.

Even though the following story has terrifying components, the feelings I wrote were in contrast to them: "Great reassurance. No matter how many vectors are aimed at me, how much needling or slow torture, I am saved from ultimate Evil." This is an example of the importance of including on the dream tablet the feelings of each dream.

Jul 4, 1987
Escaping from Evil

> A woman dressed in white agrees to show me directions. Immediately we're surrounded by young thugs. She and I stick together, walking as if we're confident, but she's wearing rather high heels, so we can't move quickly.
>
> Now the thugs disperse in all directions. They see a man who's powerful, maybe demonic, coming straight toward us. This man not only has power, he's extremely intelligent—he knows higher math and can send missiles toward us from many angles [the way a billiard player banks shots and does amazing maneuvers].
>
> I don't know what the missiles are—poisoned needles? insects? They pierce and cause great pain and some loss of blood, but not death. Maybe he wants a lingering, painful death and for us to plead with him. I tell the woman, "Take off your shoes and run. I'll play interference."
>
> What I do is relax and pray to the Most Holy One: "Into your hands I commend my spirit." Now I am drawn at an accelerating speed—on my back, feet first—toward the evil man, then above his head. There's a whoosh, and I waken.

Flying to Orgasmic Heights

Jun 29, 1978
Flying into a New Dimension

> I'm reaching orgasm without intercourse . . . without masturbation . . . I'm flying, but more than that, almost exploding into a new dimension. It's not just another burst

into another planetary system, but more like emerging from the birth canal into a whole new dimension of living.

REFLECTIONS:
1. I'm remembering professor Lowanne Jones' remarks as we walked through a red-carpeted tunnel at the New York airport–about the birth canal, rites of passage, and our emerging at the other end as new women. I hope this bursting dream is prophetic of the future that I envision.
2. I'm surprised at the timing of this dream, a full week after my return from Europe. Why not then and there?
3. The release of tensions that have been building for months may have been accomplished in this wonderful dream.

INFERENCE:
I don't need to fear a letdown after intensive work on a manuscript, or after a PITS residency, or travel, or whatever. The letdown can be as pleasurable as it is necessary.

Here are two more examples of orgasm reached during a flying dream:

Mar 4, 1985
Suspended Animation

> I'm hovering above the bed, suspended, and my spirit is aware of this. There's light, as if sunlight is breaking through clouds. Beams or rays like that, golden. I'm uplifted, not by willpower but desire. This feels like sexual orgasm, certainly a peak, and I'm not frustrated, even though I realize it's just a beginning.

May 14, 1998
Flying Associated with Sex–Three Times

> First: It's scary because I don't know who is in bed with me or how he got into the house.
> Second: There are many hands and feet fluttering over and on me. Like Cupid and other cherubs–from infants to teens to one adult man.
> Third: There is JOY, ebullience, a swooping as if on a roller-coaster, and we're together when this

occurs, in brightness. Again the man is anonymous, yet this time I give and receive total acceptance.

Flying to Spiritual Realms

Here is an example that includes family relationships during a spiritual experience:

Aug 8, 1975
Believers Fly

> An elaborate, colorful, marvelous dream that could only be a dream unless it's a mystical state.
> I realize that only believers such as Daddy and Stevie [my youngest child] are experiencing part of what I am. I'm flying in grayness near the ocean. I can't tell if those are cliffs? or sand dunes? Are there drop-offs? In the haze I think, This is what people mean by a curtain of fog. It hangs in gentle draping and moves like sheer curtains in a breeze. Sunrise comes gradually and gloriously–an ecstacy for anyone who witnesses it.
> I do a gradual and complete circling off the warm, golden sand, and then return. It would be nice to do this again, but I'm more desirous of going above the water. Now I float in air, and now I roll back the water–tuck the land over the water like the edge of pie dough around a pie plate. I descend to the ground, satisfied and safe.
> Now I see images of persons I don't know but am sure they are friendly. Daddy asks for corroboration, "Are they real?" I say, "Yes," even as I see them vanishing or dissolving. Now I see another sprite of white light, like a cherub. It comes behind Stevie and hugs him. They are playful, the sprite riding Stephen's shoulders instead of the reverse!

In another variant of flying to spiritual realms, I am "flying on my own, yet under Divine Providence, who liberates me by degrees. I'm flying face-forward, very far and fast, so fast there are no landmarks. I fly through galaxies, not much concerned with heavenly bodies in my lateral vision. I think, Infinity is all right, I'll never be afraid of that concept again. But oh, how cold stellar space is! I wonder, Am I heading for death? or from death toward eternal life?" (May 1, 1976).

At the end of 1976, in a single night, I had a phenomenal flying dream beyond my understanding at the time. I chose to honor it by transposing it into a poem. It is only now in the 21st century, while sorting through stacks of flying dreams, that I appreciate how this early dream provided a visual repertoire of images for many subsequent dreams.

Learning to Fly

I hang-glide over rough terrain
    seemingly alone. Yet somewhere
    bettors, a cheering crowd

Next I sweep through spun-silk air
    like a trapeze artist in spotlights
    Below: drum rolls, fanfare

Perfecting loops in my bio-plane
    open to the wind, yet in command

I sky-write
    interlace rose-window clouds
    design my own mandala

    In orgasmic lift and climb
I burst through gravity and time
    In the ultimate spiral, breathless, electrified

I travel out of body
    beyond imagining

I reckon
    that black is not extinguished light
    but absolute brightness beckoning

Comparable to that outer-space journey is one to inner space:

Feb 28, 1979
Inner-Space Journey

> I'm in an auditorium about four stories high [like the Civic Auditorium, where circuses performed], above the crowd on the ground floor. I fly for a long while. when I think I can't endure the intensity anymore, I drop my head on my chest. Now the blood racing to my head counteracts my giddiness.
>
> Now I dive headfirst from this great height. Now I decelerate and touch the ground with the crown of my head gently, as if in greeting, and float up again. I'm not in a spotlight [as in many dreams] and this is not an outer-space journey.
>
> I'm flying in my inner space, yet not contained, not confined. Self-satisfying. I don't need ohs and ahs from other people.

REFLECTIONS:
1. My flying four stories up indicates flying in the realm of hope and possibilities.
2. The "touching of the ground gently" with my crown shows promise of my linking the Spiritual Level with physical grounding in my future. This I do hope for!
3. This dream may be a reiteration of the magnificence of the Brahms Requiem that we've been rehearsing. In my mind is the lullaby from it, "Rest thou softly / Softly rest."

After my near-death experience (NDE), flying dreams took on a new character. [See the section "Beyond All Boundaries."]

– Thirteen –

Opposites in Play

In its simplest form, a dream of opposites juxtaposes unlike persons, animals, or things for dramatic effect or for the sake of argument. The following example concerned a bird, who in my dreams invariably represented a high Being, but who in this instance caused emotional and physical pain!

Oct 3, 1978
Coexistence of Beauty and Pain

> In semi-darkness I'm outside and see blossoms on trees and unusual birds in trees. One bird looks like a Christmas-tree ornament. Each time I think I can identify a bird, it eludes me–it flies away, or blossoms obscure it, or the light fails.
> Another rare bird is an oversize hummingbird, like crystal. It's blue in the dusk, hovering in front of 1904 [a neighbor's house]. Someone wants to get a photograph but needs a flash attachment. He calls to me to keep an eye on the bird. I couldn't do otherwise, it is gorgeous.
> Now the bird and I are close, near the south side of the porch. I feel its long beak [stabbing] like a dagger–a hurt as well as a surprise. Yet we stay close, not exactly attached, even though I'm feeling pain.

REFLECTIONS:
1. Hearing PT Bird singing in the morning has left me crying. Such perfection! I'd like to think that he sings from joy, but how could any bird be ecstatic in a cage? He sings of being a canary and does to perfection what his nature allows.
2. I cry because this is a passing moment, even though he's been with us six months and I've tape-recorded his singing several times.
3. There is pain in beauty. I'm not convinced that there is beauty in pain.

An obvious dream of opposites occurs in what I call a Yay-Boo dream. An explanation is warranted here. One of the books that all my children recall was the story of a boy who learned to fly (Yay). One day his plane had engine trouble (Boo), so he had to use a parachute (Yay). When the parachute did not open (Boo), he landed in a haystack (Yay). The haystack had a pitchfork in it (Boo), and so forth. So, too, my dreams alternate between problems and possible solutions, or between one attitude and the possibility of another. This can happen in one night, as when "due to steepness of ascent up a hill, only disturbed persons are qualified to climb" was followed by "the steepness of the loft in a cathedral makes me decide to leave the Church" (May 16, 1978). Most often, though, alternation of views happens within the space of a few nights, as when "at Camp Coitus I have sex with several men consecutively" (Mar 6, 1976) but a week later, "a man is assigned to a woman for a love affair, and I am glad to be shuffled free from him" (Mar 13, 1976). Such Yay/Boo pairings remind me of Tevyev in *Fiddler On the Roof.* In the midst of daily tasks or in the middle of the night, I weigh in, "On the one hand . . . But on the other . . . "

A more attention-getting dream of opposites shows a friend acting or speaking in an uncharacteristic way. Such an occurrence makes me wonder if I have underrated or exaggerated certain qualities in that person or, worse, am in waking life projecting some of my Stuff on him or her. An example occurred in two scenes of the dream "Anti-Johns"(Oct 10, 1976) when my friend appeared as a teacher in the Clerihew School [a clerihew is an insult poem using a person's name satirically]. He was unjustly making an issue against me in a sarcastic and accusatory way. In the morning's Reflection, I recognized that John's image was replacing those of nuns who had reviled me–Sister Mary John in eighth grade and Sister Joan in twelfth grade–and that I should not let any critique of his concerning my writing upset me because it was well-intentioned.

On a deeper level, when a dream person's opposites are pronounced *throughout* a dream, I ask myself: To what person or issue am *I* in opposition in waking life? Conversely, when the entire contents of a dream, including feelings, are in opposition to my waking life, they may illustrate how congruent in thoughts, words, and actions I am presently when compared to previous years or previous lifetimes. An example of a dream of opposites occurred in two installments one night, about an hour and a half apart–the first with almost no positive feelings, the second with many:

Oct 3, 1983
I'm an Outcast from History

> In history class I don't even have a syllabus and don't know work is due. I think I can bluff my way this time by reading the [assigned] book tonight, making a report, and typing it neatly. Not like the few scribbled papers of persons who'd done the work on time. [But] A fountain pen leaks–globs–on my new autumn skirt and tweed coat as well as all over my books.
>
> On my way home [to the dorm], I accidentally drop my notebook and folders. They slide down the hill about 50 yards into a bowl-shaped area. Now I slide down on my seat, crying loudly, "My books! my books!" They aren't to be seen, seem to have been plowed under the soil and garden growth.
>
> At the bottom of this bowl-shaped area are some English cottages, and I'm afraid that gardeners or townspeople will come after me–like MacGregor after Peter Rabbit–with garden tools, fence boards, maybe even guns. Yet losing my notebook and folders and missing my assignments is more traumatic than the possibility of being punished or jailed for trespassing.
>
> My legs pained me before and completely betray me now. I sink into the earth, feeling like lead allover.

FEELINGS:
Ashamed, dispirited; sad, despairing; in pain, defeated; fearful, burdened.

REFLECTIONS:
1. "Dropping my notebook" resonates with the manuscript of *Opening Night*, which I've dropped and is as good as buried now.
2. The books go downhill like the Gingerbread Boy, as if of their own volition. They plow under growth and bury themselves, as if in opposition to my caring about them. Don't I care enough?

3. "An outcast from history" illustrates a sense of alienation presently that I can't account for. Considering that my papers and books have been sought and accepted by the OSU Library Special Collections, I am anything but an outcast.

Here is the dream of opposites that same night:

Oct 3, 1983
Winning a Woman Award

> The newspaper columnist never did say woman of What, and the captions on the front-page and second-page article just say Woman Award.
>
> I've been a finalist among five or six women, for several days or weeks. Now, on a busy Election Tuesday, when I've gone out early to vote, the journalist returns for a final interview. She talks to my husband and children but not to me as she brushes past, exiting when I enter.
>
> I'm wearing the original, classic Symphony Chorus gown and am concerned that the hem will be dirty from my walking to and from the polls.
>
> Now, looking in the morning paper, I see the announcement has already been made, the column typeset prior to the journalist's final visit! But the very first item is wrong—a fact and not just an inference or journalistic liberty. It begins, "Margaret Honton, twice married, is the winner of the Woman Award. Her previous husband was Edward Haunton [misspelled]." I can hardly read the rest. How can I keep this paper from Ed? Or has he already seen it? I have no intention of remarrying and I have no lover.
>
> The article describes me as "dramatic," tells how "with a turn of the head or by holding gold lamé fabric to her cheek, she becomes the role she is playing."

FEELINGS:
Uneasy and a little suspicious, but mostly surprised and pleased; competent and outstanding; appreciated and elegant.

REFLECTIONS:
1. Even within the dream, I wonder who chose me and on what basis.
2. "Haunton" suggests I'm haunted by my husband.
3. I would like to play a role that has so many positive feelings!

At its most complex, a dream featuring opposites may express a paradox in waking life or, as in the following, set up a paradigm that I had never before considered seriously:

May 7, 1982
Breaking through a Time Barrier

> I'm aware of flying just before a whoosh sensation. A stream of cool air forms around my head and shoulders as my speed increases immeasurably. It's a break-through, perhaps through a time barrier. Yet I haven't the sensation of outer space, it's more like the earth's stratosphere, and I see light, brilliant, as if coming through clouds. But there aren't clouds . . . or maybe? Either way, the light is important.
> Most extraordinary is, I'm carrying, or linked to, or intertwined with an ungainly body—a girl, almost skeletal.
> At the end of this flight, I present the child to a society. Now the skeletal girl begins to re-shape into a more Oriental build and visage and becomes a boy! [He is] A warm body, with nothing grotesque now. My immediate response is, "So this is reincarnation!"

FEELINGS:
The semi-lucid flying is glorious of itself, with no effort on my part, no attempts at control. I know I'm flying but make no experiments to test for lucidity or to heighten my personal power.

REFLECTION:
This morning I feel reassured about a personal relationship with Divine creative power, with an ordering principle that lets me believe that illness is "the problem of illness" and evil is "the problem of evil" and that both will be overcome, no matter how many lifetimes this may take.

REALIZATION:

When I took this to Dreamtalk, group members listed numerous opposites in this dream:
- flying fast → yet entwined with another body
- breaking through a barrier → yet remaining within Earth's influence
- brilliant light → coming through clouds
- girl → boy
- distorted body → well-formed body
- Caucasian → Oriental
- awkward burden → gift to society

DELAYED RESPONSE:

It was only then that I realized *this dream as a whole presents something I am strongly in opposition to:* the very idea of reincarnation.

Ten years prior to this dream, when I began writing dream notes, I was under the care of Juanita Burke, a physical therapist at Riverside Hospital. She gave me prompts about reincarnation by loaning Richard Bach's *Jonathon Livingstone Seagull*. After I dutifully read the book, she asked, "Would you like to return in another lifetime to share with other people the compassion you've learned in this lifetime?" My answer was emphatic, "No, once is enough!" But in this dream the concept arises again, powerful enough to be considered "a breakthrough, perhaps through a time barrier." Along with the whoosh and my speeding away from earthly constraints, there is a brilliant light, an illumination gradually coming through.

– *Fourteen* –

Anxiety Dreams

My anxiety dreams exhibit images that readily identify an issue that I need to face. This contrasts with images in nightmares that are usually *disguises* for an issue. A typical anxiety dream occurred just prior to my participation in the choral movement of Beethoven's Ninth Symphony. There was agitation because of my being "late to get my seat assignment, rattling a lunch bag, can't find a pencil, have kicked off my slippers and now my feet are cold." Actions like that could occur during a rehearsal, but the dream's shifting from sheet music to an answer sheet jolted me. "I've lost the packet containing the answer sheet and need paper for figuring the math section. People next to me have a page full of answers blocked in before I begin. Even so, I finish the first part as soon as they do, with as few mistakes. The other applicants are complete conformists and I pretend that I am not" (Oct 9, 1975).

My strongest anxiety dream is that of being tested and it is always a waker-upper. There is a sense of urgency, often stated explicitly: *I can't afford to fail this course.* My repeated use of the word *course* hearkened back to counsel given me by maestra Antonia Brico in the late 1970s, "Do not be deflected from your course!" Ergo, it was incumbent on me to figure out what in waking life feels like a test; whether it is something that I have burdened myself with, or someone else has imposed on me; whether I choose to follow through on it; and what preparation may be necessary if I so choose.

Taking Tests Forever

Beginning with 1975, dreams of being tested occurred on average three times per year. During the aftermath of the NDE in 1990, they occurred 11 times in a single year. Since 2001, they have presented only on rare occasions.

It was understandable that dreams of being in classroom situations occurred during the years I spent earning my degrees. And it was not surprising that when I was engaged in Poets-in-the-Schools Program, facing a new class every 45 minutes, my anxiety would reference the tests I had already been through. But it was mystifying that, seven years after I left the Music School, I was still enduring in dreams the most demanding of tests—music auditions and faculty juries. Later on, when dreams of testing were provoked by medical tests and diagnoses, many were emotionally loaded because there seemed to be no ready answer or easily accessible solution.

Here are three versions of testing that occurred within a three-month period. First, "Along with multiple-choice questions, there are essay questions like these: What is energy? What is a megacycle? What is more valuable: (a) the beauty of a butterfly's wings or (b) the strength to fly? I say that flying is of infinitely greater importance. The teacher disagrees, but says the question was worded poorly" (Oct 24, 1975). Second, what could have been an easy fill-in-the-blank test was made difficult by the requirement to write the answers in Latin. Yet I was "very self-assured, surprising myself" (Nov 20, 1975). Third, a flashback occurred with all the intensity of my oral exam for the master's degree. "In a loft, above a divided, narrow, steep staircase, a crowd of students to take their Orals. The English Department chair and his office manager my examiners. Such aloofness! It will be as awful as the Music School fiasco was" (Dec 21, 1975).

A year later I was much more assertive about the whole concept of testing.

Oct 25, 1976
Psychological Testing at a Console

> I worry about my every move—how it might be construed. Some of the questions seem to be about information, though. The Tester (a man) has a console and I have one similar but not identical—a cross between a typewriter, a cash register, and a voting machine. He gives me a spoken cue, I look for it or some response to it on my console

and push a button or key to answer or to counter his question. There is a delaying key, also a key that makes the previous question reappear and hold momentarily while I supply the answer. But the Tester must have a key that advances instead of reversing, thus overriding my key. I run the risk of having an entirely new question appear.

The question that I finally "flip" over is visual–written on a black ground, with black letters that I can barely make out. The oral cue is, "Knights become what?" I toy with ideas and with images, but keep coming up with [inappropriate] words such as kiss and kink. Now, king, which is appropriate but insufficient. All the while I'm wondering, What do these tell of my psyche? At length I have an answer to the riddle: "Nights become THINGS." But the Tester thwarts me by rolling ahead to new questions.

I explode at the unfairness and begin telling him of my experiences with testing. A young attractive woman comes in. I infer she's also a Tester and ask [her] if she wants to hear this emotional story? "Yes."

I go back to my first computer-graded tests etc. etc. and don't even get to the math test at OSU [that placed me in calculus, where I did not belong], or to the speech proficiency test [that was actually based on the wrong textbook]. Somewhere in my recitation the woman asks, "Why do multiple-choice tests bother you?"

I say, "Because we shouldn't have to reduce possibilities to one right and all the rest wrong. You seem to be making that a major premise: 'Most of the following are wrong, can you tell which approximates being correct?' A better educational philosophy would be: 'Most of the following are correct, can you spot the one that is wrong, harmful, or likely to cause trouble?'

The woman exclaims, "Aha!" as if I were expressing a guilty conscience rather than asserting a multiplicity of possibility.

A few months later, after two appointments with Dr. Q relative to marriage problems, I was still arguing about testing: "I'm passing a test involving math thought problems. In step three you're supposed to check everything with a probe that's like a vacuum cleaner or a mine-sweeper [mind-sweeper?]. I say the probing is part of the problem, yet important in arriving at any answer at all. Now the probe is on its side, like a fallen dragon or a huge piece of road-grading equipment [an emblem of my husband]. I ask about righting/fixing/caring for it. Am told a new model is to take its place" (Feb 7, 1977).

A year later, "I give up on the whole idea of testing and re-testing. People will have to accept me without those scores" (Jan 12, 1978). Nevertheless, testing continued in dreams. "After one hour of a two-hour test, I decide to proceed with the phonetics/linguistics section and forget the analogy/analysis section. Now there's a problem of reading an Oriental menu, and I simply ask for help. Now I realize that THIS IS THE TEST–how willing a person is to ask for instructions, help, guidance, translation, suggestions" (Jun 25, 1979). It was a year later when I was given help in a test dream by an understanding male teacher:

Nov 18, 1980
My Answers Are out of Order

> I'm about ten years old, paying attention to the teacher because he's talking about a test. I can't find a sheet of paper that doesn't have someone else's name on it. My desk-mate bothers me with elbows and questions. I move to another desk, now to an easel with a huge sheet of Manila paper.
>
> In the test itself, I'm unsure if the responses should be to the time before fourth grade? or to any time in my life, including today? Some of the questions are, "Do you sing? Where? Do you stand on street corners and sing and tell stories?"
>
> Oh, I've got my answers out of order! I'm on #19 instead of #20! The teacher gives me one last chance: "Make up as many excuses as you can for why you didn't do well on the test, or how you could do better. You will get credit for each one you list." I begin, "If there's one thing I can do well, it's write. If there's one thing I can do better, it's sing."

Now I feel confused. This doesn't lead anywhere.
Why don't I just list excuses? Because that puts
me on the defensive. Yet it's easier and quicker
to make excuses than to praise my abilities.

REFLECTIONS:
1. This is the first dream I recall in which I am an age other than my present age. There were dreams set in elementary school, but in them I was my present age and aware of the discrepancy and the regressing.
2. The male teacher wants me to get a decent grade and–more important–he uses a test mostly as review and as a refresher, which pleases me.

Shortly after that, the dream setting was high school, I was an adolescent, and the teacher was female and heartless. To free myself of memories similar to that of the dream, I exorcized it by writing this poem:

Heartfelt

I'm back in high school, on opening day.
An old nun glares at Will and me,
then brands a blood-red **F** on my brow.
I think, Flunked, but not a flunky!
I say, "You have no cause to act this way."

Like a judge in a black-and-white movie,
she shouts, "I hold you in contempt of court!"
My immediate retort is,
"You hold us in contempt of love."

Will tells me to ignore her rants.
"She can grade us, sure, but she can't score . . .
what does she know of love or romance?"
I protest, "But . . . flunked *in advance?*

That's a bad omen, it could even become
a self-fulfilling prophecy."
He kisses my effing-red forehead,
a lovely way of shushing me.

Gradually I overcame the fear of "being flunked in advance," especially during the 10 years when I had contracts in the Poets-in-the-Schools Program and the one year of separation from my husband. Two weeks before the divorce was decreed, I had a very optimistic dream:

May 31, 1985
A Test I Can Answer with One Word

> A large life-affecting question is posed in three parts of a test. The odd thing is, even though the content and construction of each question is different, I can answer all three parts with one word: YES.
>
> I'm surprised that there weren't general instructions to this effect: If NO, why not? If YES, how or why? Yet I recognize humor in answering all three questions the same way: YES YES YES and not explaining how or why.

REFLECTIONS:
1. Rainer Rilke says that "in living through the questions" we most likely find the answers. If I live through my experiences, don't just put in time in the Master of Social Work curriculum or in any other function or capacity, the YES answers will come gradually.
2. The three big questions to which I choose to answer YES are these:
    - Will my health and energy sustain me, without episodes like the mononucleosis and Meniere's disease when stress was high during graduate school?
    - Will I find work that is satisfying and for which I am paid adequately?
    - Can I develop new friends in new areas and have sexual relations with someone who cares for me as a whole person?

The next dream, a very lengthy one with equally long reflections, occurred one year after my near-death experience, when I was focusing on major life issues.

Apr 17, 1990
A Test on Red Tissue

- Questions are on red tissue paper—long and narrow horizontal strips that get tangled, crushed, and torn. Answers are to go on white papers that are folded vertically, something like computer pages. But some of the white sheets have holes at crucial spots where I'm supposed to put my answer.

  I keep losing my place because there are so many sets of Q's on each page. I put the answer for #12 of one set in the place of #12 of another set and am terribly upset about this. There's no explanation at the beginning and almost no form to the test. Am I supposed to use a pen? or a pencil? I don't know if this is a time test. I don't know why I'm stuck in a classroom to take this test.

  I'm my adult size, sitting in a small school desk. I'm very uncomfortable and change my position many times. This classroom is like the 5th grade and 6th grade rooms at St. Francis. The boy behind me leans over and crowds me, and the boy in front reaches back and crowds me. I have only a few inches of work space. Papers get intertwined and dangle over the edges of the desk. Frustrating!

  This must be a psychological test. The teacher tells me, "You can't fail this test," but I wonder how I can even get through it.

  After a long while, John Kneisly comes into the room. Without speaking, he shows me a way to organize the papers—using a green paper to mark page 21 of the red sheets, because that's where the Q's begin. But this means I have something more to deal with! I fling myself against his left arm, crying, "Oh, John!" He of all people has seen me panicky and yet remained calm and helpful and reassuring. Why doesn't he speak now?

  In front of all the kids, the teacher tells me, "We'll talk later. You can let out all those feelings." I think I'm supposed to check in at a mental health unit of a medical complex, but can't find the correct buildings. As I walk along, I ask directions of one person after another. Each one is sure, yet vague. "Over there ... down two ... up there." Which way is up?

I keep walking. The day gets colder and I get colder. Finally I lie down on the sidewalk. Maybe I'll freeze, or maybe someone will come, it doesn't really matter. A hand pounds my shoulder. I say over and over, "I'm so tired."

Maybe it's that person who takes me to a medical unit. I'm given a white regulation nightgown. I wonder about tomorrow: What test or treatment is to be tomorrow?

I think about the red tissue-paper test. The teacher must have been watching my behavior, and THAT was the psychological test! She wasn't interested in my answers at all. I sense duplicity and betrayal.

INFERENCES: This dream illustrates that I fear:

new situations (not just tests)	not having directions
fragility, especially tearing	crowding
pushing, especially by boys	time trials
misdirections	coldness
brain-washing	nonsensical questions

FEELINGS:
Frustration, bewilderment, panic, despair; reprieve; anger at the teacher; fear.

REFLECTIONS:
1. Throughout the dream I have an awareness that this is like a nightmare, and I wonder, who is in charge? I think, If this were a nightmare, I would take charge of parts of it.
2. There's something terribly important about the red tissue. The red globs and the red tissue paper suggest menstruation, miscarriages, deliveries, episiotomies, other surgeries.
3. I wonder now, as I write, if my hymen was broken when, before age five, I bruised myself in a tricycle accident.
4. What if the dream refers to a physiological disturbance in me at present—say the relationship of red blood cells to white blood cells? What about tissues themselves? "There are holes in some crucial spots where I'm supposed to put an answer" might refer to osteoporosis (relative to that, I'm having a bone density test next week).

In 1992 there was a string of testing dreams that displayed anxiety because "too many tests ahead of scheduled time" (Jan 29, 1992), "insufficient time allocated" (Feb 9, 1992), "difficulties writing my own ticket" (May 26, 1992), and "filing a Herculean task" (Jul 21, 1992). The final blow was "an exam on a non-course that has no objectives, taught by a non-entity–a non-nun" (Jul 24, 1992). It was in that year that I suffered indignities from more than one medical professional. At a time when I was tested by a rheumatologist I stated within a dream, "The judging of any of my lifetimes and of all scenarios, is up to me and not to some male authority figure. I'm not in competition with any other person at any level. I don't have to live up to my reputation or live it down" (Jun 28, 1993).

The next variant of Taking Tests Forever, though complex, included humor.

Jan 22, 1996
A Literary Exam that Requires an Imaginative Response

> The question is; "What does the Countess do after the Count dies and in the intervening years before we learn of her being a model for that famous painting?" I'm writing in pencil so I can erase if desired. The room becomes dark rapidly (sunset?) and I wonder how much time is allowed for this question. I know what it is to not have two pans to cook in, two coins to rub together, a word to call my own.
>
> I begin, "The Countess learned how to make block prints, taught girls and women the alphabet and spelling and reading, wrote pithy essays and had them printed, developed a new style of plainsong more lyrical than straight chanting, encouraged females to sing in harmony, experimented with low-fat recipes and embellished them with herbs that stimulate the immune system, invented the first comfortable commode for a privy and the first donut cushion for carriage rides of any distance."
>
> I don't know if I'll have time to support my thesis from texts we've studied, rather than have it be sheer speculation. I wonder, Is it possible that the Countess could develop along these lines in a mere 10 or 12 years?

FEELINGS:
From hesitant to confident and imaginative.

REFLECTIONS:
1. The Countess was a Renaissance Woman! I wonder where my feminist commentary came from?
2. Is it possible that in the 11 years since I divorced, I have developed in noticeable ways? Yes, in my roles as writer, editor, teacher, artist, and healer. Yes, in manifesting some goals. Though I did not get to Japan when invited by Hiroko's family, eventually I was able to fly to Joe in California and EJ in Oregon, and later to attend Angelyn's wedding in North Carolina.

Though variants on the theme of Testing continued, there were longer gaps between them; it was 14 years before the next dream occurred (Jun 24, 2010). In it the focus changed somewhat, with my looking less to the past ("My grade-school teachers would be proud of this penmanship") and more to the future ("I'm delighted that my composition is moving so well"). This dream asked to be set in verse. I adhered to the dream notes except for narrating in third person and injecting a few rhyme words:

Taking an Entrance Exam for the Dozenth Time

Not SAT, not ACT, not GRE
but of equal importance
and essay questions, all.
She writes fluently, serenely,
and amazed because
under duress she never writes this well.

She caps the inkwell and pauses
to admire her handwriting.
It might yet please Sister Isabel–
the loops and diagonals
confounding the Zaner-Bloser manual,
yet lovely and legible.

Uh-oh, the 15-minute warning bell!
No time for self-congratulation.
Breathing deeply, Pearl composes
until someone stops her with a question,
"In reference to publication . . . ?"

That, too, rings a bell:
no professor, far less a publisher,
will read handwritten pages,
regardless of their elegance,
the word *manuscript* over the ages
having lost its significance.

She leaves off mid-sentence,
and moves to a word processor
aligned as a fare-thee-well
at a checkout counter.
Here her Inner Critic, quick to belittle,
argues about every jot and tittle
and skews the whole examination.

Lacking freeform loops and leaps,
wanting something (apex? parallel?),
Pearl wobbles.
Bereft of inspiration,
she trembles for what may already be
utterly lost in translation.

The question remained: How can I achieve greater cooperation between my Critic and my Creative Child? I must have felt beset by criticism from outsiders, too, because there appeared on my dream tablet this verse:

my desk is clear the first time this year
an inkling of my thinking about
what I want to whisper   yodel   write
   model   plant   trample   shout

Three years later I was still longing for joy and inspiration.

Oct 8, 2013
Facing a Final Exam or Project Unprepared

> This is a short course, maybe a summer term. Without a finished project, I won't get an Incomplete but a Failure grade. But I'm not able to present a project, not physically or time-wise. I can't do an invention or a replica, can't paint a picture or illustration though I know exactly what colors are right. There's no sense drawing stick figures.
>
> Now I realize that I've overlooked a skill–my writing ability. I go to the prof and plead for my project to be creative writing about the era. He is doubtful about the very idea and about my ability. I say, "You'd be amazed at what I can create overnight." He relents, "All right, overnight it is. Hand it in 24 hours from now."
>
> As I write, colors become very important [as if bonding me to consensus reality]. Though I feel the sky should be a brilliant blue, it becomes increasingly paler, down to a light pastel.

FEELINGS:
Anxious, uninformed, unprepared, hopeful, assertive, productive.

REFLECTIONS:
1. My first consideration in the morning is about the fading of the brilliant sky and my inability to prevent it. I'm concerned that my brilliance (a descriptor that Laurel Richardson, both a friend and a sociologist, has applied to me) is fading.
2. Though my professional aspect doubts that I can succeed, my student self is confident about my creativity and follow-through.
3. This dream is commentary on my proposed collage–a diptych. It may be a warning not to let *critique* overcome *creativity*.
4. The opposite of "stick figures" is well-roundedness, fullness, which I need in life as well as in collage.
5. The title of this dream suggests the final phase of my life *and* that I haven't prepared for it adequately. That may not be a fact, but it is my present assessment.

Recently, though still pondering many questions, I was reassured about answers being inherent in the questions posed:

Sep 17, 2016
Filling in Ovals and Making Music

> The ovals become musical notes and, as I fill in the answers correctly, a melody appears! This looks easy. But I soon realize there are several staves on a single page—probably not a full-orchestra score but at least an SATB choral score. The ovals show not only interweaving of melodic lines but also the harmonic structure.
>
> I must answer many questions correctly to begin to apprehend how this music sounds and how rich it is.

REFLECTIONS:
1. I recently filled in ovals for the annual survey of the Women's Health Initiative, which I have participated in for over 20 years.
2. Yet I feel that the scoring and the musical score here relate to the themes of *Dream Encounters*. If so, this is reassurance that there will be interweaving of themes within the larger construct *and* that the result will be harmonious.
3. I must be patient in answering many questions before I can begin to apprehend how rich the composition of this book actually is.

Undergoing Telltale Deaths

Apr 21, 1984
From Dismemberment to Disembodiment

> I don't know how my legs were injured, but they were mangled, then amputated. My whole body may be decaying.
>
> A doctor wants to use some of my body parts to restore me [making me the organ donor for myself]. I protest that the flesh is corrupted and I don't want putrid stuff laid on me. Somehow the doctor persuades me that the flesh is beyond decaying and is sterile now.
>
> He lays sheets of my remaining body on my lower legs. No grafting or stitching! I'm still doubtful. He

says, "This will do it, if you are a believer. Do you
believe in Jesus Christ?" I snap back, "Of course, I
believe," though I don't know now what to believe.
   Now he scatters on my legs small pieces that look
like parchment dipped in iodine. I'm at a vantage point
above the surgery, and somehow I know that these
pieces are from the body of Christ. I wonder how many
persons have been treated in this bizarre way, and why
I've been chosen to grow new legs. For the rest of the
day, I have to lie still. The next day I'm able to walk,
and soon my legs are flexible and "weller than well."

In the next variant, two months later, Death appeared in female guise. "A woman I'm accompanying draws a heavy black veil or shawl over her face. It's like drawing the final curtain on a play. I think the covering itself will suffocate her [a persistent fear of mine since birth]. I'm distressed that something I've said has triggered this withdrawal in her" (Jun 12, 1984).

One month later, with Death again pictured as a woman, the setting and the tone were quite different, as was my total involvement:

Jul 30, 1984
Formal Recognition of the Darkness

   In a social gathering, everyone dressed in formal black, one
man and I react to a simple suggestion, "Would you care
to lie down?" We laugh until our sides ache. We almost die
laughing, but no one else gets the joke the way we do.
   A woman says, "It's time to say your goodbyes." I kiss
him goodbye, on the lips. It becomes a Chagall-type kiss
that lifts us both off the ground. Our bodies don't touch,
not even our arms in embrace, it's just this wonderful kiss.
   Now the woman kisses each of us in the same way. The
three of us are sealed in as deep a relationship as when the
two of us were laughing together. There's a sense of rightness.

FEELINGS:
Hale and hearty laughter; total acceptance; a final and full goodbye with the sense of "What a way to go!"

REFLECTIONS:
1. The feeling of Death prevailed, even before I read the quip this morning, "We almost died laughing."
2. In Symphony Chorus we referred to our black dresses as "shrouds," and that's how my formal black dress feels in this dream.

A year later there was another dream in which I myself died. Peacefully! In the morning there was a feeling statement, "There's something fluid about this dying, like a choreographed scene, with awareness and acceptance" (Nov 16, 1985).

The next dream about the possibility of a violent death had a surprise ending. Yet deeply-felt questions remained unanswered.

Apr 1, 1986
A Plane Bursts into Flames

> Charles [my brother] and I are in one plane with about 50 passengers, and there's another plane the same size going in the same direction. It bursts into flames and begins falling. I feel the same thing is happening to us [in our plane]. My life does not flash before my eyes. Rather, I'm thinking of Mother–what a shock it will be for her to lose two children in one incident.
>
> I tell Charles, "At least we'll die on impact and won't suffer being burned." As we drift down, I send a few messages to God: "Thanks for the good times, I did my best, etc." Fatalistic but not terrified.
>
> Our plane does not crash! We lift up again, like a hang-glider on a chimney of warm air. I realize our plane is not on fire, either.
>
> What's left for me to accomplish in this life? I have difficulty re-adjusting from active acceptance of death to acceptance of more years ahead.

FACTUAL NOTE:

This dream is a delayed response to the near-hit of a TWA plane on March 22, 1986, nine days earlier. I was among 141 passengers routed to St. Louis. In that instance, there were four or five military planes headed toward us. *We missed by an altitude of 100 feet!* I heard no murmurings in our plane and wondered how few persons saw what I saw. I was not frightened in that moment, did not realize the implications, was surprised at the plane's size and terrific speed.

REFLECTIONS:

1. The frequent conflation of waking life events and dream experiences leads me to question Patricia Garfield's statement, "Death in dreams is usually a metaphor for 'non-functional, inactive, as if dead.'" The realism in some of my dreams of death far outweighs the metaphorical content.
2. Joan Windsor, in *Dreams and Healing*, holds a more encompassing view. "Usually this theme [dreams of dying] symbolizes the death of outmoded patterns of thought accompanied by rebirth of new ideals and changes in spiritual direction that will eventually result in the advancement of the soul. A minority of death dreams do, in fact, foresee the end of one's human existence and herald the rebirth of the soul into a higher dimension."

In 1987, at a conference of the International Association for the Study of Dreams (IASD), a presenter asserted that we do not allow ourselves to die in dreams, that we pull ourselves out of the dream state before that can occur. I begged to differ and scheduled an appointment with her to discuss this. I argued that participating in death within a dream was at the very least a rehearsal for the occasion itself. Moreover, enduring death within a dream–not passively but with active acceptance–enhanced one's integrity and courage in waking life. She remained unconvinced. For one thing, I did not have with me the relevant dream notes of June 2, 1987 that countered her premise; for another, I did not have the credentials of a psychologist or other professional counselor. Yet I went ahead and narrated part of the previous night's dream:

> A bomb has been thrust in my hand, something longer than a hand grenade. I can't loosen it—maybe it's handcuffed to my wrist. I jump through an archway to an alley, trying to get away from the high-density crowd, to save a few people. But the explosion kills hundreds, and collapsing buildings crash on thousands. I am not guilty of this destruction, yet I am a carrier, against my wishes.
>
> A black woman is pushing the remnants of my body in a wheelbarrow— thinking to bury her grandmother? When she recognizes me in the remnants, she's glad at our momentary reunion. We have truly loved one another in this lifetime.

One response to this dream from the presenter seemed like a compliment; but when she said it a second time, it was a challenge, "You put the welfare of others ahead of your own safety and welfare." I asked, "What else could I do with a bomb handcuffed to my wrist?" She said confidently, "It's your dream. You could have shaped it in many other ways." But I wasn't just an observer, I was in the thick of the events. [The entire dream is processed in section 19, Me and My Shadow.]

Two years after her assessment, I found, in *Dreamtime and Inner Space* by Holger Kalweit, an entire chapter on dismemberment in the experiences of shaman apprentices. Kalweit helped me look at my awful dream image as "a metaphor of inner change; [an] allegorical and culturally oriented symbol for an introspective psychic rebirth."

A likely antecedent of that bomb scenario was an incident ten years prior, when I was in the Music School. The race riots had been tempered, but there were still special-duty police on campus, barricades to prevent any through traffic, barricades near the Administration Building (two doors from the Music School), and general unrest. One day in music theory class, Mr. Vedder did not arrive. Unheard of! While the class waited for the required ten minutes before "bolting," we wondered about an unclaimed black bag near the door. Considering its size and shape—as big as a bowling bag—we joked that it might be a bomb, then became more serious about the possibility. As my classmates dashed down the stairs, I picked up the bag, put it in a metal wastebasket, and carried it half a flight to the staircase landing before I booked out of there. My overwrought imagination feared that the bomb would blow up the elevator that freighted harps, bass violins, and other large, expensive musical instruments; better to have it blow out a window far from the elevator. I was about a block away when the realization hit: *That was crazy!* The class learned a few days later that the black bag had been left unattended by a visiting professor and contained only musical scores.

In the next dream of my dying in a violent way, "I'm electrocuted and revived. A miracle, and charted as such. Why didn't I see visions? I tell someone, 'I was gone a while,' and he agrees" (Apr 18, 1988).

The last entry I have relative to anxiety about a violent death is very short, and without a specific date for 1989. This time it involves fire. "I'm huddled, like a black heap of charcoal or furnace coal, in the corner of a large porch of a white frame house."

FEELINGS:
Rather like "The Little Match Girl," I'm huddled, forlorn, dying unattended.

REFLECTION:
My becoming charcoal is a more vivid image of what occurred in one of my earliest recorded dreams (Dec 24, 1975): "My obituary states DEAD FROM THE HEIGHT. Not from the heat of the raging fire, not the hate of an assailant, but the height from my point of observation, where I could not escape the flames."

A likely antecedent of this dream was an incident when my seven-year-old brother and a friend of his tied me (age five) to a pole and lit a fire at my feet. It sputtered out and did no physical harm, but from "the height of my point of observation," there was emotional harm.

Being Unseen/Unheard

In the first four years of my note-taking, I recorded 51 instances of calling out within a dream. From those I usually wakened myself and often wakened another person. Of those calls, seven were for help, nine were commands, and eleven were exclamations in anger. In 22 instances, I was calling the name of one person or another. There were only two calls exulting in joy: "*Alleluia!* I say as I'm greeted in France with kisses of respect on my fingers" (Sep 2, 1977). Later I exclaim, relative to meeting the female troubadour Marcelle Drutel in France, "If it takes a miracle, then it's a miracle we'll have!" (May 14, 1978).

Prompts for dreams that had me calling out were what I called "daymares," actual situations in waking life that took all my strength to cope with. The following poem highlights daymares that eventually erupted in a single dream:

Meltdown in Aisle 14

Upon recall of a generic prescription,
I go to my doctor for the genuine item.
But no . . .
my PCP overrides me
with yet another substitution,
which brings on itching, head-to-toe.
Needing the genuine item,
I return, reminding the doctor to sign
Dispense as written.

A robot calls to say,
"Your prescription is ready,"
Hooray! I drive to the pharmacy,
only to hear, "Wait . . .
there is a discrepancy."
So I wait, and I wait, until
a tech behind a grille states solemnly,
"Your insurance won't pay."
I know.

"Oh . . . we have only 50 of the 90.
Do you want to wait until tomorrow?"
No, I'm needing it today.
"Well, if you say so . . . That will be . . .
one hundred-twenty-seven-fifty."
I know.

"Okay, your wait will be . . . "
The floor rumbles,
capsules explode, vials tumble,
and a counter gives way
as a lone voice bellows
N-o-o-o-o-o

In daytime I felt a non-entity when people ignored me as if I were invisible; also when what I said went unheard, unheeded. Replaying such situations in dreams, I would waken myself calling, "Didn't you hear me?" One time, I was so upset with a family member that a dream shaped up as a *verbal* protest; the next morning I honored the protest by giving it a title:

The Unkindest Cut

>all this interference
>all this cutting into dreams
>is like a double-bar in music
>or a chord that won't resolve
>a gong exploding the Grand Pause
>an iron curtain clanging down
>before the red velvet one is drawn

Regarding the following anxiety dream, a bit of explanation is due. *Quodlibet* in music occurs when all the instrumental players and singers perform simultaneously, each with his own song.

May 24, 1976
The Quodlibet Poetry Reading

> I'm giving a reading in an auditorium at noon. I intend
> to start with "Spring Sequence," but someone asks
> for "On Green Wings." Another person chimes in,
> reading a poem of mine, which I don't mind. But, not
> understanding it, she reads poorly, which I do mind.
>
> Now the emcee calls on a petite woman, who starts
> reciting an epic poem, beginning with, "When dooryards
> last in the lilacs bloomed." An orchestra sets up, tunes
> up, and plays but doesn't drown her out. I insist, "It's my
> reading, truly." Finally the woman closes or is shut up, and
> the musicians quit, too. I ask the audience, "Do you want
> to stay for the remaining seven minutes?" Some do.
>
> I comment, "After this program, which was
> spontaneous, unrehearsed, and I hope unique, there's no
> point in my reading anything surrealistic. So I'll read a
> few love poems . . . if I can locate them . . . " But the other
> performers have walked away with my notebooks!
>
> Now I see the few remaining people are surrounded
> by green. Not by tapestries and carpets [as before], but
> with rich natural greens, several shades, everywhere
> in an outdoor amphitheater. They themselves look
> like a pastoral scene, with persons draped by shadows,
> persons in white, like shepherds and shepherdesses.
>
> I don't need a microphone for so few [people]
> and in such a setting. I step forward, wanting to
> embrace them as they have embraced the good,
> true, and beautiful around them, including me.

In the next example, I am not even aware of being invisible:

Apr 27, 1985
Conducting an Invisible Orchestra and Chorus

> A small orchestra or combo is at my left, stage right.
> The chorus is at my right, stage left. There's a terribly
> wide gap between the two groups, and I have to turn

> my whole body, not just my visual focus and baton
> when giving cues to them. A tug-of-war for me, like
> I'm being pulled apart by the two groups. I feel the
> music will sound like a run-down Victrola record.
>
> I can see the instruments playing, but not the
> invisible players. I have a sense of ethereal bodies in the
> chorus, but see only mouths [like the Cheshire cat].
>
> I have on the music stand only typing-paper
> sheets of scribbled notes and commentary, not
> musical notes. How can I carry through with this?

FEELINGS:
I could shrug this dream as just a frustration sequence, except the pull in two directions feels so personal.

REFLECTIONS:
1. I suppose the conducting is a pun for my conduct. If so, what do I need to pull off or pull together?
2. The music happens almost in spite of me. I receive it and respond to it, even while afraid that I can't fulfill the responsibility of conducting. Thank goodness, we aren't in concert!

With hindsight, I am able in the 21st century to look at this dream from another perspective, by re-setting it as a Yay-Boo story, to wit: I am conducting an orchestra and chorus (Yay), but they are invisible (Boo). I use my whole body when giving cues (Yay), but feel torn apart by demands and have no musical notes to guide me (Boo). Yet the music happens, almost in spite of me (Yay). I don't know how I can carry through (Boo), but I do (Yay).

In the next variant of Unseen/Unheard, I was in an unfamiliar place and without so much as a scribbled note.

Jul 5, 1986
From Asking Directions to Giving Directions

> I'm searching for a summer theater. I ask directions in a
> small town that grows and grows as I drive through it and
> becomes a goodly city. When I ask, people repeat my words
> as if they're a foreign language. "Summer theater? Oh, you

mean summer stock." Or, "You mean Players Theater," or simply, "Players." And they never give directions.

I keep driving until I see a group of young women. They say, "You're close," or, "Over there somewhere." I park and go into a pavilion that's much larger inside than it looked from the outside. I tell a man at a desk, "I want to read for someone."

Several people are milling around, and a woman asks me for a [reader's] cue. I give her an upbeat, but she doesn't understand. Now an upbeat and a downbeat, but she still doesn't get it. I illustrate, conducting a few measures of 4/4, and now she asks me for a cue for syncopation! I think she knows a lot more than she's letting on. Now another young woman who's been watching joins her. I find myself conducting them, not reading for them! This isn't what I came here for.

FEELINGS:
Lostness, unheard; annoyed by non-answers; angry that the young women are taking advantage of me; angry at the mockery of people who are gawking; quick on the uptake.

REFLECTION:
I waken with my right hand in the air, conducting 4/4 time, and wondering if I can suggest syncopation with my left hand.

The next example of Unseen/Unheard has all the elements of the previous ones, though with a different emphasis:

Sep 20, 1989
Without My Detailed Notes for a Presentation

I'm in a large meeting room or small assembly hall, with about 200 women present. I have my super-size poetry notebook and a couple of slim books, but my two pages of detailed notes, are not here!

I tell myself, I will not panic. But I do panic and can't pull out of this state. I tell someone, "I'm going to my room to get the notes," hoping she'll use some delaying tactics.

Outside, I can barely walk. I slip, fall to my knees, throw my arms forward to balance myself, get mud on hands and cuffs and hem of mint-green dress. I hold my hands up in supplication, asking for help in getting up. Two young black women in elegant clothes pass me by. One of them says sarcastically something like, "Pull yourself up by your bootstraps until you're in a socio-economic bracket where you can help yourself."

In my hotel I'm bewildered—can't find my key, am not sure of the room number, and have no I.D. because I've left my purse in the meeting hall. I decide to return.

Back at the meeting place, when I'm facing the audience a second time, I see there are only about 20 people left. I hope I can quickly locate some appropriate poems about women as role models, but I still haven't located the first poem and have no focal point around which to develop my presentation.

INFERENCES:
1. I need to "find my key," to be in tune with my Self, whether the audience is 200 people or only 20.
2. I need to rely on my intuition more than on cross-referencing in a logical mode. I can rely on both past experience and inventiveness.

After my near-death experience I never again felt a non-entity. But, ironically, my longing for reunion with the Divine distracted me from completing everyday tasks. Among my dream notes I found a parcel of free-writing (15 pages!) about incompleteness and completeness (Jan 14, 2012). Possibly that free-writing forestalled any more dreams about my being unseen or unheard.

– *Fifteen* –

Nightmares

Some dream researchers, such as Professor Ernest Hartmann at Tufts University School of Medicine, have made a clear distinction between a nightmare and a night terror. They classify a *nightmare* as a dream, often long and complex, whose images leave such an imprint on the dreamer that it is remembered for a long time, for months or years afterward. With even greater intensity, the *night terror* causes the dreamer to waken suddenly, often screaming, in awful fright with accompanying physiological symptoms.

Over the centuries, in daily parlance, there has been a distancing from the deeply personal "The night mare has me," with a spectral horse hovering near the sleeper, often in the company of a beastly incubus. An illustration of that is the frequently-published painting, "The Nightmare" by Henry Fuseli (1781). Add to that the expression "the night mare and her sevenfold young," and it's terrifying indeed! Gradually the concept has become more generalized, "I have a nightmare," yet physical responses such as pounding of the heart or paralysis of the limbs have not abated.

Of my nightmares, I present two themes with the strongest feelings: Threat of Rape, Murder and Mayhem.

In dream groups that I led or participated in, and especially in workshops at dream conferences, I've been occasionally challenged this way, "Why didn't you change the ending of the nightmare?" My initial response was, "Because I wasn't lucid within the dream." A few dream workers insisted, "You can do anything in a dream! Give yourself prompts in advance to change a scene that is uncomfortable. Also, you can practice ways to become lucid." But such pieces of advice went counter to my belief that my Unconscious would bring up issues only when I was ready to deal with them. *I had no desire to exercise control over the content of my dreams; I desired to learn from the situations they presented.*

Later I found support for my practice in Thomas Moore's *Care Of the Soul*, which I paraphrased on a dream tablet: "Care of the soul is about experiencing and learning, not sailing through life. We take *care* of the soul, we don't expect to *cure* all." For me that amounts to staying in the moment, comfortable or uncomfortable, not wishing to be elsewhere or to behave in an idealistic way.

That many of my Reflections have ended with questions does not faze me now, though it may have early on. Gradually I developed half a dozen ways to follow the questions posed. For instance, there is a technique called "re-entry," which challenges me to visualize changing an image or an action of the dream—whether at the beginning, in the middle, or toward the end—and to observe what results. This has proved fruitful when done in the light of day, engaging Consciousness with the dream material presented by the Unconscious.

Nightmare Theme: The Threat of Rape

From dreams in the period 1975 to 1995, there were 12 related to the threat of rape. I found none after that. The progression began with the following:

Dec 19, 1975
Attempted Rape

> I wrestle with the man and finally get on top of him. His penis is erect and between my legs, but he can't ejaculate. Anyway I'm wearing slacks and am partially protected. I bash his head, his mouth bleeds, [there are] broken teeth, too.
> Even so, he has great strength, and I have to force his arm down. Doing this, I break some bones in his hand. His strength re-surges, and I have to muster mine. I call for help, but no one will aid me. I realize there's no kindness in the world, certainly no justice.

FEELINGS:
Assaulted, struggling, abandoned.

REFLECTIONS:
1. I am strong, with an un-guessed strength.
2. Yet this is a stalemate, with neither of us a victor.
3. Even though I seem to be on top, there's no satisfaction, no feeling of power, no triumph, and no support from others.
4. This man is no one I know, so must be allegorical–probably representing male authority figures on campus.

The next scenario showed me extremely vigilant. Again, no one helped me out.

Jul 17, 1978
I'm Accosted Multiple Times

> In a classroom situation, a young black man announces, "I will have you before this week is over." I say, "You will never!" It's not a matter of prejudice, but I am NOT to be had. The class knows, the principal and teachers are alerted, and policemen are in the halls. Yet he accosts me on a fire escape, in a long hallway, and other places.
> One time a teacher lets this boy/man go to the same room I'm in because the guy was castrated in an accident when he was a youngster. That he "has no balls" does not prevent his attacking me, whether it's technically rape or not! I think, even in my terrorized state, Finger-fucking could be rape if it were done forcibly, even if the girl/woman technically remained a virgin.

FEELINGS:
When I wakened, I got up immediately to shake the terror.

COMMENT:
A prompt for this is the book of "new psychology" that I've been reading. It states over and over that illness, violence, and poverty are the result of *attractions by the afflicted person to persons who comprise the threat in society*. This is fallacious and another way of blaming the victim.

In a dream less than a month later, I did know my assailant:

Aug 9, 1978
Confronting My Attacker

> [I waken myself shouting.] "You couldn't arouse me. You couldn't please me. You Slob!" This is directed at X, who is clawing at me, scratching my buttocks and rectum. I confront him with his meanness, but he's ever so sure of himself.
>
> Now his hands are at my throat, trying to choke me or suffocate me. I can't call out because of laryngitis. He's maddened by my seeming calm, apparently wants to hear me scream. I say quietly, "God knows about this and all the rest."

FEELINGS:
Threatened, assaulted, voiceless; confrontational, trusting in God.

It seems that I tabled the issue for six years, which included my move to an apartment.

Dec 24, 1984
Another Cry for Help

> [I waken myself shouting] "Help me! Someone help!"
> A man has slipped in bed with me, now putting his hands on my breasts and locking his body against mine. I'm caught completely off guard and immobilized.
>
> I'm in bed here in this apartment and aware that it's nearly Christmas. Did I leave the door unlatched? Has someone made a copy of my key? I want someone to rescue me. Maybe my voice is muffled under these blankets?

FEELINGS:
Helpless, victimized, in terror.

REFLECTIONS:
1. The man might be a metaphor for memories creeping up on me, my past overtaking me. I hate having this reminder on Christmas Eve.
2. If anyone in the upstairs apartment heard me, no one investigated. In a similar situation, I might not either, even if I knew that someone lived alone and might actually need help.

Two years later, my written account showed strong resistance to dealing with the issue. Yet I admonished myself, saying, "According to the first rule of dream work, if something is getting through to my Conscious, then I'm ready to face it. Am I? How?"

After another year had passed, this theme was presented in an extreme version:

Nov 8, 1988
I Am Being Crucified

> I'm perched on a cross so my knees and lungs don't collapse. There's an awful pull in my shoulders, yet the worst pain is in ribs and upper belly. People are shouting and mocking. I have at least one advocate, who would have me taken down from the cross. It is a woman lawyer who considers crucifixion a form of rape. Later, in court, she maintains that the victim is innocent and the state is guilty of a heinous crime.
>
> I'm almost anesthetized–in shock? Someone is nailing my fingers (not wrists) and gets the nails between joints without shattering the long bones. In my stupor I wonder how this can be.

FEELINGS:

Helpless, innocent; shame at being almost naked in a public arena; nailed, in shock, stupefied; befriended.

REFLECTIONS:

1. Regarding *stupefied*, two inferences: First, it resonates with how I felt when hearing the results of the national election. Second, I may need to check possible side effects of the prescription I'm taking for pain.
2. I felt myself as male in this dream! Not "identification with Christ and the Divine" that Catholicism recommends, but identification with maleness.
3. In most dreams in which I'm naked, it feels positive and indicates openness, but quite the opposite here.
4. My recent questioning of inculcated values may have triggered this dream, which shows how wounded and weak I feel.

5. I am grateful for an advocate, literally "one who speaks out" for me.

The final episode concerning Threat of Rape occurred about five years later. At the end of it, I showed more confidence when harassed, but did not change the situation:

Jan 10, 1994
Immobilized, When Tormented

> I'm lying on the berm, almost into the street, in front of United Dairy. I see a slim woman with graying hair walk into the store. Now I'm aware of several young black men. The shortest of these men swaggers toward me, dangling from his fingers my ring of keys. "Recognize these?" Yes.
> "Want them?" Yes, of course. Where did you find them?
> "They were handy." He slips them onto a finger of mine and holds my finger tightly. He could snap it in half if he wants to. He taunts me, "What do you say?" Thanks very much.
> He's more threatening now in body language. I'm still on the ground, and he throws himself on top of me. I wonder, Does this mean rape? In daylight and in front of witnesses? But I don't move or cry out.

FEELINGS:
Immobilized; tormented; in mortal fear, retreating out-of-body. I'm amazed that I did not carry those feelings into wakefulness.

REFLECTIONS:
1. This is how I responded in my childhood–retreating, leaving my body to the tormentor and moving my consciousness elsewhere.
2. The unanswered questions in the dream itself, and my ability to wake from the dream experience without having a cloud hang over my day, suggest that this dream presented a past-life experience. If so, the "bleed-through" was my being left in a gutter to die.
3. The lesson for me presently is to stay in my physical body when under duress and not retreat (through a tear in my aura above my left shoulder, so a psychic tells me). This may require all the strength I can muster.

Nightmare Theme: Mayhem and Murder

Long ago I read that in research labs 80% of the nightmares involved being chased. I don't know if I doubted that at the time or merely accepted it without questioning. Recently, however, when sorting through my boxes of dream notes, I found only 10 in the category of Nightmare: Chased. That seemed too low a number, so I decided to group Chased and Escaping along with Murder, in the theme of Mayhem and Murder. There were 20 such dreams in an 18-year period. I have included excerpts in most instances and have avoided repetition of very similar dreams.

In the first instance, I was warning a friend of the dangers of assault and rape. Even within the dream I realized, "All this has something to do with poetry submissions" (Sep 21, 1975). In the next instance, a year later, I was deeply involved during the dream but had no idea of what prompted it.

Oct 25, 1976
I Gun Down the Opposition

> Troopers come up the steps one at a time. I "pick them off" with a big gun, one of those repeater things with a belt of ammunition. Someone helps me drag the bodies up from the landing and stack them in the attic hallway. Soon so many are jammed in, there's no room for me.
>
> Now I want to know how to dispose of them [the bodies]. They're a health hazard, will putrefy, and stink. Someone says, "Bury them at sea." I try to arrange for a helicopter to come, to dump them into the sea. I can't get the phone number of the U.S. Air Force or Army Air Force, but finally the Navy.
>
> Now someone says, "One of the bodies is not dead, just in a coma." I think this is awful and I don't want "it" to die of suffocation in that heap of bodies. So I shoot it point-blank with a pistol, even while thinking, This is outright murder! Now the full implication hits—that all my "picking off" is murder—and shock sets in.

Apparently I was following the advice given by Patricia Garfield in *Creative Dreaming*, to this effect: If you are the victim of an aggressive action, you should become reciprocally aggressive and attack your dream enemy, to the death if necessary. Her explanation: "The death of a dream enemy releases a positive force from the part of you that has formed the antagonistic image."

Two months later, I was even more forceful, and with no regrets. "A woman kills three assailants with their own weapons, then [kills] a man coming out of a fruitcake tin with a butcher knife, then two men who start mutilating her. Everything goes black. She survives in memory as a heroine of feminists and women generally" (Dec 21, 1976).

The next dream variant was "Murder of a Man Who's a Public Figure." He's found "face down in a bowl of Jell-O at a banquet or a smorgasbord table. No signs of violence. Yet a woman comes in, exclaims over the body, and pulls out of him an ice pick! How will she prove her innocence?" (Mar 3, 1977).

A few months later, in "Fleeing from My Homeland," my Unconscious offered a warning to cancel my scheduled flight to Europe because, "One plane crashes at take-off, and the plane I'm in is barely off the ground when its rear third drags and crashes" (Jun 15, 1977). The dream was so vivid that, before fully waking, I was ready to sue the airline! To be sure, I canceled that trip and waited a full year before conditions and the people I wanted to interview were in readiness. My dream notes alluded to Rainer Rilke's saying, "Everything is gestation," and to his advice to "live along the questions into the answers."

During that period of gestation, I had a lengthy dream about escaping:

Mar 23, 1978
Three Dark Scenes of Escape

> I leave the U. of M. Hospital [in Ann Arbor, Michigan], still in a gown or robe, and drive the car all night, to Lower Monroe [in Grand Rapids]. That turns into the route with the high retaining walls by the penitentiary [in

Columbus, Ohio]. I'm going too fast for the curve and the darkness. The last thing I'm conscious of before crashing is slamming the brakes and taking the key from the ignition.

Sometime later, I'm in a dark shelter, where a milkman tries to get information from me. I don't want to give him my husband's name, but he insists. I want police for protection. I'm willing to face a trial or whatever, as long as I can get out of this place. Some ugly people have come into the shelter and are scaring me. The woman has lovely, dark eyes, but her other features are distorted. The man is a shadowy figure, very threatening.

There's another dark scene of escape before or after this. I'm on campus–a combination of the University of Michigan and Ohio State University. Everyone avoids me. I seem to be more threatening than threatened, maybe a frightening appearance? I look in a mirror and see only a smudge or bruise on my nose and puffiness around my eyes. No lacerations, no blood. A waitress helps me get to a phone. I have two dimes for a phone call, and some nickels and pennies I can leave for a tip, but I want my husband to give her a dollar tip when he comes for me.

REFLECTION:
This dream is an example of a Yay-Boo dream. Without dismissing the intense emotions I felt in the dream, I can now condense the story to read somewhat differently: A woman leaves a hospital and drives a long distance (Yay), but she drives too fast on a dangerous curve and crashes (Boo). She revives and finds shelter (Yay), but some people intrude and scare her (Boo). She isn't injured (Yay), but looks frightening (Boo). A waitress helps her get to a phone (Yay), but the woman has too little money to give her a good tip (Boo). She thinks her husband will come get her (Yay).

After a five-year respite from Murder and Mayhem, there were–on one night–multiple threats and scenes of violence. The setting was a psychiatric hospital where I was visiting. "Every time I turn around, someone has a weapon—a saw, a pipe, knives. Now a heavyset man puts some leather thongs to my throat, and I know the next step is to use razor blades or a barber's razor. I call for help, but no sound comes because his hands and the thongs are gagging me" (Sep 2, 1983).

There was another recess before violence erupted again. In a scene that resembled the Tarot 10 of Swords, "Several long fencing swords are stuck in me, mostly in my chest." The next scene is even worse, because personal and sexually aggressive. "A man comes toward me with swords sticking out of a wide, black belt. He does pelvic rotations, and the swords come at me. They hit not in the genital area, but higher" (Dec 6, 1988).

The next variant of Murder and Mayhem was six years later:

May 4, 1992
Powerless Against a Killer

> A dark scene, indoors, upstairs. I've called 911, but got no answer. Called a second time, no answer. A man is trying to kill me. He comes up the steps. Has a gun, a hand grenade, is armed to the teeth with knives.
> He runs a fine metal cable around my neck.
> One move from me will slice my throat.

FEELINGS:
Terrified, helpless. I waken screaming for help. Dry mouth. Still gasping. I need water but can't get up for a drink.

REFLECTION:
I've made an immediate connection between this dream and the riots in Los Angeles: the helplessness when crying out and trying to escape, also the fact that police do not help but are a major part of the problem in government and in neighborhoods. And the police were acquitted after the Rodney King disaster!

Six months later there was another example of how "the political is personal."

Nov 12, 1992
Escaping and Being Harbored

> There's a tremendous fire in an upper story of a large building, and I suspect it was set to smoke me out. I don't know why I have been singled out, but I do know that this political hunt is specifically for me. I must escape from pursuers.
>
> I get to a lower story and eventually to my own level of apartment. In my corridor, half of the flooring is red. Is it charred? It feels like an omen, something like the Old Testament's splattering of blood on doorposts so the angel of Death would pass by. I have a single key, not on a chain. I take only a few items from my apartment—passport, other I.D., some layered clothing.
>
> There are young people to help me—EJ, Tony, and possibly others from AYH (American Youth Hostels). I know I must move on, not to endanger their lives.
>
> I'm traveling light. I don't have a physical handicap or pain, yet I move slowly and deliberately.

FEELINGS:
Though innocent of political intrigue, I am pursued by an enemy; threatened, yet deliberately calm.

The last dream of this series is important for its quality of redemption:

Oct 26, 1995
Huge Snowplow Threatens

> Accumulated snow is heavy and deep. Possibility of an avalanche. A lull in the storm. I'm stumbling across a road that has only one lane cleared. I see a bright light approaching, like a searchlight on an emergency vehicle. But it's the headlight of a huge snowplow—as high and wide as a combine—coming right at me! I wave frantically. I make eye contact with the driver, but he doesn't stop or even slow down. I fall on my face and force myself to roll over on my side [like a movie heroine in the path of an oncoming train].

FEELINGS:

Frantic, endangered; heroic, relieved, but in shock.

REFLECTIONS:

1. The high-intensity headlight is one positive image. It isn't a *head* light in the sense of intellectualizing, but refers to the light of faith.
2. The driver seated so high up could be my ego self, frightened and frightening. It might also be my High Self, seeing the larger terrain of time, space, and events, and plowing ahead, no matter what risk is involved.
3. "I'm thinking about my life!" is a protest but also an affirmation.

– Sixteen –

Bedtime Stories

Sometimes my Unconscious has used the diversionary tactic of story-telling to break up patterns of sadness or obsessive thinking. I regarded the stories as entertainment; they led me away from introspection and gave me a lift throughout the day, which was a blessing. These stories occurred near dawn, which is why I was able to retrieve details as well as a plot line.

Household Tales

Folktale

Lately I've been dreaming about the comforter that Great-great-grandma Baugh set aside to go to the hospital and die. It's like an archaeological find. Irregular pieces of the under layers are studied as if clues to a lost language, threads of the linen cuff analyzed to find whose faces it had touched and how many of those children sucked their thumbs. Sometimes jewels or manuscripts have been hidden in the quilt's cavernous insides. Sometimes the gold embroidery stitches swirl on calling cards of caring persons who might yet visit me (circa 1980).

Fable

I ride bareback a large horse in considerable traffic. Oh, a parade! Now I move the horse into a freight elevator [of the hotel where I work as a chef], all in one circular movement, like an old-time movie comedy. The horse enjoys the game as much as I do.

The woman manager of the hotel tells me she will keep the horse as a mascot in exchange for heaps of rich, non-smelly manure for her gardens. A horse is a horse, of course . . .

Soon there are crowds of wealthy people who come to this hotel for the novelty of its mascot roaming the public rooms.

A taxi draws up in front with five chauffeurs in it, the Marx Brothers–Groucho, Harpo, Chico, Zeppo, and Gummo. A man waiting at the curb calls out hopefully [like the lisping boy in "The Music Man"], "It might be, yes it might be, something special for me!"

I hope the taxi will give the man a lift. But what happens is, the door opens slightly, and Daisy [the mixed-breed dog in old Blondie and Dagwood movies] jumps into the taxi. Away they go–five chauffeurs, one harp and one dog–to a night at the opera (Feb 28, 1982).

Historical Romance

The King of England chooses me "to wife" [conditioned on] when I become a widow and he is free. I'm my own person in the meantime, with no titles or responsibilities yet with some honor. This is a king, not a prince or consort. At a costume ball, he's impeccably groomed in tight black pants, formal jacket, and white ruffled shirt. He wears two gold studs in his right ear and an ebony ring in his left ear.

There's warmth to his bodily presence and his smile. I'm only slightly put off when, in his public declaration concerning me, he says, "I'm not sure why I've chosen Margaret unless for her music." It's as if he has been drawn to me by fate, and he knows and feels enough not to resist.

Though he touches me only with handclasps and, in the formal declaration, on my shoulder, we both know there is to be a mature love relationship eventually. The music suggests "making beautiful music together" [sex] as well as enjoying the arts together.

I'm not troubled about the imposed waiting period or my future widowhood. I sense "all things in good time" and all good things in this lifetime (Nov 14, 1985).

Fairy Tale

I'm walking on a construction boardwalk, and now over debris, to get into a shoe store. At least three grown daughters are with me, sometimes trailing behind. Soon we're on a spot where the earth dips down or else has been cut away. Down this embankment are plants–weeds, briars, a few flowers. At the bottom is a three-strand wire fence, I think barb wire.

Cathy goes scooting down the hill, gets clothes caught in the wire, her long hair, too, and maybe her skin. I think about the fairy tale "Sleeping Beauty," where a wall of thorns grows up as protection for her and as a challenge for Prince Charming. Call this adventure "Waking Beauty."

I go down a more gradual incline. I need a hatchet to cut away branches that are shading fruits, flowers, and some lovely peach trees. All I have are my rose clippers and I must reach overhead to do the work, a strain on my shoulders. I wish I could go barefoot, but thorns and barb wire are hazards.

It's important to let the sun shine into this area, so I clip as best I can, also break a few large branches of a massive vine that's choking many things. I toss some pieces over the fence and, for the first time, notice there's a ditch on the other side and a road, maybe a highway, beyond that.

I wonder, Is Cathy happy? Is she mostly curious, as I am, about this terrain and its possibilities? Or does she long to get past this and join in the traffic beyond? I think she can get away from the fence with minimal damage to her clothes and her skin.

Now how will I get back up the hill again? It looks very steep, and the earth is soft, and I don't see any rocks for footholds. I may have to use roots of the monstrous vine that I'm trying to prune! (Feb 22, 1987).

Animal Hero

At a peak moment in an oratorio, I hear the tenor John McCormack singing exquisitely the final words of the story. The final image is of a dog whose name (or breed?) sounds like "Weinachtenabend."

The dog is almost mythical, swimming beyond boundaries into darkness–like a hero on whom everyone has placed hopes. Something related to what James Hillman calls "the process of Soul-making" assuredly as "a carrier of Soul" (Dec 5, 1992).

Old Woman, Old Woman

I approach an old woman who's almost blind. She wears a bright red scarf over scraggly gray hair. Several teeth are missing. She'd qualify as a hag in a story, yet she's powerful even in her declining years. She recognizes me by touch. We hug fiercely. There are two huge dogs that protect her–one a black lab, the other maybe a huskie (Feb 5, 1998).

Maiden, Mother, and Crone

I can't decide if they represent godmothers or guardians or graces. [Or maybe three faces = three phases.] As I face them, to my left is a dark-haired woman in a brilliant blue dress with black-and-white touches, not harlequin, but a suggestion of being "out there," probably "far out." In the middle is a woman in a two-piece dress, almost formal. The skirt is well below her knees but not to her ankles. Colors are orange to russet. To my right is an elderly woman. She's in burgundy velvet, very formal. The neckline is called "sweetheart," not round, not square (May 24, 2005).

Parodies

When I began reading, tentatively, about dream theories, I read one book by Sigmund Freud before proceeding to one by Carl Jung, whom several friends had recommended. My acknowledgment of Freud came in the following poem (circa 1983), copied almost verbatim from a dream:

Freudian Slips

In the full-dress uniform of Epitome Linen,
I entered the exit
of the Country Club Excelsior to deliver
hand-embroidered towels for the spa.
After swimming 50 laps in the nude,
I was enjoying a deep massage when
the manager noticed
I was not wearing the gold bullion of a member.
"Imposter!" he shouted.

I slid off the table,
ran down a marble corridor,
darted into the nearest steam room.
But it was For Men Only.
Sigmund Freud glanced up, saw my dilemma,
and acted as a decoy–
performing flamboyant exercises
to attract the manager's attention.
I ran around the corner and redressed
in the impeccable uniform of Epitome Linen.
At the exit I exited.

My next delivery was to the Faculty Club.
But *en route*–seeing Professor Freud
in full academic regalia
ascending the steps of Old Main–
I pulled over and jumped out of my van.
At the top of the stairs he beckoned to me.
I made a quantum leap from Superego to Id.
When I reached the professor,
he flourished his robe like a magician and
gathered me inside.

Siggy and I, cloaked in total harmony,
danced and caressed.
No matter that administrators and soccer players
were traipsing up and down the stairs.
Within the robe enfolding him and me,
buttons unbuttoned and seams yielded
of their own accord.
I gathered him inside.

A partner to this dream was another playful one (Jun 9, 1986), when I was reading a book by Jung. The dream's first words were, "Outrageous! Let's do it again!" In thanks for the light-heartedness, which I desperately needed, I based a poem on it:

Jung at Heart

"To individuation!" says Carl.
"To life!" I salute.
We bound off the trampoline,
hang-glide, and parachute.
"Outrageous! Let's do it again!"
A dry cleaner bag, a shower curtain,
any such for a sail . . .

Aviator and aviatrix,
we take off from a Florida cabana,
glide along the shore–
almost to Havana before
plunking down at dawn.
Next, above a tennis lawn,
we're doing it, doing it.

Now in someone's summer home–
a mansion where
a housemaid has been furbishing upstairs.
Carl flaps a satin sheet
while I go for organza.

We can scarcely hear her cry:
"What . . . do . . . you . . . mean . . . by . . ."
We've already come
and gone–humming down the atrium,
swishing out of there.

Pursued by Mafia,
we're wary of the welcome
of a shadowy *mama mia*
offering a ride to Home, Sweet Home.
We rise to the occasion–
on automatic pilot we fly.
"To transcendence!" says Carl.
"Bottoms up!" I reply,
as we sail the Mexicano sky.

Whodunit

I have saved the most detailed story for a finale to this section on bedtime stories. The lengthy dream itself (circa 1988) arose from my reading and from watching movies, plays, and television. I offer a clue for interpretation: Freud's oft-quoted remark, "Sometimes a cigar is just a cigar," which implies that most times it is more than a cigar.

Mysteries Never Cease

Sets
A mansion haunted by so many entities,
no one is sure who's alive, who's deceased.
A parlor with inherited furniture:
anachronistic, eccentric, the seat of howling furies.
A seedy dining room needing repair:
broken hearth, downtrodden carpet, swaying chandelier.
A kitchen with appliances switching off and on,
challenging the chef to a nervous breakdown.

Places, Everyone
Milord, a philanderer, ardent for sexy young women
who seem independent.
Milady, neither ardent nor sexy, yet capable
of dismissing his mistress as if she's invisible.
A humming maid with a stunning figure,
who moonlights as a spirit channeler.
A chef who, sans butler, manages the mansion,
despite wraiths taking stock in another dimension.

Camera
Figures all the angles, from close-up to zoom,
pursues from crypt to gallery,
from parlor to billiards room,
throughout this spooky dramedy.

Action
Two specters are throwing fits
about a missing decanter
used to serve strong spirits.
The maid exclaims, "Never no more!
It's already top-heavy with protoplasm."
She is piqued by milord's antiques
more than by his orgasms.

Climax
That man of means, never far from her,
is careless when lighting his Havher cigar.
A spark ignites the broken hearth.
It shakes the room and causes such a *BOOM!*
that the chef's souffle collapses in the fray.
Neighbors arrive. One, brandishing a gun,
shouts, "Is anyone alive?"

Milady, quick to recover, notes that the maid
has passed on to oblivion,
and says, "Yes . . . more or less."
She glances at that oafish lover,
raises one eyebrow to convey "How *gauche*,"
and toasts herself with Bacardi rum
before she dials 911.

Anti-climax
The good cop and the bad cop can't seem to agree.
They race around, confounded,
trace ephemeral clues, fingerprint, accuse
every entity that has a breath of life,
interrogate everyone but the prepossessed wife,
and come to the conclusion: *C'est la vie.*

That's a Wrap

– *Interlude* –

Consulting Mirrors

Recently, when backing out of my garage, I was stopped in my tracks for several minutes by a thought: This maneuver is similar to reviewing dreams!

The rearview mirror warns:

> OBJECTS IN THE MIRROR ARE
> CLOSER THAN THEY APPEAR

So, too, objects, situations, and feelings in dreams are closer than they appear; even a replay of Old Stuff is triggered by recent happenings. I was able to shift gears in the alley and make headway to a side street, to a through street, and toward my goal, yet my musing about dreams continued. Though they are rarely straightforward, often present obstacles, and require constant adaptations on my part, dreams do lead me onward, no matter how circuitous the route may seem.

While working on this memoir, there were times when I thought. "What a perceptive remark when I was a young adult!" and there were times when I thought, "Well, *duh*, how did I miss what was going on in that relationship?" Occasionally there was a dream that read like an exposé, yet I knew it was not necessarily an accurate picture of a situation, rather my emotional response to a situation.

I appreciate that my dreams and the morning reflections on them illustrate some of the obstacles that women of my era had to overcome, and challenges that they had to meet on a daily basis. While rarely addressing contemporaneous social problems explicitly, they do provide the context of a married woman of the Catholic persuasion.

In response to Monica's caution when I undertook this memoir, "You may come to the conclusion that there is no conclusion," she is correct in the sense that dream work and dream play are ongoing until death. Yet, while I was grouping dreams according to themes, and observing a great deal of cross-referencing, I was able to weave together strands of my life that had seemed separate and inexplicable before. Such cross-referencing and weaving have helped me to integrate disparate aspects of Self, especially in times when I felt I was disintegrating, piece by piece. Now the realization *that everything fits* has healed any split in my Self, whether of intention or action.

During the work-in-progress stage of compiling *Dream Encounters*, I made the following sequential observations:

- I was afraid that re-reading the dream notes would dredge up memories that I might have trouble dealing with, that I would lose sleep over yet again. Fortunately, I've been able to read them as if they were short stories by a contemporary author.
- What has surprised me most, and reassured me, is that I can trust my memory about major events in my life. Although I fail to remember many things, what I remember is accurate.
- There are, in my advanced years, no significant changes in the number of dreams or the intensity of feelings within them.
- There is one aspect of dreams that has gained more importance over the years: a growing respect for writing feelings on the dream tablet during the night. Without access to the original feelings, I could not have proceeded beyond the first sorting of the dreams.
- That my dreams indicate very little of what was transpiring in the "real world" two generations ago is surprising to me now. All the years I was on campus, and for some time after that, I was an activist and had little tolerance for folks who sat around talking about how weird or distorted or wrong conditions seemed to be. Anyhow, I do not apologize for, or magnify, the original raw content of the dreams.
- Similarly, there are few allusions to politics, even though my husband held elected positions for many years and was involved with township, city, county, state, and federal projects, and our family worked on several election campaigns. If memory serves, all that concentrated activity brought feelings to the

surface that were dealt with consciously rather than imbedded in dreams.
- I am astonished at the anger repressed to the age of 53! And vexed that it seemed necessary, even at that age, to add a statement, "My mother did the best she could," as if I were still afraid of reprisal almost two years after her death.
- How I've managed to overlook, until the third iteration of this book, that Graduating is one of my dream themes, amazes me.
- Another theme I have not emphasized enough is that of Longing. It still persists, decades after the near-death experience, in notes like this one: "Not simply that I am a survivor, but that I am a chronicler of how it feels to straddle Time's chasm, with one foot on Earth and the other foot in the air, leaping" (Aug 16, 2016).
- I am a more compassionate person after reviewing my thousands of dream notes. Having at last learned how to be kind to myself, I can respond–in the affirmative–to other persons engaged in knowing and forgiving themselves.
- I am an active participant in most of my dreams; it is a rare occurrence when I merely observe a scene. Even then I come up with qualifiers, like this: "I'm the observer. I feel like a co-author, though, or a collector of folk tales. There's some collaboration going on, even though I'm not actively involved" (May 28, 1983).
- When I first noted an in-and-out scene, wherein I alternated acting and observing (Mar 13, 1976), I thought that the distancing indicated fear on my part. But that did not hold true subsequently. Two years later (Mar 4, 1978), I decided that "in-and-out scenes indicate my rational self getting involved, trying to set the picture straight." Later, during a meeting of Dreamtalk (Apr 28, 1983), someone offered that the distancing may be a signal to look more objectively at the *overall story*. Years passed before I felt confident that my Conscious is in constant dialogue with my Unconscious, and that intuition happily partners with intellectual discernment.
- My vocabulary when writing the dream notes is another surprise. There are words that I never use in conversation,

also a few words that have sent me to the dictionary in the morning, either to verify the meaning or to check the spelling. This verbal fluency in the middle of the night confirms my belief that *everything* goes into one's subconscious memory bank. Also, in a sleep state, retrieval is more immediate and often easier than in an awake state.

- I know that dreams have an inner logic and I've found in my dream notes a particular grammar. But I am not a linguist, nor have I read research about a grammar within dreams, so I can only mention a few features in mine: (1) mostly simple sentences, not compound or complex; (2) present tense *now*, not alluding to a past or a future with words like *before* or *next*; (3) few adverbs qualifying the verbs; and (4) an abundance of questions beginning with *Why*, a few with *What*, but almost none with *How*, *When*, or *Where*.
- For the most part, I have been highly aware during dreams, in a semi-lucid state. This caused evaluations *within* some dreams; a comical one was, "Proof-reading is not a good activity for dream life" (Dec 26, 1976). Whenever I have tried analyzing within a dream, that logical functioning caused an abrupt awakening.
- I should not be surprised by how many "big" dreams occur in the Christmas season, because I do considerable conscious reviewing in December and January. I am surprised, though, by how few "big" dreams have occurred near my birthday in mid-July, which is another time of conscious reviewing.
- Occasionally while sorting dream notes, I've found myself laughing out loud. Strange juxtapositions and non-sequiturs have me wondering, *What on earth?* I wish I'd saved more to provide comic relief for the serious dreams.
- I truly appreciate Charles McPhee's summary, in *Stop Sleeping through Your Dreams*, of qualities effortlessly displayed in our dreams: "Dreams speak an uncanny yet beautiful, uniquely personal language. They are fabulous creations, often displaying a sophisticated sense of humor." I know there is redeeming social value in entertainment dreams, whether sophisticated or slapstick.

- A statement by Elizabeth Gilbert in her book, *Big Magic*, comforts me: "What you produce is not necessarily always sacred just because you think it's sacred. What is sacred is the time that you spend working on the project, and what that time does to expand your imagination, and what that expanded imagination does to transform your life."
- About displacement in dreams, there is a parallel in a favorite puzzle that my children owned: blocks that, when stacked, could present the face of one person, the torso of another, and the legs of a third, with comical effects. In dreams, the stacking of personal features or behaviors is more subtle, not always comical, and sometimes dramatic. Dreams with displacement have shown me never to categorize a person in waking life, never to wedge him or her into a particular relationship.
- I am pleased by indications in dreams that my relationships with persons, as well as my perspective on many issues, have changed—mostly toward the gracious and the generous.

Now I include reassuring lines written on my dream tablet, relative to the images, barriers, and fears revealed in dream encounters:

Reflection in the Morning Mirror

When the laser of my intellect
bores a passage through
this trembling self-image,
and allows the electrons of my cells
to dance with the electrons of the mirror,

the barrier dissipates,
harmless as the bathroom steam
that clears each morning,
allowing me to face
what was never to be feared.

– *Seventeen* –

Erotic Encounters

It seems necessary to provide a context for the four types of erotic dreams included here. As a practicing Catholic, I faced challenges concerning sex, even when consummated within marriage; chief among them was the issue of birth control. It was understandable that during the years that my husband and I resorted to abstinence, relying on the "rhythm method' of birth control, I was sexually frustrated for a week or longer every month and had erotic dreams. It was not understandable that, after having a hysterectomy and the privilege of enjoying sex spontaneously, I would still have erotic dreams, and with an array of partners. Was I a nymphomaniac? The Church preached that sex was "for the procreation and education of children," with a parenthetical note about "the relief of concupiscence."

I was a virgin before marriage at age 19, monogamous for the 31 years of marriage, and celibate thereafter, the latter not by choice. The frequency of erotic dreams–from three to five every month–bothered me for several years because, for the most part, they involved persons I knew well. I worried, How could I even think of such a thing? Am I betraying our marriage? I needed to learn from dream workers like Patricia Garfield and Jeremy Taylor to appreciate every sexual encounter in dreams because those experiences bring about, in addition to relief of concupiscence, total acceptance of self, total acceptance of others, and spiritual encounters.

Gradually I became comfortable when involved in romantic and sexual dreams such as "Kiss and Tell" (May 20, 1977). "At a party we are pairing off, not with our own mate, and someone is scandalized by this. I go to a teller and ask her to explain that anything is permissible in a dream, that a rich and varied love life is desirable. She acts as if everybody knows this, why bother telling it?"

In advance of tracing *themes* among the erotic dreams, I offer two *motifs* that appeared numerous times: chocolate and ice cream. The first, chocolate, concerned romance in the broadest sense of the word, including friendship, love, and career. I trust these are clear in the following poem, which I transposed from a constellation of dreams:

Sweet Dreams

11:30 p.m. Reserve
not chocolate delight but torment
doubly sweet . . . dark . . . forbidden . . .
treacherous . . . and heart-rending
with calories

1 a.m.   Just Desserts
I am your spring roll, a delicacy–
rich, but with a thin skin.
When you nibble, do so gently.
You are my fortune cooky–
golden, yielding a cryptic message.
I read you eagerly.

2:30 a.m.   His and Hershey
Chef Emiril and Julia Childs
vie for the State Fair crown
while an artist sculpts their busts in butter
and an emcee rouses the crowd:
"What will it be . . . sharp or mild?"
"What did you say . . . sweet or bitter?"
while I stand paralyzed by wishes
and aching for deep chocolate kisses.

4 a.m.   Aphrodisiacs
A surprise party in reverse:
My guests eat, drink, and be merry
until–abruptly–they all pick up and leave.
Wink-wink, nudge-nudge, they josh me,

"The coast is clear, make the most of it."
I'm ready to close the door
when I see a man's form
and wonder who will materialize.
He knocks lightly on my forehead
and says, "Surprise!"
I'm so flustered, all I can muster is,
"Well, hel-lo there!"
It's Richard Gere.

He gives me violets, I serve him wine,
and conversation is what we dine on.
He brings me up to date
on all things Chicago,
and demonstrates the latest dances,
leaving me entranced.
We meld into a dazzling duo.
He draws me to, I pull him fro,
he lifts me and I soar . . .
Beyond all bounds we go,
in infinitely more
than choreography.

5:30 a.m.   Sticky Buns
In the state of bliss known as Vermont,
in a high meadow I'm sunbathing—
lulled by the lazy drone of bees,
undisturbed until a dog comes panting
and glides to a hunter's point,
his muzzle perilously close to me.
I get up slowly, gaze across a daisy field,
and see my lover—yes, the Sundance Kid.
Arms outstretched, we run toward one another,
as romantic as an ad for Faberge.
He lavishes endearments that take liberty
with facts: *beautiful . . . desirable . . . lovely . . .*
I take liberty with his clothes,

and we have a toss in the hay.
Now, as I hear him say,
Come to me my melancholy Maggie,
I come. It's that right, or I'm that easy.

7 a.m.   Sugar Fix
I waken myself calling out,
Give me liberty or give me chocolate!

This constellation of dreams included forbidden sweets, surprises, and superstar lovers. What was the *theme*? One could answer, "Wish fulfillment." A more thoughtful response might be, "Longing, because the longing is deeper than the wishing." Consider the first descriptors–dark, forbidden, treacherous, heart-rending–and the final line, which can be understood as, "If I can't have the liberty of romance in my life, then at least give me a sweet substitute." It seems odd that in the midst of the beguiling food, I don't eat any. Credit that to inhibition? to self-discipline? or to satisfaction provided in the dream itself?

The second motif closely associated with erotic dreams was ice cream. In the first two years of my note-taking, there were ten entries in my concordance featuring ice cream; the frequency dwindled after that. Here are two of the earliest examples:

Jul 7, 1975
An Ice Cream Truck That I Drive

> A man has an ice cream truck and abandons it. I try driving it home, and it's so big I almost hit a woman in a gold dress. I get it to our driveway, now open it, and start tasting the flavors by putting my hands in the big containers [deep, like at Baskin-Robbins].
>
> My husband gives me a dirty look. He puts the truck in the garage [an impossibility] and doesn't do anything about the situation but make me feel guilty, though most of the ice cream hasn't been touched.

FEELINGS:
Surprised, resourceful, eager, greedy, overpowered, reprimanded.

REFLECTIONS:
1. In a recent dream I chose "Borden's because it's got to be good." Here I choose to sample several possibilities.
2. In this dream there's anxiety about the truck driver. Will he lose his job? Can he get another job? That resonates with job searches by my husband as well as myself.
3. The woman in gold is an idealized woman. I almost bump her off in my desire for fulfillment.

Less than two years later there was a poignant scenario represented by ice cream:

Feb 21, 1977
Odd-Sized Gift Boxes All Holding Ice Cream

> My husband gives me a half-dozen gifts in odd-sized boxes. But every package, including the one that looks like a necktie box, holds ice cream. I keep looking for a surprise. It's not a pleasant surprise that every package holds the same thing.
> After opening them, I try to say something polite. I comment on the two boxes of chocolate, "One must be double-chocolate, and the other mocha." In fact, when I test the lighter ice cream, using a teaspoon, I'm disappointed—it's plain, ordinary chocolate. Also, I know that my husband will eat the rest of it now that I've started it, and I'm resentful over that.
> I close the lid, wondering how the ice cream is supposed to stay firm if it's not kept in the right conditions.

FEELINGS:
From eager to disappointed, polite to resentful, near despair.

REFLECTIONS:
1. This dream is a reflection of our marriage. Enough said.
2. How many people have a passionate craving for ice cream? For them, what does it represent? In this dream of mine, it's sex. On the plus side: sweet and smooth, goes down easily; can be licked, spooned, swallowed; can be enjoyed alone or served a la mode; is a socially acceptable treat in every instance, every weather, all over the world; is served and enjoyed in the best places. On

the minus side, it doesn't stay firm but melts easily; can drip and cause embarrassment; is consumed readily; and creates a desire for more, more.
3. The variety of dream contexts in which the ice cream motif appears, suggests that it has a more general meaning, too–the freedom to make choices.

Theme: Almosting It
Notes Prior to 1975

In one of the earliest entries on a dream tablet, I lamented, "I feel cheated of my youth, cheated of fun and freedom. If I'd had some love affairs back then, would I be crying now over a lost youth?"

In response to a dream, "Love Play with Bob Newhart," I wrote, "I could still love, with a new heart, with a different disposition than I've had before. And maybe I can love heartily, and be loved heartily, in a manner I haven't experienced before" (Dec 9, 1975).

I had been so disciplined in restraint for so many years that I was inhibited even in dreams. The following selection from a dream poem, "A Series of One-Acts," shows several constraints:

Bedroom Farce: Inhibitors Working Overtime

In my blue silk kimono and floppy slippers,
I go to the door for the morning paper.
There a male carrier makes a pass at me.
I think he won't deliver, but
he comes, questions only, "Where?"
and floors me, clinging passionately.
Yet (to my surprise) he listens when I plead,
Stop! My Conscience won't allow it!
He leaves, dragging his security blanket
and clinging to a teddy bear.

I'm no sooner in my bedroom than there's
a proposal from another man who's in
top hat and tails, with a gold-studded cane.
I kiss him, caress him, want him
to know how much I care.
It's an old refrain,
I can't, even though with you
I'd love to . . .
He disbelieves, shrugs the affair,
leaves unconsoled.
When a woman comes, I'm not sexually aware
of her female anatomy,
so caught up am I in unfolding
my soap opera existence, biodegradable love.
I do notice that she wears
my white negligee.

Almost immediately there's trespassing.
An intruder comes from behind,
imposes hands
heavily on my shoulders, mounts me, and
—thrusting—presumes to say,
"You're not holding firmly enough."
This when I'm trying to break away!
There's no rescue, either, by a Royal Mountie
while an imposed Conscience is screwing me.

Dreams of "almosting it" went from "unsuccessful attempts at lovemaking" to "caressing and awakening with a kiss;" from "gentle and thorough kissing with an unidentified man" to "almost fulfilling;" from "intercourse interrupted several times" to "almost climaxing."

Family life had to be reckoned with, even in my dreams. For example, even when I was "in my inner chamber, at heart's ease with a lover, and I had taken care to lock the door from the inside," all too often there was a tapping on my door. A child or my husband stood there and, like Poe's raven, conveyed the message, "Nevermore."

In this section I include more poems based on dreams than in any other section. Writing them brought release that was not available through sexual enactment.

Theme: Engaging in Sex Play
Notes 1975 through 1978

I never got enough playfulness in waking life or dream life, so I was delighted when "Playfulness in the guise of a pantomime artist" helped me shed some inhibitions (Feb 8, 1976).

In the beginning of my note-taking, the men were all unknowns. Eventually I learned to ask my partner's name because, "I want to be loving the real you" (Dec 19, 1976). Later, when I knew very well who my partner was, I sometimes hesitated, sometimes went full-steam ahead. In my morning Reflections, I tried to understand what had prompted the encounter, with questions like these:

- Is it a quality I admire in him and want to emulate?
- Is it a quality in myself that he sees in me and I don't recognize?
- Does the dream relate to a recent conversation? If so, to what purpose now?
- Is his presence in the dream how I perceive him in waking life, or not?
- Is this a reminder to get in touch with him? To stay away from him?

While at the university in the early 1970's, I was in my prime. That helps explain why I had erotic dreams involving fellow students, some of them poets. With two of them, I shared poems transposed from those dreams, knowing that they would understand. They did, and were flattered because, even when the dream showed me as competitive, there was a current of eroticism underneath.

Also, a professor arranged for me to partner with a poet who was probably 15 years younger than I (only five years younger if my university I.D. were to be trusted). Bruce and I alternated meeting at his house and mine to go over lines, even though my husband was terribly jealous about this. His jealously may have increased that poet's attractiveness; at any rate, the first dream in which I reported reaching orgasm was with him and was "so gratifying, with total acceptance, that it's reinforced whatever conscious caring I've had for Bruce" (Dec 25, 1975). It was several years before I let Bruce read some dreams I'd had about him. His response was typical of him, without elaboration, "I'm glad I give you great orgasms."

In Graduate School, at age 42 (though my I.D. mistakenly showed 32) I had sexual dreams involving professors, particularly the one who was mentoring me when my assigned advisor was busy getting a divorce. I did not relate my dreams to Jay, but had a few occasions to convey my feelings through some riddle poems that I was experimenting with. (In courtly love, romantic riddles were understood as *word play only*).

What Jay reminded me of–subjectively–was all that I had missed in relationships with men, and all that I did not know about literature and life. He also reminded me–objectively–of what I had to offer as a "mature student" and as a poet, and he challenged me to improve the critical essays I was submitting for publication. He had that much confidence in me, heady stuff! With him I was not inhibited, but I was circumspect.

In an undated dream note in 1975, I admitted, "Yes, a kind of enchantment, without incantation or drugs, and without intercourse." Further, "I do think that if I were to have a sexual dream with Jay, or a flying dream with him, I'd feel relief from the tension that builds when I'm with him in waking life." That release and relief did not occur until a year after my commencement, when I was on campus for another reason and visited Jay on the spur of the moment. He was as welcoming and gracious as ever and, in a dream that night, I had an explosive sexual encounter with him. Ta-da!

In contrast to Jay, in a dream of compensation, another professor and I did some square-dance maneuvers, alternating who was the pivot and who the swinger. "I say to Robert, 'So this is how it feels to stand up and be counted!' He turns to face me and says, 'Didn't you realize I'm standing up for you?' He pulls me close, to feel his erect penis, very hot even through clothing. 'I did not know,' I say, laughing and delighted" (Aug 11, 1975).

Yet another prof, whom I considered my nemesis in waking life, appeared differently in a dream:

Nov. 5, 1975
Change in a Relationship

> George says "Relax" in such a way that I go deep [into hypnosis]. Now he's lying on a bed next to mine, reaching to me, holding my hand, now arm and elbow. I curl up, put his one hand on my thigh, and go deeper.
>   Now I hear him talking to my husband, saying, "A poet—and your wife is a poet—feels and sees, registers at several levels of consciousness at once and with intense emotions. Notice how deep in sleep she is, but she knows what is going on here, in herself, outdoors, in her past life . . . and you can't stop her."

There were two music professors that I dreamed about, long after I had left the Music School, usually after having heard one of them in a concert–soaring, as in sex. There were also women on campus who were the subjects of sexual dreams, but I did not share my dreams with them. Why? I was afraid that they might consider it a come-on. For the same reason, I was careful even when complimenting a woman. In a snippet of a dream, "Passionate Scene With a Woman Friend," I was "quite overcome by her powerful feelings and attraction to me. It's gratifying, but I'm puzzled. Did I lead her on? Can she think only in terms of sexual passion?" Years later, when I had developed deep and lasting friendships with several lesbians, they encouraged spontaneous speech and hugs.

In the summer of 1977, following a sexual dream, I wrote in my Reflections about *The Hite Report*, concerning "arousal and orgasm during petting and necking that peaked higher than any experiences women had during intercourse." The author explained that this peaking was due to the *prolonging* of the intimacy, which did not occur in the "slam-bam-thank you ma'am" version of intercourse described repeatedly throughout the book.

That summer I was thinking of Bruce, about my reservations concerning a sexual adventure with him, and concluded, "Oh, the reservations are mine, about my body, not about his behavior" (Jul

24, 1977). Yet, considering that his forebears were in Scotland, and he'd always wanted to trace his lineage there, I invited him to meet me in Scotland after a conference I was to attend. His refusal was two-pronged, "You're too nice for that" [meaning a Highland fling]. Then, "I am not a home-wrecker." I asked, "Who would ever know?" He answered, "We would." Then out of my life he went, fading into the sunset. I had gambled and lost a friend.

After that loss, I perceived that many of my sexual dreams were a defense against my falling in love in waking life. At that time I thought I could choose to love, not to *fall for* anyone or anything. The following poem, based on dream images in 1978, declared my independence in the title but not in the conclusion:

Recently I Had a Dream that Wasn't about You

At first temptations were only candy
kisses, smacks, red hots, tootsies.
Then I was carried away on a pleasure cruise,
enjoying the captain's cabin and spread,
smooth sailing all the way.

Overseas, Schubert desired me
to finish his unfinished symphony.
Rodin aspired to round out my curves
through initial life studies, nude.
Yeats yearned for the dancer and the dance.

In Switzerland I was pursued
by a St. Bernard's loud pants
and ardent tail-wagging.
My petting raised his temperature
so high, he melted the snow.

At a hostel I was asked by a traveler,
"How far do you want to go?"
Inflecting French in the future,
I said, "Every breathless step, each climb,
each peak . . . because it's there."

You know the story?
Apart from my dream?
I went out alone in the alpine air,
and wakened the valley
calling your name.

Theme: Enjoying Foreplay and More Play Notes 1979 through 1987

Playfulness has such a high value that it recurs many times and in diverse situations in my dreams. The next two dreams illustrate the enjoyment of playfulness and the thwarting of it.

Oct 27, 1979
Sexual Activity Endorsed by a Docent

> In a group of adults, the last session of a course on architecture. We go into a building that's like a chemistry lab, now more like a warehouse, now like a corridor in cloisters—very shadowy, though there are windows along the left wall.
> Our instructor tells us to listen to the docent ahead of us, who is lecturing on Romanesque features. Now we're in an adjacent room, well lighted. There's some point made about a great canopied bed. Our group is completely disinterested. I don't know when or how sexual activity here begins, but it seems to be stimulated or at least encouraged by our group's docent, a woman. She's standing on a bed and undressing, as if to show us how—it's not a striptease, just an undressing. I see that she's cold—though she's almost flat-chested, her nipples harden and body hairs stand up because she's chilled.
> There's a perfectly permissive atmosphere. When a man makes an inviting remark to me, I snuggle up to him. He starts nuzzling me, and I take off my sweater and blouse. Now we're both naked, though I've slid under a sheet. He joins me, and I feel how thin he is—tall and thin but not bony—and he has loverly hands. We caress and enjoy foreplay, even with all

the other adult activity around us, as if ours were somehow a private matter. But he stops abruptly and begins dressing again, saying, "There's too much going on around here."

I'm surprised, perplexed, and disappointed. I say, "We can find another place." I feel desirable, an even stronger feeling than desiring. The man isn't rejecting me, he's rejecting the confusion all around us.

Apr 6, 1981
Expansiveness and Love in the Attic

I'm talking with a contractor who's finished the walls and rafters, giving the attic a feeling of lightness and expansiveness. It's understood between us that the present moment is a culmination. This is a time for caressing, as if the plans included this. We don't call one another by name, though.

He tells me to relax when I've just begun to tingle. He explores my lips and tongue with his tongue, delicately, gently. Now his tongue is like an artist's tool–a feather, a gentle swab. There's a giving on his part, and for me a soothing that I must be needing, and he knows it somehow. No single move seems preliminary to another, but is efficacious in itself and undemanding.

When we have intercourse, the same feelings prevail–exploration, caressing, soothing–as if his penis can fulfill needs I don't even realize I have.

FEELINGS:
Light, expansive, cherished, fulfilled.

REFLECTION:
Seemingly I have greater freedom regarding my future than I've dreamed of before.

In September of 1981, I had several dreams about a dear friend and confidante. It was John Kneisly who had told me, when I was in a vulnerable state, "Everyone in Montage [a poetry performance group] respects the others, but there's one person we all love: Margaret." That dreams about John were erotic did not surprise me;

by then I was aware of the many levels of union in such dreams. I include here only the beginning of one, for its humor. "John is dressed elegantly for work. After one kiss he says, 'There goes work for today!' and begins undressing" (Sep 17, 1981).

After establishing that "I have a right to mixed affection" (Dec 1, 1981), I went ahead and had "an intimate conversation with Cary Grant, followed by rocking and intercourse" (Jun 12, 1983). His name was a pun for a "caring, granting lover." Six months later I was with a man who "looks and walks and talks like Gary Cooper–quiet, almost naive. I'm close to him physically and we kiss ever so gently. Now it's like we're breathing the same Life Force. Though we become passionate, it's the original kiss that I remember–a mutual giving, not a taking, nothing possessive about it" (Feb 17, 1984).

At that time I read an article, "Sex, Intimacy, and the Older Woman," in which a medical doctor, Domeena C. Renshaw, stated the following:

> Even in the unconscious, uninhibited state of sleep, there are dream cycles (for an adult usually 4 per 8 hours) during which 80% of the time the sexual arousal and response occurs, sometimes quite normally, with a sexual dream and even a sleep orgasm.

From that statement I felt reassured that my frequent sexual encounters in dreams were statistically within the normal range. Enjoying sexual intimacy and intercourse in dreams had additional values beyond the release of biological tension or the expression of fantasy, even beyond the desire to integrate an aspect of another person or a quality I wished to emulate. It also signaled a desire to relate in a new way to an identifiable person and the milieu we shared.

There can never be too much sexual expression in dream life. Sometimes what it amounts to is a complementing of a personal quality. For example, one of my dream lovers is a gorgeous, tall, black woman with an outgoing personality–a perfect complement to my introverted state.

In a surrealistic dream, "My breasts are blooming like gardenias or camellias–fragrant, smooth, with the illusion of purity! My left breast is in full bloom, my right just blossoming. A man thinks he can draw the right one into opening by sucking on it. But it's a woman who comes to me, caressing and licking–not sucking–and has me peaking all over" (May 18, 1985). If that was surprising, the next dream was mystifying:

Jul 10, 1985
A Young Girl Sets about Arousing Me

> I go to the living room window, part the gold draperies, and look at the ravages of last night's storm. Now I feel a presence close to me. I don't hear or feel breathing, just an electrical charge that makes the hairs stand up on my neck and arms. This happens so pervasively that I'm not afraid of this powerful energy field. I reach my hand back in an exploratory way. I feel firm flesh and now female genitals–as if I've been led to the spot. But this is just a girl! What's going on here?
>
> Lights have turned back on, and I can see her body and the totally absorbed sexual expression on her face–not titillation but total involvement in arousing me sexually. Now she says a few words to someone she addresses as "Mother" or "Lady Mother," a great goddess, I'm sure. Now she says, "See how well we're coming. See these lovely pointed nipples–they won't let down for quite a while!" This girl/woman is excited and exciting, giving pleasure and taking pleasure. I am totally receptive and, however strange this sounds, during the act I form a prayer.

FEELINGS:
I feel I will burst and cream all over the sofa. This intensity is what wakens me. Yet there's something more, on the spiritual level.

REFLECTIONS:
1. The girl reminds me of a Grecian wood sprite or nymph, so I've consulted a mythology at hand. It describes nymphs as young girls who love to dance and sing and often are extremely amorous. Surprise: The Muses are a kind of nymph, "although some of them assume virtually the stature of deity." Well, if I have a

Muse overseeing my affairs, I'm in good hands! Or if this dream is an introduction to Psyche and Eros, I'm doubly blessed.
2. My prayer within the dream was, "Most Holy One, bring me a slow and careful, playful, delightful, delighting lover. I believe this can happen. I trust this will happen."

Theme: Inviting My Playmate Lover
Notes After My Near-Death Experience

Two years after my NDE, I made the inference that "dreams help me rehearse for a place and time and way to enjoy sex with a partner. Rehearsing in dreams, I can set the stage and gain confidence for acting appropriately in waking life" (Jan 9, 1992). By December of that year, I discovered myself lucid in a dream of "flying with a man. We're soaring and I don't pull out of it" (Dec 30, 1992). Near my 61st birthday, after a wonderful evening with Fred, I had a fantastical dream, "Throwing Myself at a Man" (Jul 16, 1993). A comment on it was, "I hope to be as comfortable with any man I meet as I am with Fred."

Two months later, in a dream called "Highly Charged and Released Sexual Energy," I had known a man for only a short while, yet felt "passion as urgency . . . now . . . NOW! The first time, we draw together. The second time, I'm all over him. The third time, I only look at him and he's pressing his body against me. The attraction is mutual, intense, and gratifying" (Sep 26, 1993).

Shortly after that dream and a dream workshop conducted by Jeremy Taylor, came this realization: "What I'm looking for in a Playmate Lover is a three-in-one man! Someone who: #1 totally accepts my practice of Reiki; #2 finds me sexually attractive and satisfying; and #3 knows how to be affectionate and playful. DR and Fred fulfill #1, Michael fulfills #3, but who—and when—fulfills #2?"

When there were erotic episodes in dreams that did not lead to climax, I recalled Jeremy Taylor's statement, "Unconsummated sex in a dream suggests a missed opportunity in one's spiritual development." But even after that counsel, I wanted to know the lover in my dreams (as much as in waking life) and to be known by him.

In an undated entry about that time, there were more questions about his identity. "Oh my, is the lover whose identity keeps me in the dark Eros himself? Saying that the lover is Love itself felt right when I started scribbling, but now sounds sappy. For me the point of the myth about Psyche and Eros seems to be *If only* . . . If only Psyche had restrained her curiosity, she wouldn't have wakened Eros with the melting wax of her candle; aroused her sisters' envy and malicious remarks; caused Venus' retribution; or brought about a series of trials and the necessity of helpers before she could be reunited with him. Yet there is surely something deeper than mere curiosity in Psyche; she *needs* to know his identity. That need impinges on her own identity and sense of selfhood."

A most unusual dream a few months later (Oct 3, 1994) was spelled out in three words:

LOVE
Show Me

I debated, "Was this my own prayer? or a Divine call? or a message from a potential lover? All of the above?" The answer, according to my signal system, was "All of the above." So I proceeded with more questions–12 of them–and at the end was prompted to focus on two answers to the riddle:

- Love is shown to me through dreams
- Love is shown to me through DR [massage therapist] and the healing work we do together.

The next variant on Erotic Dreams left me guessing, even more than usual, about the man's identity. I felt that he was Other. But was he a potential lover? a guide? or someone I already knew?

On my dream tablet at that time were scribbles that I was able to piece together in daylight. They illustrated a sexual dream that had a spiritual component, too:

In a Dream I Have Yet to Realize

> A Great Being—androgynous,
> garbed in violet light, or composed of it—
> drifts through my bedroom wall.
> The wall begins to pulsate violet,
> and I hear a voice of the same vibration:
> This is my beloved
> in whom I am well pleased.
>
> The Light Being turns slowly,
> now faster, faster, and hums—
> a musical top spinning bright spheres,
> a whirlpool rising, evolving into
> a double rainbow.
> One of its arcs is my Playmate Lover.
>
> Each riband of light unfurls,
> 70 times 7 strands inviting.
> Now my strands intertwine with his.
> We turn slowly, faster, faster,
> creating a series of overtones.
> Such pulsations! Such a hum . . .

As an example of my firm belief in a Playmate Lover, here is an excerpt from a letter (Dec 16, 1999) that I wrote to a friend back in Columbus:

> I fully expected both phenomena—erotic and ecstatic—to occur when merging with my Playmate Lover. When he did not materialize in Columbus, I assumed he would in Pueblo. But after I made a fool of myself, misinterpreting things that a handsome man here said to me, I gave up hoping. Well, not completely, because I did several Resonance Repatterning sessions to remove possible conflicts between my Unconscious and my Conscious on this subject.

In my dreams for many years, the man is younger, in excellent health, and always/all ways is playful. How many men are like this? How many are available? What is the chance that I could meet him?

Maybe we will be introduced by a mutual friend who knows our good qualities. This is why I'm delighted that Joanne sees in me my "bouncy child," and why I hold to the hope that a potential lover will see this quality, too.

Certainly I was aware of statistics concerning both the availability of men and their expected life-span. But I was convinced of an over-riding factor relative to the expression of love. I believed that my purpose in surviving the NDE was to fulfill three goals: First, heal myself. Second, help others heal themselves. Third, tune in to joy and carry the vibration of joy throughout my days. I sincerely believed that recognizing my Playmate Lover, and uniting my energy field with his, was part of the plan or compact or contract for my 1990 lifetime. *How* it would play out remained a mystery.

– *Eighteen* –

Here Comes Everybody

While crowd scenes appear throughout the years of my dream notes, there are also individual personages who resonate with archetypes. Regarding personal myths, Thomas Moore, in *Care Of the Soul*, maintains that it is not necessary to label one's deep, mythic stories with Greek or Roman names. Each of us can enlarge our thinking to include the mysteries at work in our lives that will never be fully explained. He recommends observing the myths "that are particularly ours as individuals . . . each of us has our own special demons and divine figures, our own other-world landscapes and struggles."

From my childhood, contemporaneously with the terrifying Big Nurse was the White-Haired Young Woman, whom I never could explain. She was always smiling and often beckoning. I deduced that she was someone from my future, or even myself in the future, though that was beyond fathoming. Early dream notes described "a 65-year-old white-haired baby sitter, very attractive" (Apr 15, 1975). Also, "My white-haired young woman rides an escalator to a shrine"(Apr 19, 1975). When I was at the university, one professor fit that image perfectly, but I never discussed anything personal with her. In recent years I have wondered if that figure represented my sister Maureen, whose hair was completely white at age 50; though younger than I, Maureen has led me to new ideas and expressions.

From age 30 onward, I embraced my Bosomy Black Woman. She epitomized freedom of movement and freedom of expression–*all that jazz*. And I loved her flamboyant hats, unique and oh so colorful. Ten years into dream work I noted: "She has previously expressed my sexuality (physical level). Last month she expressed my creativity and intellectual gifts (mental level). Now she illuminates my soul (spiritual level). I've spent considerable time trying to arrive at her name. It is Mnemosyne! She is the Goddess of Memory and the mother of all Muses! (Mar 22, 1985).

This section on personal myths shows my Unconscious reveling in juxtapositions of unlike images and characters. Yet somehow they belong together. Though sometimes I could not make sense of the jumble, I felt sure of one thing: *It all fit.*

It was 10 years into my processing of dream notes when I made two important inferences:

- It is enough to know that everything in my life does fit. While it may be desirable to integrate many figures and associations and feelings, it is not necessary, not even for an artist. Let some things be!
- I need to quit searching for the prescribed right-shaped pegs for the right holes, or the right-colored beads for a given design. I can go beyond my identity as Margaret-who-needs-to-know. I can be simply Margaret-the-yea-sayer.

This section on Personal Myths features vignettes, ranging from the ridiculous to the sublime. I have included these examples without reference to why they occurred at a particular time, or to what efforts I made to incorporate their meaning in my waking life.

Personal Myths

Artist's Model

Jack Benny is narrator. In the finale he's dressed like a female portrait by Gainsborough (Apr 23, 1975).

Dracula

In a dark castle-like house with a huge entry hall, wide, curving stairs, and the requisite sliding panels, hidden staircases, and dungeons, police come to investigate one murder and find bodies all over the lawn–dead or dying (Sep 21, 1975).

Magician

> Lou Grant is manager of a small airport. I want to fly to Grand Rapids, but he doesn't want me to. He disguises the planes as camels and elephants. What a circus! (Nov 16, 1975).

Matinee Idols

> Here are Gary Cooper, Clark Gable, and Cary Grant together, but saying and doing nothing! It's their initials that are important, and I need to settle something with C.G. in waking life (Dec 24, 1975).

Giants at Odds

> A satire called "The Man Who Came To Death" stars a giant of a woman who stands up against her giant husband (Dec 16, 1977).

Slapstick Comedians

> Laurel and Hardy in a laboratory are throwing potatoes against a wall, for sound effects, also for symbolism that the audience understands (Jan 5, 1978).

Nature Sprites

> Everything is blooming all at once–daffodils and tulips, lilies of the valley and violets, peonies and roses, daisies and delphinium. Amazing. And it's orchestrated–there's a motion to the flowers themselves, or through them, as if nature sprites have just walked through (Jan 4, 1980).

Pantomime Artist

> Dressed in silver and blue, zippered up and down two sides, he draws me. The spirit of playfulness touches me–shoulders, elbows, fingers, lips, bones to the marrow, flesh to the quick (1982).

Prankster

> A story or a ballad about Kuniyoshi, a boy with a blue bear. There's a downhill sweep [as in the story of "The Gingerbread Boy"] suggesting some mischief in the chase. We're all caught up in it, almost flung downhill, as if on a giant slide (Jun 30, 1984).

Goddess in Disguise

> An old woman flattens herself like a plank of wood and slides back into a tree at night to sleep. No one detects her there. I wonder if some night she'll slide in too far and won't be able to come out again (Nov 26, 1984).

Wizard

> I waken crying, "A wizard has me in thrall! He's more powerful than I'd imagined!" He bends a two-inch wood pole I have in my hand without my seeing so much as his hand. A Voice tells me, "He was powerful, but he is dying. This is his last effort to dominate" (Dec 27, 1984).

Prince Charming

> The race-car driver steps out of his car like a handsome young prince. He starts singing in a lyric tenor voice, a song that's as lovely as anything Brahms or Schubert ever wrote. In one phrase there are half-tones that modulate to a new key, and here his voice quavers but he doesn't falter. I wish to embrace him, but what I do is josh him, "A bit of a problem with the F# wasn't there?" He knows that I accept the lyrics as a lovesong and him as a person, not just as a racer or a prince (Oct 7, 1985).

Movie Star

> Paul Newman is playing clarinet–ragtime–at a bar on campus. At breaks he comes to me, flirting with those blue-blue eyes and white-teeth smile. I'm charmed, of course, but wary. One time he looks at my shoulders and throat and says, "You used to jump rope, didn't you?" (Mar 9, 1986).

Opera Star

> Placido Domingo appears on High Street near Broadway. Immediately a crowd gathers to hear him sing. I say, "Placido means placid? I can never remember what the name means—something like flaccid?" He laughs. Now I say, "'Oh, peaceful!" He says, beaming, "See, you do know"(Mar 22, 1986).

Jimmy Stewart Conflated with the King of Scotland

> I tell him, "I had a dream about you last night." He says, "I know, I was there." He gives me a card from the breast pocket of his velvet dinner jacket and says, "This is to remind you, when I call for a date, who I am" (Jun 2, 1986).

Gnome

> I instruct my students and apprentices, "Every time you get up to perform, even during rehearsals, always, always invoke the gnome Glockenspiel" (Sep 23, 1989).

President of the United States

> President Bush knocks on my door and asks me to do something patriotic or heroic that I can't or won't in conscience. I tell him what the priest says at the end of each Mass, "Ite, missa est." By that I mean, "Go forth, carry forth your own mission" (Nov 2, 1992).

Femme Fatale

> Elizabeth Taylor complains about the condition of my bedroom, which she's taking over. There's amazing endurance to her; she's made comebacks from terrible diseases and alcoholism. (Mar 29, 1993).

Silent Film Star

> A small man in baggy clothes, like Charlie Chaplin's little tramp, is affectionate with me. Who would guess that there's such a perfectly proportioned body inside those clothes? (Sep 3, 1993).

Comedians

> Two Hollywood actors—Danny de Vito and Bill Murray—are visiting the town I live in. They tell me, "That's Kramer over there" [Jerry Seinfeld's body-language comedian]. I nod and say, "He visits here often. This may be his home town" (Sep 7, 1994).

Hollywood Lover

> Nicholas Cage senses that I am "ripe." I respond to his kisses, caresses, fondling. Yet I'm confused. Shouldn't this be with John Travolta, whom one actress called the sexiest kisser in Hollywood?(May 20, 1998).

Geisha

> A young Japanese woman, astonishingly beautiful, is presented from father to son. She is unconstrained by her kimono and obi. She is greatly admired for her beauty rather than her artistry with inking kanji (Sep 26, 2016).

Our First Black President

> Barack Obama, interviewed on t.v., explains and demonstrates how important is a pause between a question and an answer (Dec 2, 2016).

Reflecting on this section of personal myths, I am encouraged by the counsel of Thomas Moore:

> If we become familiar with the characters and themes that are central to our myths, we can be free from their compulsions. Again, we can see the importance of imaginal practices such as journals, dream work, poetry, painting, and therapy aimed at exploring images in dream and life. These methods keep us actively engaged in the mythologies that are the stuff of our own lives.

– *Nineteen* –

Me and My Shadow

I need to re-iterate that one's spiritual journey is itself an archetype. In addition to my pilgrimage dreams, and long before I had read any of Carl Jung's works, I had a lengthy dream of journeying that exhibited several archetypes. First was a subterranean journey through a stone crypt, where I went "through an opening in a door, rather than opening the door on its hinges. There are obstacles to making any progress, but I have superior knowledge or experience or confidence and can make my way." Next there were passageways and a labyrinth. Eventually I encountered Maestro Evan Whallon as Wise Man and a woman in white as Wise Woman (May 17, 1979).

Subsequently, several of my dreams that had feelings with both negative and positive valences were so powerful that I inferred they were archetypes, and sought confirmation in the works of Jung. I have grouped a few of them according to his schema in *Man And His Symbols*, where he outlines four steps toward achieving selfhood: recognizing and dealing with the Shadow, the Animus, the Self as one knows it, and the Social Self. Jung asserts that these steps are roughly chronological, so that is the order I followed when giving the examples below.

Dark Shadow

When I was a youngster in the late 1930s, I listened to a radio program called "The Shadow." Each program began with a voice-over, a man saying spookily, *"Who knows what evil lurks in the hearts of men? Heh, heh, heh . . . The Shadow knows."* That opening set up my equating shadow = evil. In fact, my parents forbade us kids to listen to the program, which made it all the more tempting. I tiptoed from my room to the boys' room to listen, until one night the story was way too scary and made me regret I'd ever listened to it. Nightmares of a Blob, a Glob, and even a Golem sprang from that radio show, each picturing the ultimate invasion of privacy.

The intense fear generated by "The Shadow" program was undoubtedly the basis of my disallowing my own children certain television programs and many movies. In one dream note concerning "a terrific spiritual battle," I labeled a dark haze Evil because, "Though it has light at its center, it does not allow illumination" (Nov 15, 1978).

During the Great Depression, I felt a dark shadow over our country. I knew poverty first-hand and sensed the general unrest, though I was too young to comprehend the social upheaval or the political furor. During World War II, my hometown of Grand Rapids, Michigan was overshadowed by the loss of so many young men on distant battlefields. In my own family, my mother's brother contracted tuberculosis while serving in the Philippines, and one of her cousins died on a battlefield, heaven knows where. Two of my dad's brothers made landings in North Africa and Italy, and my dad traced on a huge map the military maneuvers that got through censorship of their letters. He also had a brother-in-law fighting in the "Pacific theater," a euphemism that I did not understand. I was acutely aware, however, that the Catholic practice of "giving up something for Lent" had become a patriotic practice for every citizen–giving up many things "for the duration."

In the 1970s, many years before I was introduced to Jungian concepts, I was dealing with my personal Shadow and was able to detonate some of the negative feelings by incorporating in a poem images of actual happenings that still haunted me.

Shadow

A presence felt, unseen–
  The ether mask at Children's Hospital.
  A foreboding like the underside
  of a star fish not quite dead.
  Prickles of fiberglass and panic
  when my brother locked me
  in a suffocating attic.

Sometime more tangible–
> The black veil worn by Cat-lickers,
> those nuns who stalked in pairs to throw
> lone children down the sewers.
> A coal-grimed curtain floating
> from a neighbor's upstairs window,
> like the voice of a woman pleading,
> Let me go, let me go!

Sometimes less–
> Vapors hovering over the dye vat
> in the textile factory,
> fungus in my bloodstream,
> voodoo in my dreams.
> Carbon monoxide lingering
> over our sleeping family.

A portent like this moment–
> at John F. Kennedy
> a huge jetliner crossing
> two hundred feet above
> our small plane's taxiing.
> Shadow, Old Familiar,
> you keep me shuddering.

Those threats arrived from outside of me; I had yet to deal with negativity inside me that I had repressed. For instance, in my childhood–in addition to explicit shaming–I was plagued with morality tales and Victorian verses about what marked a girl as "unbecoming." One put-down was, "Don't trouble trouble until trouble troubles you," implying that I was the cause, not the victim, in many incidents. Even a Mother Goose rhyme was used to scold me:

> There was a little girl who had a little curl
> Right in the middle of her forehead.
> And when she was good, she was very, very good,
> But when she was bad, she was horrid.

I would have loved to be horrid occasionally! But, considering the punishment for small offenses, I was afraid of doing something big. The following dream is illustrative:

Jun 28, 1985
A Little Girl in Trouble

> I've been pushed too far emotionally, and I scream at a woman whose relationship I'm not sure of, only that we've lived together for many years. "I can't take this any longer! I won't!" After my shouting, she makes it clear that I have poisoned the relationship, it can never be restored, she has no wish to continue it at all. The trigger [for my shouting] was her accusing me when I'd offered to go to the deli for some special food she might like. I just described what I saw [in the deli] yesterday, and their prices as indicators of quality. I was not begrudging her, just wanting to buy the right stuff.
>
> Yet she riles up, "You just want to deprive me of a little pleasure." On and on, a tirade. I feel more and more like a little girl despised. I cry out, "You don't know what it feels like not to have any space for yourself, any privacy, any private thoughts. How it feels to be brought up where there's kicking and cursing and insults all around, and you're used as a ploy in arguments. How you don't dare speak up, and you're accused of being sulky, sullen, stubborn if you're quiet."
>
> I go on and on about an unhappy home life, then say, "So I try to keep quiet and cheerful with you. But then you're demanding and accusing. You blame me when I'm trying to be helpful. I can't stand it any longer! I won't!"
>
> There's no pleasure in my shouting and no satisfaction afterward. "I can't keep pressing this Stuff down!" I tell the woman. "I'm not a little girl, but you make me feel like a bad little girl, and it's hard for me not to be hateful. I can NOT live with hate."

On the same night as "A Little Girl in Trouble," I had a dream about Big Nurse. I had utilized an audiotape by the dream worker, Diane Keck, in which she guided the listener to encounter a

Shadow figure and then meditate on it. I had chosen Big Nurse, a very large, dominating woman who frequented my dreams. I was in anguish immediately, and there were no explanations forthcoming. Nor could I request a gift from her, as recommended by [dream researcher] Patricia Garfield.

Big Nurse epitomized the Public Health nurses who came to our house with big needles as well as the hospital nurses who loomed over me. This dream may have been my first awareness that in some way she also represented my mother.

REFLECTIONS:
1. On waking, there was an internal message that these dreams are complementary. All I can fathom is this equation: in trouble = troublesome = troubled.
2. I could not confront Big Nurse because that would only confirm that I was guilty for being sick and guilty for causing others distress. I felt that being sent to the hospital [where at that time no visitors were allowed] was punishment for "my fault, my fault, my most grievous fault."
3. Today I'm thinking about Mother's tale of woe concerning the intense care she gave me for a whole year–through the kidney failure. If it actually was that long a siege, then the mastoid surgery was less than one year later. That, too, was a severe drain on Mother's limited emotional resources; that, too, produced guilt feelings in me.

One year after "A Little Girl in Trouble," came a dream called "It Takes My Heart Away." In it I arrived at a startling conclusion and, speaking to my Mother, I declared, "Each time I get a little closer to what's bothering me, and now I think I'm onto it. As far as you're concerned, I'm your shadow, even when I'm not there!" (May 30, 1986). Functioning as her shadow meant that I myself was a non-entity.

Notes for a half-dozen similar dreams are not necessary to include here. That I finally acknowledged that my situation had truly been precarious was an accomplishment. That I acknowledged (in the Reflections) how much negative Stuff I had carried into the marriage verged on the heroic.

Too often, when I have had a black woman in a dream, I have heard someone declare, "That's your Shadow." I thought not, because our family had been involved for many years in efforts at integration with blacks. We built in a "changing neighborhood," for which banks would not give us a loan. The architects of our house, Angel and Ransom (wonderful names!) were black. And at our open house, there were enough black friends that someone in the neighborhood, in retaliation, attacked our house–first with eggs and then with shots through the front windows.

Yet one version of the black woman in my dreams did qualify as Shadow–the inattentive mother that I chose never to be. Rather, I vowed to be superior to her in every possible way, even to being concerned about children who were not my own and feeling responsible for their welfare. That was a fact of life for me from age nine onward, when I took over many of my mother's duties–not only doing the household chores but also attending to her two youngest children. Here is an example of that Shadow:

May 3, 1984
Rescuing a Black Baby

> I'm in a women's hospital, the maternity wing. In this room are six beds in a row, and at the end is a platform affair–well, it looks like a giant high-chair. On it is a black woman who has just delivered a baby. The baby is naked, though cleaned of blood or any birth particles, and is standing up, as on the tray of the high-chair. "This is the strongest baby I've ever seen," I tell the mother, "though I've had bigger babies than this."
>
> The woman isn't even holding the baby, just gazing at it. Now the baby does a backward dive or somersault, flinging itself from a height of 8 or 10 feet. I catch the baby, like a heavy football, and clutch it to my chest as if to run for a touchdown. But I don't run, I just stand here, looking up at the mother, wanting to lecture her. I do let her know that the baby would have been killed if I hadn't been there to catch it. Now I feel a heavy responsibility. What if the baby is as intelligent as it is strong?

> Now the mother comes down off the high-chair or throne? or judgment seat? to the floor level where all the beds are. I'm not elevated and she's not demoted, so we see face to face and focus on the baby as the center of attention.

REFLECTIONS:
1. I may be in my infancy as far as development of creativity is concerned. In this dream I am more closely related to the child than to the mother.
2. The Creative Child has "tumbled" for me lovingly, has flung itself at me. Such trusting!
3. This dream may also refer to this year of separation from my husband, noting that if I hadn't made the move, my Creative Child might have died.
4. What if I am as strong as I am intelligent?

Another example of that Shadow woman suggested that at the age of nine I felt like a slave.

Jan 18, 1987
Catching a Black Baby

> A black woman has left a six-month-old baby in a small crib, like a doll's crib. The baby pulls himself up, and I think he could easily climb out. In fact, I catch him as he goes head-over-heels to the floor. Now an older sister of his (age 2 or 3) demands my attention. I'm just getting the baby settled down–his eyes are closing and there's a sweet smile on his face—when the girl tugs at the crib and wakes him.
>
> The black woman comes in and out of the scene. I keep telling her, "Take the children and all their belongings. Take them out of here before the auction begins!" She ignores me.

Bright Shadow

Another perspective on Shadow is the denial of personal gifts and good qualities, to the extent of stifling energy, enthusiasm, and spontaneity. This is referred to as Bright Shadow. A succinct definition of it is given by Frank Ostaseski in *Discovering What Death*

Can Teach Us about Living Fully: "Sometimes what we repress is not our raw sexual energy, our shame, or something we feel guilty about, but rather our innate goodness."

From my childhood onward, I was an expert at "hiding my light under a bushel." The corollary of that was just as stifling: shining my light merely to gratify other people. From my earliest years, there were adults who spoke of me as "Sunshine," and I felt obliged to put on a happy face for them. In Catholic schools, too, a smiling response gave me security, even when I was seething inside. At the university I was freer, with a range of verbal responses that led to authentic facial expressions and body language.

In the late 1980s, I encountered the work of Alice Miller, a psychotherapist and ardent supporter of the rights of the child. While studying her *Pictures of a Childhood*, I was grief-stricken by her thesis concerning the stifling of creativity in children by adults, including parents. In her attempt to rescue herself from exploitation, she "went underground" and, not until she was a mature adult, did her delight in creativity spring forth again. In the following passage, Alice Miller could be speaking for me:

> The creation of a work of art has often been compared to giving birth, the artist identifying with the mother by bringing a "child," the work of art, into the world. Yet as I envision the creative process, I do not identify with the mother giving birth but with the child struggling to be born. This holds true for my writing as well as my painting.

For me, abnegation was a defensive tactic. If I did not declare any power, I could not be robbed of what I had. Here is a dream that illustrates Bright Shadow:

Jul 5, 1992
A Reading of My Aura

> A Being on a higher plane reads my aura and lectures me because: either I don't realize, or else I don't acknowledge, the brilliant purple. He asks, "To whom will you bequeath the purple?" As if that's a possibility!

> I'm puzzled because the purple that I sense is a very narrow band swirling in an odd arc–from my mid-thoracic area, across my back, then to eye level on my left side. Even if I could bequeath a certain energy field or virtue or disposition, to whom would I give it? I think of my children and how many gifts each of them has, I think of students. Maybe I'm looking in the wrong direction? Maybe I should be concentrating on the fact that something brilliant is part of my makeup.

Ironically, any self-denial of my brightness was a distortion of true humility. Yet I was still in denial at age 73! At that time an advisor said flat out, "You need to avoid speaking in neutral ways. That's betraying the brilliance and richness of your experience" (May 24, 2005). Only one other person had ever commented on my brilliance (I almost typed "alleged brilliance"). It was the sociologist, Laurel Richardson, who pronounced it on several occasions, yet each time I had difficulty responding to the very idea. It was only when I became a Reiki practitioner that I was able to tap into the Energy that she called brilliance. Then, recognizing it in myself, I could also see it in clients, a gift for all concerned.

The Collective Shadow

As I was working on this book in the 21st century, when the Collective Shadow hangs over civilization as we know it, I discovered that there were 10 dreams of large-scale disaster in the first two decades of my record-keeping and only one in the next two decades. Though this is a small number for such a large theme, the intensity of feelings almost required that I include them in this book. Yet I debated about including them, wondering not about their relevance but whether they might have "redeeming social value" for readers. Society–as we have come to know it in our country–is in such tumult that I do not wish to give more energy to factions. Therefore, I follow the lead of Christopher Perry, who, under the banner of *The Society of Analytical Psychology*, gives a brief summary of the Collective Shadow:

> In the deepest areas of the shadow, we find manifestations of evil as a dynamic in the world, to which we need to relate with collective guilt, responsibility, and reparation: privatised water, the arms trade, famine, torture, Guantanamo Bay, etc.; each of us will have such a list.

Here is my list of dreams about large-scale disasters, several of them provoked by human interference with Nature:

- Volcanic Eruption
- A Wave of Filth over Animals and People
- Day of Judgment of Living Corpses
- Flooding of the Known World
- Surviving a Tornado
- Surviving an Earthquake
- Annihilation with Few Survivors
- End of Our World Due to Nuclear Disaster
- End of Our Civilization Due to Violence
- An Attack by Armed Invaders

I include one example of the Collective Shadow in its entirety:

Jun 2, 1987
Unending Horror

> Four dreams, horrific in themselves, have a cumulative effect.
> <u>1 a.m.</u> Legal constraints by executors of wills are not followed through. Posing and trickery involved, a mockery of the judicial system!
> <u>2:15 a.m.</u> A sense of disaster and doom. A stock-market crash, the wreck of the *Lusitania*, a dirigible in flames, mass hysteria, wildness overall. A downer for me to even write about.
> <u>3:30 a.m.</u> Unending horror. Old films of destruction of Jewish ghettos and of extermination camps run before my eyes. Now I'm in the streets, seeing and hearing and smelling the stench.

> Now viciousness in a black neighborhood–police brutality. I'm here for a concert by a black musical group that's performing on a stage of polished wood, floating in a cove or channel. They are slaughtered.
>
> I am a victim, too. A bomb has been thrust in my hand, something longer than a hand grenade. I can't loosen it, maybe it's handcuffed to my wrist. I jump through an archway to an alley, trying to get away from the high-density crowd, to save a few people. But the explosion kills hundreds, and collapsing buildings crash on thousands. I am not guilty of this destruction, yet I am a carrier, against my wishes.
>
> [There is a replay.] It's more awful because this time I know what's coming. The sight of a bass violin and other instruments ready to be played in the concert is heart-breaking.
>
> [In the next scene] A black woman is pushing the remnants of my body in a wheelbarrow, thinking to bury her grandmother? When she recognizes me in the remnants, she's glad at our momentary reunion. We have truly loved one another in this lifetime.

REFLECTIONS:
Trying to shake off the violence, I wrote in my journal until 4:30 a.m. There hasn't been this much violence in my dreams *totally* during the past 12 years, and there's no sense of release. I protest this overwhelming onslaught of images!

CONTINUATION:
The onslaught continued when I went back into the dream:

> <u>6 a.m.</u> A daughter of mine has been evacuated from a dangerous area, maybe from the hospital where she was just born. Angelyn, kindergarten age, is sent home from school to get parental consent for immunizations. A black girl of Angelyn's age has just witnessed the shooting of her father in the street. She's in shock but otherwise unharmed.

That these dreams occurred while I was at a conference of the Association for the Study of Dreams (ASD) encouraged me to share parts of them with conferees. Bob Ruhl stayed with me after supper because he'd heard the distress in my voice during a workshop. Bob was a photo-journalist in Vietnam and "learned to remove somewhat from the *pain* of events while staying in the *reality*." He saw nothing wrong with my distancing devices "as long as they are done consciously and are not total denials."

I worked with that dream, "Unending Horror," for many months. In October I read parts of it in Dreamtalk, where members spoke of the courage in the dream. That was solace for me, yet those scenes will never leave my awareness.

The most recent large-scale disaster in our country has been the rise to power of the man who became our 45th President. I refer to him as The-Man-Who-Would-Be-King, one who would never yield to the will of the people. His name is not uttered in my house, lest I slide into a reactionary, hateful mode. Nor will his name be respected in my writing; consequently, I have kept only one snippet of a dream about him, which occurred within three days of his ascendancy. Attorneys General of several States had, that quickly, filed lawsuits regarding actions of his that were unconstitutional.

Jan 24, 2017
A Billionaire President

> After three days in the presidency, he declares the country bankrupt and tweets, "No agency to pull us through, dangling over the edge of a participle."

From his first days until his last, he kept everyone dangling–the press, the populace, policy advisors, and powerful leaders of countries that had long been our allies. During his reign he kept every violent faction in our country dangling over the edge, as to when and where their fascist or neo-Nazi groups could do the most damage. Among his heinous acts was his repeatedly inciting violence. That played out in an attempted *coup* by well-organized fanatics who attacked the Capitol Building during a joint session of Congress.

His avowed intention was to overturn whatever Barack Obama, our first black President, had accomplished, and he set about doing that with vengeance. Within a fortress constructed of lies, he seemed invulnerable; his claim to fame may be that he survived two impeachments by the House without being censured by the Senate.

Another disaster, the Covid-19 pandemic, occurred in 2020, during his final year as sitting President. Due to his original denial of the facts and his lack of leadership thereafter, citizens died off by the thousands–many of whom would have survived if he had followed the advice of epidemiologists and other scientists.

Foreshadow

Much has been said recently about the legacy of violence that we are leaving to our children and grand-children. Not as much has been said about the legacy of violence that we inherited from our forebears, all the way back to the Founding Fathers of our amazing country. The history of the United States is one of violence, and we are reaping what our forebears sowed.

Abraham Lincoln, in the midst of the Civil War, questioned whether "a nation conceived in liberty and dedicated to the proposition that all men are created equal" could long endure. That we come to grips with that question, and honestly face our Shadow right now, is crucially important to civilization.

– *Twenty* –

A Hitch in My Get-Along

A bus driver proved to be a most persistent Trickster in my dreams. I understood that the bus was not only a vehicle of transportation but also a vehicle for communication; the bus driver thwarted me on both counts. There was an obvious correlation with bus drivers in my waking life, some of whom showed meanness as a power play.

The situation was, I had to take a crosstown bus to get to High Street and there transfer to get to the OSU campus. The route of the crosstown bus was like an almost-round balloon with a long string, the string leading down a hill to Riverside Hospital. At my end of the round, I could go south on the hour, or north on 20 minutes after the hour, or south on 40 minutes after the hour, or north on the next hour, etc.. There were no schedules posted or handed out. If I were on the wrong side of the street when I saw the bus approaching, I could sometimes run across the street, to board. But if the driver wanted to thwart me, he jolly well did.

One of my earliest written notes about this Trickster was when I was 43, "The missing-the-bus sequences are so frequent, and have been for years, as to be pathetic and almost boring" (Aug 1975). Six months later, I questioned, "What is it I wait for that seldom comes on time, often passes me by, takes me on wrong routes, and drops me at unwanted destinations? *Opportunity* seems to answer these questions" (Jan 2, 1976). Such dreams gained intensity and, on the rare occasions that I boarded the bus, the Trickster was still powerful, as in the following:

Aug 29, 1984
Trying to Leave the Bus

> I recognize that I'm near my bus stop, tell the driver it is soon, and ask him to go easy. I gather books, food, and clothes and try to fit them in a brown paper bag with no reinforcement.

> Though the driver has been just coasting, still he's passed Griggs St. and I'm anxious about Burton St. [my destination]. He lets me off at Burton without making any smart remarks or giving [unwanted] advice! I'm grateful.

FEELINGS:
Anxiety followed by relief.

REFLECTIONS:
1. As I wrote *Burton*, I thought *burden* and, like a "bag lady," I'm still juggling my burdens at the end of the line.
2. The coasting resonates to my decision not to register for the course, "Women's and Men's Issues" in the Master of Social Work (MSW) program.

Later on I had to face, in one dream, *three* versions of the bus driver/Trickster.

Jul 7, 1987
Three Bus Drivers Pass Me By

> The first is the Burton bus, going east. The second is the Madison bus, going north. The third is the downtown bus. It's daytime, and I'm standing right at a bus stop, though each time it's in the middle of a long block, not at a corner.
>
> The third time the driver is alerted by a passenger that I'm standing here. He makes a stop-and-start action, so I think maybe he'll wait until I catch up with him at the corner. But he doesn't. I am furious! If cursing would help, I would curse.
>
> I'm crying now, out loud. I decide to cross the street, get on the bus going south, and ride it to the end of the line. There the driver will have to turn around and go north and he can't mess with me again.

In retrospect, I can account for the dream's "long block" and the "run-around": I had a year-long siege of viruses and infections that culminated in depression.

The next variant is the obverse of a bus driver's passing me by; here he passes my destination:

Oct 9, 1989
Two Instances of Overshooting the Mark

> I get on a bus ahead of friends, and the door closes. Too fast! I'm stuck with all the gear—a painter's drop cloth, a microscope, a camping bag, and a pillow. The driver doesn't let me off because I'm slow in gathering all this stuff. On he goes.
>
> A new driver, young and friendly, thinks to help me by taking me closer to my destination. But he's gone two blocks past it before I can get him to understand.
>
> The day is darkening, almost evening. I see a place where people can rent a booth to sleep. But I must get back to the transfer point to meet my friends.

FEELINGS:
Stuck, misunderstood, more and more alone.

REFLECTIONS:
1. This refers to my trip to Oregon, for a work holiday at the site of the home that EJ, his friends, and our family are building. I "overshot" my abilities while staining boards and—worse—got so much grit in my eyes that I had to be taken to a doctor in town, 30 miles away.
2. The "transfer point to meet my friends" resonates with the second half of my trip, when I went on to San Francisco and met Hiro's mother and several of her aunts, who were visiting from Japan.

The Trickster was not to be ignored. As the title of the next dream indicates, I needed greater assertiveness when dealing with him, with whatever he represented.

Feb 10, 1992
The Longest Wrong Bus Ride in My History

> The next Burton bus won't be by for 40 or 60 minutes, and I can't get a taxi here, and I can't walk the three miles home. So I get on the next unlabeled bus that's going west. [But] It turns after a couple of blocks.

> I'm worried right away and ask the bus driver questions. The more agitated I get, the slower and more enigmatic his answers. I'm furious and tell him, "Let me off the bus!" He can't because we're going among some cattle. They're so close that their tails brush in the windows of the bus, and we're choking on hair and dust.
> Now the driver is in a middle seat, lolling and grinning. The bus is lifted onto a truck, guided by remote control, and we're moving through a heavy-industry area. Miles and miles of it.
> The driver assumes that I've never been to a big city. When we get near downtown, he points out the tall buildings, telling their names and who built or endowed each one. All I can think of is reaching Campau Square [in Grand Rapids] and taking a different bus home. I say, "I must get home before dark!" The bus driver laughs as if I were a child, a "fraidy cat." I tell him, "I need to be able to see some landmarks. The city is unfamiliar after so many years."

FEELINGS:
Disoriented, alerted, alarmed; assertive but ignored; ridiculed, terrified.

REFLECTIONS:
I sense a lost soul–I mean a wanderer, not a person condemned.

In the next variant of Negative Trickster, I lost my driver, as opposed to his losing me.

Jun 9, 2006
I Lose My Driver after a Conference

> I've been at a weekend conference at a hotel, and I did a presentation yesterday. I throw my belongings in a huge duffel bag and now stand in a long line to turn in my key.
> Cleaners and waitresses are setting up the ballroom for the next event. I ask them if they've seen my driver, but they misunderstand me. One woman offers me a paper cup of juice and some crackers, as if I'm a street person she wants to get rid

of. I wonder if there's a Greyhound bus that runs on Sunday and I ask, "How far to the bus station?" About four blocks . . .

My duffel bag gets heavier and heavier until I can hardly drag it. I start to unload it–there's an amazing amount of stuff that I don't remember packing. I feel sure that my ID and money are somewhere in the bag, I just have to keep looking. My pockets are loaded with small change, and some [coins] fall onto the floor.

FEELINGS:

Accomplishment; eagerness to get home; increasing anxiety; weighted down.

REFLECTIONS:

1. The missing driver may indicate that I'm afraid of losing my drive after the demo I am scheduled to do on Sunday.
2. The duffel bag represents my excess baggage on both the physical level and the emotional level. I am aware of how heavy my Stuff is, and wish I could unload it.
3. The dream's small change resonates to the small change noticeable in my general health. Yet the dream does say, "loaded with small change," so there may be effects that I'm not aware of.
4. Most important: I do have my ID [identity] and money [wherewithal], even when I am lacking in drive.

If I ever had any doubt that the bus driver qualified as the archetypal Trickster, his changing clothes and appearance several times in this final dream clinched his identity:

Dec 8, 2016
Bus Driver Goes the Distance

> I see a bus at a curb, get on, and take a seat. Now I realize, I have no money! Other folks get on and don't pay, either. The driver comes and I tell him, "I don't know the territory." He says mockingly, "You Don't? We'll see about that."
> He drives past gorgeous cliffs, also valleys–each one could be a national monument. It's as if he's trying to prove something. I admit, "Oh, I have seen that," or, "I have been there."

He stops only occasionally and doesn't say that it's a rest stop, so we [passengers] all stay in our seats. Sometimes after he has a rest, he comes back wearing a different parka or jacket, and even his appearance changes. Nothing uniform about him!

The longer he drives, the farther I travel into unknown territory. I'm more than worried and uncomfortable, I'm scared and tell him so. He sneers, "You asked for it." NO, I did not!

FEELINGS:

Eager for a tour; awed by the beauties of nature; scared, trapped, abducted.

REFLECTIONS:

1. In this dream I'm taken for a ride in the negative sense. It's far more scary than commuting [communicating] in an established pattern.
2. That the bus goes on and on indefinitely resonates generally with life's journeying and particularly with my living on and on so many years after the near-death experience.

– *Twenty-One* –

Hello, Long Time No See

In Feminist Studies at OSU, I learned that the injustices I felt when my three brothers got preferential treatment in clothing, sports equipment, educational opportunities, and more, was not unique to our family; it was the norm throughout our country. When at age 54 I saw how bitter some of my young classmates were, I tried to temper my anger and discouragement. Nevertheless, my own Negative Male aspect was easy for me to spot—awake or asleep.

Negative Male Aspect

In a dream so extraordinary that I have included all seven scenes, I met seven representations of my Negative Male aspect, all of them challenging me:

Jul 18, 1986
Trying to See the Principal/Principle

> [One] In my own house, at a party that's gotten out of hand, students are taking drugs. One of them assaults me with an ophthalmologist's device—he jabs it into my left eye. The pain is sharp and I'm surprised he hasn't blinded me. I hope there won't be permanent damage. When I order him out of the house, he scoffs, so I force him out bodily.
>
> [Two] At a school, some of these kids are getting ready for a field trip or a picnic. One guy is lipping off about "all the whores we can get." I tell him to report to the principal and, absurdly, think he will.
>
> [Three] I go from one classroom to another, trying to find my way to the principal's office. Another woman, black-haired, not quite as old as I, who was assaulted at the party, too, is a teacher here. We agree to approach the principal together, this very morning, even though

there's hubbub about the class picnic. But we can't get through and, even worse, we get separated.

[Four] In one classroom just above the basement, a man is hollering in exasperation, "For the love of God!" And he continues ranting and raving to 5th or 6th graders, like someone in a missionary band. He tones it down slightly as I walk through, find my way to an exit, and go up some iron steps.

[Five] Now I'm in another building, like a clinic or hospital or maybe a jail. Two black men dressed spiffily in pastel suits with matching hats leer at me through a half-glass door. I'm struggling to pull on clothes in an examining room.

[Six] In this prison-like place is another awful sight—a man or youth who has shrunk and curled to a snail of about eight inches, hardly human, mostly a mouth that's open wide and shows ulcerations in it. I talk to him soothingly, believing that his distress will be relieved shortly and he'll uncurl into a whole person again.

[Seven] In this building there's another man who opens his sliding-glass window (like a ticket window) and speaks directly to me in a burlesque, high-handed manner, "There's something you need to realize. Your smiles and endearing manner won't win me over, I'm not such an easy mark."

I think but don't say that my "smiles and endearing manner" help me regulate MY feelings and activities, MY day, MY life. I make a calm rebuttal, "You've made that clear twice before. I'm surprised you don't remember telling me so."

FEELINGS:
Pained, shocked; active, persistent; separated, incarcerated; struggling, embarrassed; hopeful, assertive.

REFLECTIONS:
1. I've had experiences similar to these in waking life, but haven't been aware of the cumulative effect as spelled out here.
2. Even the principal's absenteeism or ineffectiveness contributes to the Negative Male aspect.
3. The two leering black men, spiffy in pastel suits, are in direct opposition to my Guides who always appear in tailored pearl-gray suits and are unfailingly helpful.

Jul 8, 1994
Unresolved Conflict between Two Men Who Want My Attention

> Or maybe I'm wanting their attention? They're John Kneisly and a tall black man as handsome as Denzel Washington. I've halfway agreed with each to an excursion. There's a matter of their bringing me a coat to wear. John brings a zippered jacket–designer styled, with colors and stripes, almost new. The black man brings a very expensive "great coat" of a period movie–not appropriate for the occasion.
>
> The black man decides that I'm going to ride a horse. He will have me mount by putting my foot into the palms of his hands and hoisting myself onto the saddle. I know this will not work. So he calls a lackey, and together they propel me onto the horse–a very large one that I can hardly straddle. Now the black man tells me to ride ahead of him, that the horse knows what to do. But the horse is headstrong and gives me trouble from the first moment, doesn't even let me hold onto the reins.
>
> Now I see John approaching. I don't know how to explain what's happened, what I'm doing on this horse, or where I'm headed. I introduce the two men, though I can't think of the black man's name. He extends his hand, and he's huge compared to John. But John refuses with an odd gesture because his hands are covered with oily black stuff, probably from cleaning a fire pit. It's an awkward moment for me.

FEELINGS:
Up in the air; inappropriate, uncomfortable; awkward, unbalanced; excited.

REFLECTIONS:
1. This morning I think, In a cowboy movie a rough-and-tumble man might have shaken hands, oil or no. But John is a gentleman, not a cowboy.
2. Both men have great potential, including an aesthetic sense. And both the coats [roles I can put on] are attractive.
3. The conflict is between my being carried away or exercising some control about my purpose and direction. This may be a

life-change issue. Do I want to proceed slowly with a person and/or values that I know? Or do I dare go off, bucking tradition, to try my strength and balance?

Positive Male Aspect

It took me 15 years to recognize my Positive Male aspect. Here is an example:

May 31, 1985
A Man Released from a Task or Ordeal

> After I have a sexual encounter with a "socially acceptable man," a second man comes to me. He's been lost? or kidnaped? or gone on a voyage? for so long that most people have given him up for dead. He comes across a crowded room, straight to me, and I'm overwhelmed by love and loyalty and friendship and rightness and belonging.
>
> We hold one another, a full embrace, for many minutes. I'm taking deep breaths at first because of dizziness. He's not the conquering hero type, but he's been released from an arduous task or ordeal. He doesn't look like a bedraggled survivor, but a together person.

FEELINGS:
Befriended, loved, released, hopeful.

REFLECTIONS:
1. This second scene was not romantic wish-fulfillment, but a portrayal of love based on mutual respect and friendship. The feeling was not erotic, but a sense of completion and fulfillment.
2. This aspect of Self reveals something about the survival of my masculine qualities, and that they can express as great a love as my feminine qualities do.

One year later, on my 54th birthday, "At a conference, maybe at a health spa, a gentle man sits to my right. He puts his left arm on the back of my chair and his right hand on my right thigh. Maybe I've drawn him to me, anyway now my right hand rests on top of his. I lean against him ever so slightly, yet this is wonderfully intimate. I'm thinking, Behind every successful woman is a man" (Jul 19, 1986).

After a recess of six years there came a startling dream that showed total acceptance of my Male aspect. "I have male genitalia, very large, an encumbrance. At first I wonder about being an hermaphrodite. Now I'm totally IN this body. I recognize this is not a dream and tell myself, Oh it must be a past life! My penis is very large, even when flaccid. Every move I make, I'm aware of it. I'm not wearing trousers, thank goodness, but something free-flowing, like a short tunic of ancient Romans and Greeks. I have a very wide leather belt that may protect my solar plexus" (Nov 23, 1993).

Three years later, in "Partnering with My Male Aspect" (Feb 12, 1997), *play* was again the generating factor, and the merest touch created a flow of Energy:

The following example of four-foldedness was unique, in that all four representations were men. (In most instances of four-foldedness in my dreams, there have been three women and one man.) In this "big dream," the men clearly represented four levels of my Self:

Aug 7, 1998
Creating My Own High

> [One] At a night school with mature people who've had experience in a variety of careers, someone inquires about Ed Moore's going for a Ph.D in his fifties. That's remarkable because he had been designated a slow learner in elementary school and had to overcome physical handicaps, too.
>
> [Two] A black man lounging in a chair comments on the academic degree system in the United States, "This small university might rank rather low compared to expensive, prestigious schools. Yet the degree, that piece of paper, is so important to some people and corporations." I agree that life experience is very important, "Yet the pursuit of knowledge is worthwhile anywhere, anytime."
>
> [Three] Now I'm talking earnestly with a young man—dark-haired, wearing glasses—about an experiment he's doing in a lab. We love one another.
>
> [Four] Now another man comes into the lab. He's tall and slim, lanky and graceful. He comes directly to me, and

> I nuzzle near his right ear. I blow gently on his neck, and he responds with romantic words and passionate kisses. Now I'm straddling his erect penis and feeling his heat.
>
> But the earnest man interrupts us. He insists that HE is my desired and deserving partner, that we've known one another forever and are meant for each other. He's eloquent, and I'm drawn back to him. Yet he's still sitting at his lab bench, and I wonder about his priorities.
>
> Now I'm in a chapel on campus. I've just eaten some apple slices, therefore will not take Communion. I decide to achieve my own high, or to invite ecstasy in my own way, by rising above the heaviness of gravity. I float peacefully for awhile. Now I bounce exuberantly and touch the ceiling with my hands. Now, deliberately and gently, [I touch it] with my head. The reaching is effortless and the touching delightful.

FEELINGS:
Belonging, worthwhile; intellectually stimulated; earnest, observant, loving; from romantic to passionate; from elevated to peaceful.

REFLECTIONS:
1. Quite a repertoire of feelings for such short scenes!
2. I didn't feel frustrated in the dream or upon recalling it, even though not sexually gratified. The sense of deep love in the earnest relationship may have held precedence.
3. The four-foldedness that I see and feel can be summarized according to levels. Ed Moore represents my physical level; the black man, intellectual; the earnest man, spiritual; the romantic man, emotional.
4. That I am alone while achieving ecstasy indicates individuation.

Negative Female Aspect

As several sections of this memoir have already indicated, my dreams are replete with female images that have a negative valence. Sources in waking life were my mother, nurses, teachers (especially Catholic nuns), and professional women who had no time for, or patience with, other women. In the following dream, there are echoes of witches in books and movies in my childhood:

Apr 12, 1994
Beautiful Woman with Black Shopping Bag

> She's at my side door. I'm indoors, stooping to pick up or rearrange something. I see her with one foot in the door [literally]. She's tall, slim, black-haired, and carries a black bag with a white swirl design that suggests a cat. I don't like the feel of this—her intrusion. I push my back against the door, but she pushes forcefully against me. Now I turn to face her. On her right shoulder is a pink creature that looks like the chick of a buzzard, very ugly. Now this beautiful woman's face turns witchlike, every dramatic line of eyebrows and eyes and mouth exaggerated. She's like the witch in "Snow White."
>
> I tell her, "I don't like that cat." She sneers, "There's no cat, just the illusion of one." I repeat, "I don't like the cat-ness that I'm feeling here." She curses me and says, "Then feel these CUTS!" She makes two lines, a big X, in front of me. I feel the first diagonal on my back, but not the second. I make the Reiki power symbol, saying, "Go in peace." This may be why I don't feel the second cut—because I'm not entering into her space, but releasing her.
>
> She gets on her bicycle, with her buzzard and shopping bag and other gear, and leaves. I don't even care if she's stolen the bicycle. All that matters is my being at peace in my own home, in my own Self.

FEELINGS:
Invaded, threatened, cursed; surprised, wounded, recovered; relieved, at peace.

REFLECTIONS:
1. The cat-ness resonates to the problem of cats destroying my seeded yard and my rock-garden plants. There's a suggestion of cattiness, too, but it's the viciousness that scares me.
2. The refrain, "In my own home, in my own Self," picks up Dorothy's chant in the "Wizard of Oz," "There's no place like home."

3. All right, what do I need to confront here in my own home? The buzzard suggests carrion, and I leap to G. M. Hopkins' assertion, "I will not, carrion comfort despair, / not feast on thee." I've been too close to despair the past two or three weeks. Now I pledge: *I will not feast on despair, and despair will not feast on me.*

Positive Female Aspect

It is time that I focus on my Positive Female aspect.

> I visualize change as a 3-D model,
> almost architectural:
> observable, measurable, tangible,
> well-defined, not an abstraction.
> I want to turn it over and again,
> like flapping a golden pancake
> or flipping a valuable coin,
> giving both sides equal attention.

When I was a teenager, there was a song whose chorus went like this: "Accentuate the positive, eliminate the negative, latch on to the affirmative, and don't mess with Mr. In-Between." I can't guess how many positive images I overlooked during the years when I was trying to "eliminate the negative"! Here are two examples of my Positive Female that left me pondering:

Aug 26, 1986
In the Deep, a Woman Calls My Name

> I've descended willingly into semi-darkness, guided only by a voice behind me, a voice I trust. In a deep sub-basement, a woman calls my name as if she'd never uttered it before, as if her pronouncing it stablishes a strong bond between us.
>   Although she's been guiding me, I've preceded her into these rooms. When she calls my name, I turn around to face her. There's a sense of unutterable love. Even though my mind questions what is my relationship to her, there's total acceptance.

> I don't speak her name. Well, I don't know it.
> All I say is, "You know I love you," as if this needs
> to be declared aloud for a sense of completion.
>
> We kiss on the mouth and I'm more aware
> of the kiss than of our bodies embracing. This
> isn't romantic, this isn't erotic, so what is it?

FEELINGS:

A marvelous sensitivity and acceptance of Self *as is* that overrides all the questions.

REFLECTIONS:

1. Repeatedly, when I've listened to meditation tapes, I've not been able to visualize my ideal Self. This dream implies that it isn't necessarily a visual image; rather, it is a *feeling* of total acceptance and love.
2. That this dream occurred immediately following my ex-husband's re-marriage seems a rite of passage for me, too.

Oct 31, 2001
A Vision within a Dream

> I'm staying overnight with a woman who may become my friend. She's very caring, also beautiful, with long, dark hair.
>
> There's a flash   flash   flash   series of images, black-and-white, crisp but of such short duration that I can't focus on each one. A man's face is repeated and seems to be changing–the way computer graphics can make a face look older or younger. I'm sure that he is the cause of trauma in a past life. Now the face of a French man is very clear.
>
> After seeing these flashes–like mug shots–I have the sense, Oh, this explains it all. But I've gasped at the images many times and may have called out while viewing. I've wakened the beautiful woman. She says something complimentary about my breasts. I wonder how she can have even a vague idea of them because I'm wearing a winter flannel nightgown. Oh, the top button is undone and the placket is askew.

FEELINGS:

Cared for; unfocused; curious to fearful; relieved, flattered.

REFLECTIONS:
I assumed that the flash flash flash series referred to flashbacks. Yet my Signal System indicates they are also flash-forwards, anticipatory!

A light-hearted example of what Jung calls the Social Self occurred in the following dream of four-foldedness:

Jun 25, 1979
Four-square and Desirable

> I see several women, including [neighbors] Mary Alice Cua and her daughter Vicki. All the women are dressed in black–several in chiffon, at least one in lace. I comment on their clothes, saying "stunning" or "elegant," but not on their person.
>
> One woman gives me a quick once-over and says to another, "We could say she's pretty." I'm wearing black, too [never in waking life except in Symphony Chorus], so I take "pretty" as referring to my person. I think, They don't know the real me, I have beauty. That's not protesting, just stating a fact.
>
> [Later, at a square dance] One of the men likes me particularly. He says something to me about my 64. I'm puzzled. That's not my age [I'm 47 now]. It's not a perfume number like Chanel No. 5, yet it is a highly desirable quality [4 x 4 x 4).

REFLECTIONS:
1. Will I develop some "highly desirable quality" by age 64? Or meet a highly desirable man then?
2. I wonder what Jung would say about the number 64 in this dream. In *Man and His Symbols*, he expounds on how "individuation tends to be based on the motif of the number four" and "manifestations of the center are characterized by four-foldedness–that is to say, by having four divisions or some structure deriving from the numeric series of 4, 8, 16, and so on."
3. Square-dancing is four-dimensional, if one considers time as the fourth dimension–a fact in dance and in music.

4. In square-dancing, while squaring the circle and circling the square, moving in and out of the center, all eight of us relate to one another. There isn't anything mystical about this, but it's certainly an expression of the Social Self.

– Twenty-Two –

Goodbye: God Be with You

Dreams have permeable boundaries; they let us go wherever we wish, whenever, in whatever role or guise, and meet whomever we wish, for whatever reason. Dreams prompt us to let go of imposed beliefs and taboos. And dreams are like archeological sites, with layer upon layer of personal and historical artifacts that we can uncover and examine.

This section has been the most difficult for me, presenting emotional challenges in every stage of its development–from sorting to assembling, condensing, and proof-reading. It begins with dreams that illustrate my difficulty in carrying through on advice offered by friends, "Let go and let God." Following those are dreams that only approximate my feelings when letting go of religious proscriptions and medical prescriptions; a desired career; my children, husband, and home.

I had just entered my fifties and there was genuine fear involved. "My awareness seems to be a holding power. I keep the family together somehow; it's only when I let go that they all come apart" (Apr 4, 1981). There were many times I felt that I myself would come apart. I had to develop new strategies and new skills, as suggested in the following dream:

Feb. 17, 1983
Letting Go through Automatic Writing

> I'm doing automatic writing, putting down whatever words come into my head, regardless of syntax or sense, believing I'll make poetry of this with only slight revision. My pen is wide, a felt-tip, making the words look and feel important. Now I'm able to let go of all control, let my hand shape the letters and words–each a revelation, and most a surprise to me. It's slow-going at this phase, though I'd expected inspiration to flow more readily.

> There's a sense of power, not a feeling of being in another's control. After all, it is I, my Inner Self, doing the writing.

REFLECTIONS:
I think of a 19th century woman novelist who wrote whole passages with her eyes closed. My eyes are open in the dream, yet I have perfected the letting go.

Two weeks later there came a dream with seven scenes, several of which referred to my letting go of control (Mar 2, 1983). In a graphic scene, the problem was passing shit and the comment was, "I can't control my bowels = I've got to let go, let nature take her course." In the final scene, about my future and flying into it, "I wish to take control once we're in the air, not as responsibility but as playful activity with the feeling of freedom."

In another dream situation, I needed to let go of perfectionism, relative to refinishing wood storage shelves. "I'm in conflict about letting go or not, because I did the best work that I could. If I attempt to sand down the defects, that might reveal other defects or problems!" Yet my conclusion was, "Letting go is not defeatism, it is a form of assertiveness" (Oct 1, 1988).

Years later, after a workshop with Peter Inman, a healer, I had a dream that came directly from his work. Its lengthy title was one of Inman's precepts that I needed to integrate:

Apr 20, 1993
Releasing the Need to Expiate for Any Offense – Real or Imagined

> In India, I'm going to a temple or some other magnificent place. An elephant walks into an outer area that has arches and domes. In the roofed area, it's dark and cool. It feels like a sanctuary, but may be just a storehouse of treasures?
>
> Something about a Prince and my bringing a boy and girl (or youth and maiden?), perhaps relatives, to him.
>
> Now I'm a go-between and am at risk – in considerable danger – because of my loyalty to the Prince. I write a letter or document, a formal declaration of my intent to be free of this

> [overly responsible] role and these dangers. I begin with, "I release the need to expiate for any offense–real or imagined."

REFLECTIONS:
1. The "expiation" may have occurred already, during the Buddhist Healing ritual a couple of weeks ago. If so, it occurred through the wishes of the Enlightened Ones and the Supreme Divinity, as well as through the desire of fragile humans.
2. It's ironic that my point of reference is a Buddhist ritual and not a Catholic one. But Easter is so closely associated with the fall-and-redemption form of religion that the natural cycle of death-and- rebirth is tainted.

One year later, I "let myself go" in a forward manner, toward a goal: the possibility of residing at the Gesundheit Institute, Patch Adams' healing center in West Virginia. The dream required that first I must get past the feeling of being muted:

May 8, 1994
I'm Playing a Muted Piano

> At first it's like playing a drum, but using only my fingers on the lid of a grand piano. Now I make tone clusters, all five fingers of each hand plunking onto that surface, then onto white keys. Now, it's chords, now progressions of chords.
>
> There's an African man who resembles James Earl Jones in "Field of Dreams". He leads me, with rhythmic patterns, to believe that a 3-beat is what I want, not a 4-beat. The theme is life and death, or maybe life-in-death, or death-in-life. My right hand hurts when I stretch for the 7th chords, and this wakens me.

FEELINGS:
Freedom to experiment; ponderousness; frustration; physical pain coupled with disappointment.

REFLECTIONS:
1. I feel the need for resolution. The 7th chords are more than passing tones, they lead directly to home key.

2. What is my home key? Healing myself and others. What is my chord that leads to home? Strength and stamina in pursuit of a goal.

AFFIRMATIONS:
I let myself go on this trip without anxiety. I let myself go, expressing concerns, hopes, and desires. I let myself go, aspiring to the highest possible good.

Letting Go of My Children

Bidding farewell to my children was more difficult than I had imagined, considering that they have, from their early years, acted independently. They joined (or did not) Scouts and Brownies; participated (or did not) in competitive sports; played a musical instrument or played with ceramics and weaving; pursued a variety of summer jobs; chose specialized curricula at the university (four in-state and three out-of-state); and pursued very different careers. Their decisions created many partings that affected me more than them. For a while I was tongue-tied when saying goodbye to anyone, even for a short term. It was not until I myself left home that I could say goodbye to my children without giving way to tears.

One of the most dramatic farewells occurred in 1976 when my older sons bicycled the entire Bikecentennial Trail, one starting on the east coast and the other starting on the west coast. A third son bicycled with his dad from a midway point to the west coast. Even though they had prepared months ahead for their trips, I was not prepared for the letting go, as indicated in this dream:

Jan 8, 1976
Missing One or More Child

> Trying to regroup the family, I want to put an ad in the newspaper and on the bulletin board of the police station. I go to the phone book and try to read maps, but the yellow pages are all mixed in with the white.
>
> A young man offers to show me the way to the police station. He starts riding his bike, but I can't

get mine to move, even downhill. I try to get the
pedals moving, but there's no rubber on one pedal,
just a single bar, and my foot keeps sliding off.

FEELINGS:
In the dream everything resists me. In waking life I feel as disregarded as the past-bloom amaryllis and leftover Christmas decorations.

By June I was concerned enough about the bikers that I dreamt about Joe as "in a marshy area and not making contact with home." I fretted, "Maybe I want to tuck the children in, to offer them warmth and security? I haven't done any such for many years, what with Stephen being 11 now." (Jun 7, 1976). A month later, the bikers well on their way, I dreamed there was a report on EJ: "He's okay. He reached the peak of Mt. Everest all right." I cry, "Alone? That's foolhardy!" The man says, "It's crazy" (Jul 21, 1976).

At the same time, I was concerned about my daughters, too, and had an occasional comeuppance due to their independent ways. A dream showed me "sorting closets, giving away 90% of the clothes—for example, a half-dozen pinafores that daughters have outgrown" (Aug 13, 1976). In my dreams, clothes represent roles; therefore, I needed to recognize that my daughters had outgrown some roles and relationships. But I was not prepared, nor was their dad, for some of their sexual partners. This unease was dramatized in a dream about Angelyn's boyfriend at the university. I wakened myself calling out, "Wrong One! Wrong One!"

Shortly thereafter, "I am caring for our two foreign students [Beatrice from France and Frowin from Germany], along with Chas, Stephen, and my mother in a wheelchair. What a combination!" (Sep 4, 1976). That dream was verbal, with emphasis on the words *nourish* and *cherish*.

A few months later, I was in the role of observer in a dream that comically illustrated the complexity of our family life: "People are to play at a card table as many as four games simultaneously *on one board*, following the rules of each game. For instance: Monopoly, Clue, Careers, and Risk. I don't understand the game or who, if anyone, could be declared the winner. Yet it may be a lesson in gamesmanship" (Mar 10, 1977).

An actual shock to me, occurred when a son became involved in a cult. When he was able to escape, it was Cathy who talked him down from the experience.

In rapid succession, and with considerable variation in the venues where they celebrated, the children married: one in 1976, two in 1980, one each in 1982 and 1983. The others occurred later, in 1986, 1992, and 2007.

Considering all the children's comings and goings over the years, it was no surprise that a volatile dream, "The Worst Dormitory Experience Ever," was set in a dormitory rather than in the family home, long since vacated. By that time, five children had dispersed to other States. Here are some responses to that dream and to my situation:

REFLECTIONS:
1. The sense of the dream is: All gone. There's nothing here for me, nothing at all.
2. The thefts of clothes and furniture = my old values are up for grabs.
3. Putting things in storage = conserving old attitudes and beliefs. They are somewhat accessible if I ever want or need them.

Letting Go of Marriage

In one of my sortings of dream notes, I wrote on a post-it, "This one may summarize, and I can drop most of the other dreams about leaving the marriage." Here it is:

Jun 4, 1976
No-Go Counseling

> A parish priest is in his office, drowsy. He doesn't criticize my husband, but he does criticize me. Typical! Ed begins quoting poets, philosophers, the psalms . . . I pound his chest and say, "Tell me what you're trying not to. Tell me now, or I'm leaving you, leaving for good." He's shocked and says, "Not now when I'm in such a condition."
> "What IS the problem? I ask, shaking him. "It's my yob, shob, zhob," he moans, and spells out the last for emphasis, z-h-o-b.

> He says there's a conspiracy against him. He doesn't get to reap anything he sows. People see only the straw and rubble, not the asparagus or other crops. People don't appreciate him.
>
> Even so, I offer that we can go to another county and begin life there fresh.

REFLECTIONS:

I'm not threatening to leave him because of any loss of job or respect, but because of his pitying attitude and his cringing. (The children refer to it as PLOM: Poor Little Old Me.) He's deceived me too many times, so now I half believe (or believe half) of what he says. I also question his motives in becoming a power figure.

In election years particularly, Ed caused too much stress on our family life. There were times when I was so caught up with checking voter registration, cross-checking addresses in city directories, and preparing mailers that I even *dreamed for him*. Here is a series:

Political Sportscasting

I rarely dream for someone else
But here I am:
My husband in the primary.

In the season's opener,
After the call, "Play ball!"
I am safe at first.

In scrimmage I thirst for power,
Kick off and carry . . .
Anything for the big hurrah.

But now I can't spot a long shot.
There's a figure-8 hoopla
Quaking the backboard.
Have I scored?
What's the tally?

> Am I still in the running?
> My manager slaps my back,
> Says, "Not to worry,
> You'll clobber them in the rally."
>
> Next season: the big time, the majors.
> But now I've contracted athletes's foot
> And can't even scratch a jock-strap itch.

There followed several dreams in which I was packing and moving out, and more than one dream in which my husband was furious over the loss of heat [sexual ardor] in the house and was blaming me.

Dream images did caution me about the challenges I would have to face if I were to divorce. In one dream, divorce was portrayed as surgery (Dec 8, 1982); in another, it amounted to my dropping out, not having fulfilled requirements (Oct 13, 1982). There were threats of freezing (Oct 13, 1982), an explosion (Nov 6, 1982), and a head-on collision (Nov 8, 1982).

I began appointments with Ron Kerkhoff, MSW at a neighborhood clinic called "Families in Transition," to prepare myself emotionally and practically for letting go of the marriage. Neither Ron nor I could have guessed the number and severity of issues that would arise when we were discussing the challenges of my living alone and finding work to sustain me financially. Here is a dream from the night prior to my initial appointment with him:

Dec 10, 1982
Testing My Ground

> I'm driving the '32 Ford up a steep embankment, but seem to have got off the usual packed-earth roadway. I decide to walk the rest of the way. When I'm within 10 yards of the top, I find the earth beneath my feet separating. Now there's a ridge, and I'm straddling it. Now it's a chasm, and I've got to get both feet on one side or I'll fall straight down 20-30 feet!
>
> I look for help. Someone on my right seems to be making progress. A person calls from above, "Have you tested your ground?" I look at the earth and see it is loose material. I

> wonder if the person to my right will dislodge it? Can I reach the outstretched hands of the person above me?

FEELINGS:
Confidence dissolving into fear; desperate yet hopeful that the person above will help.

REFLECTIONS:
1. The '32 Ford [the year of my birth] represents my old self as brought up with my parents' values.
2. The ground shifting under me = doubts about how to proceed with the divorce.
3. The helper above me may be Ron. "Have you tested your ground?" = my beliefs, feelings, desires, and goals.

Six months later I moved to an apartment for a year's trial separation. In my second day in the apartment, my Unconscious utilized similar imagery, while ratcheting up the intensity of feelings and doubling the persona. There were nine scenes that night, of which I include the seventh here:

Jun 15, 1983
Soft Red Earth Collapses

> There's been excavation of soft red earth, part of it in the roadway, with no barricades or warning lights set up. A woman in a rose-colored dress and shoes approaches me. I tell her, "Get out of the way!" [because] There's a car speeding behind her. In the shuffle, we're both on the ground and perilously near to falling into the hole. It's 15-20 feet deep!
>
> Somehow I think my husband is to blame. I imagine both of us women falling and covered by tons of earth that will suffocate us. Earlier I tried to get barricades and lights from his field office. But he wouldn't supply them or order them. And now he goes riding off on his bike, carrying bike signs [for one of the routes he's designed].

FEELINGS AND REFLECTIONS:
1. The earth feels raw, especially the way it was dug by some huge machine in just a few cuts, the "rape of the earth" by technology.

2. The chasm of red earth feels female. I'm not as afraid of the chasm itself as of an avalanche of tons of earth suffocating us.
3. Suppose the chasm = rawness from the deep cuts during marriage. I fear that if I were to fall into bitterness, or if my husband were to push me over the edge, my emotions would suffocate me.

After nine days in the apartment, I had a dream with such uplift that it countered the previous scene about the chasm:

Jun 23, 1983
Balloon Man

> There's a balloon man who says I can fly by holding a balloon. He puts one about eight inches round in my hand. I think, I can't fly with this! and the balloon immediately deflates. Anyhow, it's yellow and I'd never choose yellow for myself.
> So I go back to the man. He assures me that I can fly with such a small balloon and says he'll give me another one on Monday. He says, "It's the end of the day and the week now, and I need rest."
>
> I think, The balloon could go only on faith, and I wonder–his faith? or mine? This isn't magic, I tell myself. There are questions I need to have answered:
> 1. How high will I go–will it be out of sight? and will I need oxygen?
> 2. How far away will I land? If it's late in the day, I need to allow time to walk home or find a bus driver or taxi driver who knows where I live.
> 3. How shall I come down? There's no ballast and I surely mustn't pop the balloon or I'll crash.
>
> The balloon man answers like an oracle:
> 1. As high as desirable.
> 2. As far as necessary.
> 3. Gradually. Don't worry about coming down, you haven't even gone up yet.
>
> Now he is lying on a park bench with me. Maybe we're BOTH "resting until Monday." It's not a sexual arrangement, and I don't feel crowded.

FEELINGS:
Desire to fly, curiosity, concern whether my faith is strong enough.

REFLECTIONS:
1. The desire to fly refers to taking off with my career as much as it does to fleeing my marriage.
2. With the many questions, I am looking ahead and taking precautions.
3. Right now I don't know where to place my faith. That there's no ballast is scary.
4. I am physically tired and do need rest.

By the end of that summer, when I was 51, a dream showed determination and optimism on my part:

Sep 6, 1983
Wrinkled Road Map

> I'm traveling from a town called E I O to Athens [Ohio], via Rte. 2. Athens will be the debarkation place for the greater journey. I take many wrong turns due to heavy traffic, poor signage, construction underway, and other hazards. I'm driving a small boxcar that has to be pedaled to get it going each time.
>
> Between my starting point at a parish school and [the on-ramp for] Rte. 2, a college boy/man gets in my boxcar, ahead of me. I don't protest until I have to pedal doubly hard. Worse, he wants to steer from the front and doesn't go the direction I'm bound to. I have to counteract his superior strength. When I show him the wrinkled road map with the route I have marked, he acquiesces.

REFLECTIONS:
1. This is like a life review. I go from a parish school and parochial thinking to Athens, a university town set on a hill and resembling ancient Athens. From that seat of culture, I will debark on the greater journey–the spiritual journey.
2. My husband is the college boy/man, who finally acquiesces.
3. Unconsciously, "The direction I'm bound to" is supported by (a) Jung's idea of free will, that one is free to live one's fate joyfully,

and (b) the Catholic stance, that one is not forced to choose or act against one's calling.
4. Consciously, I don't have a route marked for me. I feel called in certain ways, but they could ultimately be detours or byways.

In late December 1983, my mother died. Maureen and her husband, Gino, drove me to Michigan for the funeral. My husband brought some of the children in the van, and others arrived by bus or train. Sensing my vulnerable state, my husband did not let up with various ploys to get me back. Those attempts, and my older brother's interference, were so obvious to other family members that my priest brother offered his services in canon law and my attorney brother offered his in civil law. A month later a dream with a comical title illustrated a serious story:

Jan 30, 1984
Turtles as Gossips, Possibly a Committee

> I've been swimming in dark water. Now, resting on a raft, I see the shoulders of a huge man emerging from the water. No, it's a turtle, now three or four turtles with their backs to me! They're churning the water and turning it murky. I wonder if I'm safe or the raft is safe.
>
> I hear one of those creatures addressing another, "Look at that woman. What does she think she's doing? Where does she think she's going?"

FEELINGS:
Independence and strength; curiosity; alarm and defensiveness.

REFLECTIONS:
1. The first turtle resonates to my husband, who lives within a protective shell most of the time. Though he has his back to me, he is making waves that disturb me and my life raft.
2. The other turtles suggest his lawyer friends. If they are encouraging him to fight the divorce, they are "turning things murky."
3. What constitutes my "life raft"? Is it the friends of mine, raised in religious homes, who have had the strength to carry through with divorce? Is it psychotherapy? Is it dream life, which I rely on to prompt me to action in waking life?

In October of that year I had a dream in which I was expected to be the "fix-it person"(Oct 7, 1984). A Reflection on that dream stated, "Here's what I wish to emphasize: the carry-over from my confidence and action during dreams to the same abilities in waking life. I do not panic. I don't even instruct myself not to panic. Today I appreciate that my husband has not harassed me since his original outburst.

Even with temporary alimony, a savings bond worth $1875, payment for occasional substitute teaching, and a few honoraria, I was short on money. I had several dreams in which an ATM swallowed my card; also a bank teller disputed my identity or otherwise refused to give me cash; and a bank manager took his sweet time in verifying my account. There were a couple of scenes in which I appeared as a bag lady, who was disregarded as a real person.

I had hoped that my share of my mother's estate would, if well invested in that time of high interest rates, provide me with $100 per month. But the amount was closer to $50 per month, and too soon I had used up the principal, too. The divorce was decreed in April 1985, with arrangements for alimony to continue after Ed's retirement and his death. He remarried a year later. Melodee, his new wife, was a wonderful companion for the 19 years before his death and has remained a benefactor to the children and grandchildren.

Very recently, 11 years after my ex-husband's death, I had an unusual dream that was a send-off, or at least a send-up of an idol who will never die:

Nov 16, 2016
A Glimpse of My Ex as a Very Different Man

> My ex is dressed in a sparkling white outfit with
> a wide white belt and silver buckle. He dives,
> fully clothed, into a pool of clear water.

FEELINGS:
Surprised at his appearance, astonished at his diving in.

REFLECTIONS:
1. Considering that I dreamed this up, it may be that I see my ex, or his life, or our marriage clearer now. Although he is still the

center of attention and making a big splash, I don't mind in this instance. That's a turnabout in me.
2. This dream may have been prompted by Stephen when I complimented him on his parenting of three little girls (sisters) whom he and Judith had adopted. He said, "Dad was only 22 when he became a father, but I was 48 and more mature. Dad's non-involvement with the first child set a pattern for the rest of us." I grant that my ex-husband had no modeling from his father, other than absenteeism. And I grant that men in the 1950s did not participate in child-rearing to the extent that some men do now.

Letting Go of Our Home

Our house on Eddystone was designed by an architect specifically for the needs of our large family. It was built on the only remaining lot that backed onto Kenlawn Park, a city park large enough for playground equipment and a recreation center but not large enough for leagues of ball teams.

We took possession of the house before Halloween, 1964. Angelyn, our first child, celebrated her 12th birthday in our new home on November 5th. Stephen, our last child, was born on November 26th. The house on Eddystone was the only home in which all of our children lived (the older children having moved from two previous houses), and it is what I think of when the word *home* comes up in conversation.

Our home was aesthetically pleasing; its exterior was stucco with two sandstone elevations near the entrance, an outdoor fireplace on the east side, and a patio beyond a sliding glass door on the south. Both the front and back of the house had walls of windows, floor-to-ceiling. The interior featured a 12-foot sandstone hearth in the living room. The wall across from the hearth was paneled in mahogany, as was the entryway, and there were hardwood floors throughout.

After ten years of living there, enjoying the house and neighborhood, I began having dreams in which my husband either took over the house completely, or sold it without consulting me, or razed it—all methods of squeezing me out. In one dream (Aug 13, 1977), there was an extreme situation of his building a new house without even showing me the blueprints, far less the construction of it. My response to that dream was, "I want a new house [a new concept of marriage] without lots of old furnishing tucked in and pet peeves making themselves at home." Yet concurrently in waking life, I was squeezing him out, not showing him my tentative plans for a trip to Europe.

Five years after that, I began having dreams about adding on "a room of her own," or moving to an apartment or else building one, or completely renovating the home we lived in. Clearly, *something had to give*. By that time I knew what each level and each room in my dreams represented, and that a house as a whole represented my marriage. The following dream is the first to show my desire for letting go of house and home:

Mar 21, 1979
Lego House

> I call out in jubilation, "A Lego house!" It's built near the church hill. It's white with orange trim, and the garage is orange with white trim. As I stand admiring it, one of the carpenters indicates the difficulty of having the roof-peak high enough. Now a wind lifts the whole roof off. I wonder what shape it will be in and how much damage it will cause when falling.
>
> When I look inside, there's no staircase. The house goes up three stories of emptiness. It's airy, and I figure that in due time the carpenters will finish the construction.
>
> When I enter, I see that the carpenters are living in the house while they build it. There is food in the kitchen and clothes on the backs of chairs.
>
> Now several of my children climb into the house through a window opening. I want them to leave before they're discovered. I belong, but the children do not.

FEELINGS:
Jubilant, admiring; agreeable to waiting; belonging.

REFLECTIONS:

This is a Yay-Boo dream. I find a house where I can let go (Yay), but now a wind lifts the whole roof off (Boo). The house is airy and goes up three stories (Yay), but there's no staircase yet (Boo). The house is livable, and there are provisions (Yay), but I don't want men staying there (Boo). Several children climb through a window opening (Yay), but they do not belong (Boo). I do belong (Yay).

Most of the bright memories of Eddystone involved Stephen's growing up. We played games at the dining room table, and I even tolerated "Uncle Wiggily" and "Candy Land" because he liked them. I recall with pleasure driving Stephen and the Hetterscheidt girl to kindergarten and later walking them there, to be sure they knew the way. I recall driving up and down the entire Kenlawn Park subdivision to see azaleas, rhododendron, tulip trees, rows of peonies. I remember driving the hills on Henderson Road, our coasting down one and coaxing the car to crest the next.

The following dream featured a teenaged Stephen, angry enough to destroy a photo of the house that I cherished. Considering that this was *my* dream projection, I must have felt that I was breaking up *his* picture of hearth and home.

Oct 17, 1984
Stephen Destroys an Irreplaceable Photo

> He's alone, by the front walk on Eddystone, and
> has dropped some small nuts and bolts. I help him
> retrieve the pieces and now see that he's taken
> apart a toy. No, it's a picture of our home.
> I say, "The frame is apart, but where is the picture?"
> He says, "Smashed with the glass."
> "The photograph itself?"
> "I cut it into little pieces."
> "Why, Stephen, why?"
> He shrugs it off lightly with, "I didn't like it."
> Surely he knew that I liked it. I framed it, hung
> it, treasured it. Now there's no way I can relocate
> the negative. Why, oh why, this destruction?

FEELINGS:

Heavy-hearted; sense of loss and destruction; dismay at Stephen's not understanding.

REFLECTIONS:
1. I tried the technique of "active imagination" regarding the dream, but couldn't move to a resolution.
2. All I understand is that the greatest happiness in the house on Eddystone, the 18 years I spent there, was experienced when the children were youngsters: our reading together, working in the gardens, baking cookies at Christmas, decorating birthday cakes.
3. The picture I had of marriage emphasized Ed and me as lovers. Now I've "smashed the framework" by divorce action, and I'm dreading the final "tearing into little pieces" during negotiations for a settlement.
4. Though I don't have the full picture anymore, this dream reminds me (a) that there are many happy memories and (b) that I had better not take them all apart–not analyze all relationships in terms of a marriage that held little happiness.

There were 13 more dreams about destruction of the house and/or the landscaping in violent ways. They concerned the marriage, not the lovely house that we had built. A few months prior to the divorce decree, I had a dream about the house itself that referred to my love of its architectural structure and my sadness at the loss of it:

Dec 26, 1985
The Landscaping and Facade of Our Large House Destroyed

> Someone pulls out some roots–thick roots, interwoven, like basket-weaving. Bulldozers come and strip another layer, down to enormous black coils. Tons of earth are moved until a smooth sub-stratum is found. This leaves the house on a bank about 15 feet above the cut.
>
> Now a man wants to shore up the house or do something to the porch with poles, ropes, and pulleys. The whole front [of the house] pulls away from the other walls. I think of the "walls of Jericho tumbling down" and am sure many people will be crushed.

FEELINGS AND REFLECTIONS:
1. My hopes are not crushed, not even during the holidays.
2. There still is a push-pull about the house and Ed's plans to sell it. I don't expect anyone to be hurt in that deal except me and my gardens.
3. In this story, it's the house itself that is letting go!

Magdalene and Stephen, the two children still living at home on Eddystone, left before the house went up for sale. Maybe their letting-go was less painful than if they had waited around for the closing.

I still had keys to the house and did what I could to "stage" it for selling, even to restoring the front garden and planting a few annuals. Then I said goodbye to each room individually and to each tree. That the house sold for far less than it was worth is another story and was a source of sadness. I thought it deserved greater respect than having a buyer haggle over it, with no appreciation for its special qualities. I wanted to say something to that effect when we handed over the blueprints and specs, but restrained myself. I turned away and never looked back.

– Twenty-Three –
New Levels of Awareness

Although the theme of reassurance occurs throughout the decades of my record-keeping, it is rare when compared to the great number of disruptive dreams. A reassurance dream is light and uplifting, and I consider each one a gift, coming as it does when I most need a boost in waking life. Certainly I have not been able to conjure a reassurance dream through conscious attempts. For this section I have selected a reassurance dream from each decade of my note-taking. The sequence of levels addressed is: physical, emotional, aesthetic, mental, spiritual, and integrative.

On the **physical level**, a reassurance dream often concerns a survival strategy, whether within the body itself (exercise, digestion) or without (at work, in social exchanges, during travel, or through attempts to go beyond known boundaries). Several of these themes appear in one dream:

Jan 20, 1979
Helped and Advised

> I receive a five-page letter, handwritten. It is a rejection, beginning, "You appear to be very young, too young and waif-like, to be attempting these subjects. Suggest you live awhile." I am 46. How old must I be before I can communicate? Since when is age the measure of communication?
>
> Now I am trying to cross an area in a dark courtyard or a basement. Now I am trying on skis—rough and wide as orange-crate slats and without laces. A man (a furnace tender? a blacksmith?) tells me, "Push forward anyhow, and friction will keep your feet on the skis."

FEELINGS:
Hurt, angry, surprised by the rejection letter; responsible; struggling; helped, advised.

REFLECTIONS:
1. Trying to cross in darkness = a spiritual struggle, one that I'm not consciously aware of.
2. Though I lack faith in the present doctor and meds, I still believe in a restorative power, God's creative power, coursing through my body and my life.
3. Furnace tender or blacksmith = reference to my *Take Fire* manuscript, especially to the concept of "a woman's love tended well by men."

A reassurance dream on the **emotional level** credits a dear friend with instructing and encouraging me:

Feb 22, 1986
Dream of Exaltation

> Meg urges me to ready myself for the experience of double-rolls and triple-rolls. I'm reluctant, even doubtful. What good would come of It? I'm not a thrill-seeker. Meg assures me, "There are deep and lasting effects." Someone in the room is levitating, not showing off but lifted in ecstasy. I think of the word exalted.
>
> I don't know how the next event happens. I'm picked up, eight feet or higher. Lying on my back, I barely miss the ceiling. Now I'm plunked down on the floor and I feel punished. It's not a case of my doubting a Higher Power, but of wondering how I fit into the scheme of things.
>
> Now I'm swooped up again and whooshed backward–out of the room, down a corridor, and a turn to the right. Now I'm in a dark sky, infinite sky above me and surrounding me. Stars are strewn like grains of sand. IMMENSITY, INFINITY, AWE.
>
> I feel myself being moved very far, yet there's a sense of timelessness, which seems a contradiction. I don't know when or how I've turned from backward motion to forward. I return through the corridor, face-forward, and make a mental note that it's a right turn again.
>
> This is unlike any previous flying dreams, even the outer-space ones. I am transported.

NEW LEVELS OF AWARENESS

FEELINGS:
Doubtful, reluctant; perplexed when I feel punished; transported, in awe.

REFLECTIONS:
1. The right turns suggest that I am on the spiritual path that's right for me.
2. There's a sense of *person* throughout: from Meg Hoskins, to me as viewer, to me in a small group. Even when I am seemingly alone in infinite space and silence, someone like a Guardian Angel is with me, a presence more powerful than Meg, yet assuredly as loving as she.
3. This dream emphasizes that I am in the hands of a Higher Power. I haven't merited this loving care or this demonstration, it's been freely given.

A reassurance dream on the **mental level** progressed from frustration to resolution:

Nov 22, 1991
A Test in Music Theory – A Review after Many Years

> There are two mimeographed pages handed out. The first two lines state the melody, and chord numbers are given on the first and second pages. All I need to recall is which inversions are represented and possible variations in voice-leading. Space is allowed for fill-in of passing tones and embellishments. The final chord is based on E, but the key signature is not four sharps. It's no sharps or flats, key of C.
>
> When I begin writing, I'm pleased to make big, rounded notes, each with one stroke of a special pencil. I proceed without reference to rules, just watching how the notes look, making patterns.

FEELINGS:
Eager; anxious; playful, successful.

REFLECTIONS:
1. That last chord could be the tonic in 1st inversion and might be a sign to modulate to a new key, to a new thought pattern or behavior.

2. The key may be playfulness. "Proceeding without reference to rules," watching to see how patterns reveal themselves, is what I choose when making collages.
3. "Recalling the voice-leading" resonates with the whispered voice in a recent dream that asked, "Margaret, are you ready?" The need to recall "possible variations in voice-leading" may apply to my desire for greater awareness of Angels and Guides.
4. The word "tonic" suggests that when I get back to toning [orally, on specific areas of my body], that will be a tonic for me.

A reassurance dream on an **spiritual level** occurred about eleven years after my mother's death and nine years after my divorce. I processed this dream (Aug 21, 1994) in the way recommended by Thomas Moore in *Care of the Soul*—staying with the images and honoring the mystery without rushing to interpret. Annotations came much later, as did the following poem transposed from its images:

Recollection

Standing on the back porch, gazing over her yard,
she sees in the mid-ground a child
bearing armloads of brilliant flowers—
like gladiolas but stripped from a bush.
Her stifled gasp turns to grieving.
Over blossoms? Surely not.
Over lost time, summers, decisions?

She herself would have made those blossoms last—
carefully pruning, cutting, arranging,
a few at a time over a much longer time.
To caution the child now is pointless
and would spoil the thrill of abundance.

She leaves her shelter, goes down to the lawn.
Smack in the middle, her ex-husband sits
at a small table, concentrating on balancing
a very tall glass with a chip on its base

that sets everything around it a-kilter.
If its bright yellow contents (a compound? an elixir?)
were to spill, he might lose
the contract, a fortune, his career.

She turns back toward the house.
Over the door bends a small tree, leafless but fruitful.
Five or more apples, each a different variety,
dangle and sway on bare branches.
One rosy-gold fruit, elongated like a squash,
counterbalances this mobile.
She sees letters incised in each fruit. Like initials
carved long ago on a tree trunk, these have healed.

She considers picking all the apples,
heaping them in the heirloom silver bowl,
a welcome to family when they come indoors.
Reaches but stops, recollects the children,
envisions each daughter and son pulling on a branch,
exclaiming over a particular, rightful fruit,
without quarreling,
everyone knowing whose is whose.

She steps over the threshold, empty-handed,
moves quietly into her kitchen
where the heirloom bowl rests undisturbed.

FEELINGS:
Disappointed about the stripping of the flower bush; dismayed over the passage of time; curious about my husband's challenge; surprised and pleased at the yield of fruit on what seemed a barren tree.

REFLECTIONS:
1. The tree is prompted by our family tree and the family anecdotes I've been compiling for my children.
2. Leafless yet fruitful = stripped down to essentials, my childhood (and that of siblings) yielded singular fruits.

3. The five apples resonate with me and my siblings. The possibility of more than five resonates with my eight children.
4. The unusual squash = the part of me (and possibly of all my siblings) that was squashed during childhood. Its rose-and-gold tones suggest spiritual development. Its elongation suggests that over time, relationships have stabilized.
5. The heirloom bowl from my mother's grandmother = what I have inherited and what I have passed on to my children. Its resting undisturbed alludes to regenerative power and likely to reincarnation.
6. The bright yellow compound or elixir = something sunny and shining that everyone would like to have.
7. The chipped and weighted glass seems to be a looking-glass for my ex-husband. While trying to balance responsibilities, he's oblivious to everything related to me and the children.
8. Yet this dream as a whole is reassurance about my balancing interior and exterior demands–those that I myself have created, as well as those instilled by my progenitors.

A profound dream when I was 80 has given reassurance on an **integrative level,** correlating dream information with waking-life experiences that needed to be resolved.

Sep 22, 2012
An Old Monk and a Young Monk

> I'm searching for something that gives/lends/shows purpose to my life. An old monk asks several questions, to which I say No or Not really or Not quite. When I mention that my husband and I were enrolled as Benedictine Oblates decades ago, the monk lights up like a cartoon figure with a light-bulb over his head.

REFLECTION:
The dream in its entirety is so rich in details that I've transposed it into a poem with the same title.

An Old Monk and a Young Monk

I've been booted out more church doors
than most folks have visited.
Yet here I am, in a monastery,
in silent retreat from media's dread.
An old monk leads the way, takes me
*by the hand so gently that I go,
not knowing if I wish to go or stay.*
He walks me past the refectory
(too late to eat) to the polished doors
of a stupendous library
which might yet be my sanctuary.

But no, a young monk takes over
and, wordless yet officious,
circumvents the chapel and choir,
where I might have sung in unison,
*Now, O Lord, you may dismiss
your servant in peace.*
Down labyrinthine corridors,
in unfathomable darkness, he
boldly goes where few have gone before.

I follow blindly until I stumble into . . .
a primeval baptistry?
Without warning, the young monk pours
a pitcher of ice water on my head,
quelling any thoughts he'd disallow.
He leaves me at my cell, disquieted
by that uncalled-for, egoistic liturgy.
Comes the dawn, I shake myself awake
and vow: *I'll get me to a nunnery instead.*

REFLECTIONS:

Taking each image as a self-image, this dream gives reassurance regarding my form of spirituality.

1. It's okay to develop my own liturgy and theology.
2. As an oldster I still have bright ideas.
3. Darkness of itself doesn't always signal danger.
4. I'm willing to follow leads of someone younger.
5. This is a reminder that more than one past life was spent happily in a monastery.
6. This recalls St. Meinrad's Abbey in Indiana and compassionate Father Blaise, who died too young.
7. This also recalls my being denied entrance to the library in the abbey at Einsiedeln, Switzerland. I didn't "go to a nunnery instead," but went walking in a meadow filled with the music of cow-bells.
8. Spirituality–though not necessarily religion–does imbue my life with purpose.

– Twenty-Four –

Wrestling with Religion

For this section only, I veer from the usual formatting. Instead of using the dreams as my primary source, I use the Reflections on them. These can be read like journal entries about the struggle I was going through: to leave or not to leave the Catholic Church.

At the beginning of this series of Reflections (which continued for 13 years) I was 43 years old and searching for a spiritual path that felt right and could sustain me. I hoped to build on what was valuable to me as a "cradle Catholic" and to expand, to be more inclusive, especially regarding the roles of women in a worshiping community.

Reflections

Sun Mar 16, 1976

In a realistic dream, I was working frantically to get tables ready for an adult's Communion Day and welcoming. Silverware still had to be laid at some of the tables, and no one was helping me. Yet I stopped to watch the liturgy. The procession was lovely–so much beauty in the faces and movements and orderliness of the gift-bearers.

Thu Dec 30, 1977

A dream concerned a visiting priest who wore a black-and-red suit that looked like something from "Guys and Dolls." He found a large cross to carry in a procession, and an altar boy had our American flag. Off they went, and I was left to clear the sanctuary.

Candles were threatening to burn up the floral arrangements. Under foot were tiny Christmas tree bulbs–some on strings and lighted, others stepped on and shattered. I thought, Being in the

Altar Society doesn't amount to anything more than being a cleaning woman. I'm not a co-celebrant in the Mass itself, only here for clean-up.

Wed Mar 1, 1978

I came across that word again, "auseinandersetzung," which I'd thought meant setting oneself against another person or belief. But in *Dreams, God's Forgotten Language,* John Sanford says it means a taking apart for clarifying, as well as a confrontation: "Two psychic principles (Conscious and Unconscious) are having a running conversation, and the result is a dialectical process in which they influence each other."

I seem to be struggling with the dream world and the spirit world concurrently. And with the same vocabulary! I'm terribly frustrated when I can't deal with dreams or meditations or writing blocks to my satisfaction.

Sun Mar 5, 1978

There's some redecorating underway at church. I noticed there was no sanctuary lamp at the Blessed Sacrament altar where I was kneeling, but there was a paschal-sized candle at the altar of the Blessed Virgin. It would have been ridiculous for me to move. The Lord is in the tabernacle, light or no light. He's in this church and he's in me. (As I write, I don't like the use of the masculine pronoun. Sigh.)

Fri Jun 9, 1978
At Beatrice's house, outside Lille, France

There are gargoyles everywhere! They raise questions about the Creator as also Destroyer.

I'm trying to deal with the destructive elements in our marriage and not place blame outside myself. Yet I will not assume "guilt" anymore, just try to understand the destructiveness and minimize its effects on my life.

Thu Sep 14, 1978

I stepped into a church to get out of the pouring rain. I couldn't believe my eyes–the priest was a woman! Episcopal, I guess. I let my surprise distract me and missed receiving Communion. Then I rationalized that my intention was to receive; therefore, graces would come anyhow. A woman priest!

Sun Nov 19, 1978

Back home after a PITS residency in Jackson, I wanted to resume volunteering at church, prior to Stephen's Confirmation. That triggered a dream in which I was polishing some silver pieces, and even carried a gold reliquary from the altar to the sacristy–casually, just another object in my armload. Someone decided to take inventory, and I had to call out what each piece was. I did not like such a public announcement of wealth.

It is accumulated service, not objects, that has significance for me. The most valuable thing I've ever entrusted to our children was–and is–my modeling of a value system. Not the system itself, but my adherence to it.

Sat Sep 29, 1979

In a lengthy dream, I was admonishing some quarreling women. Yes, me! It went something like this: Eventually you will eliminate or bypass all theories and get to an elemental place or moment when you meet ESSENCE–maybe in a star, maybe in a stone–and you say, *I believe*. I myself believe there is a Creator who designed and continues to create our world, humans and animals and all. I believe in our interrelatedness.

I waited for the women to state their beliefs, but got no response. So I went on, mostly talking to myself: There comes a time when the question of greatest importance is not Why? It is How.

How am I going to deal with my belief system? How am I going to reinforce my faith and live accordingly?

Aug 6, 1980
In a Retreat at Grailville

I feel a separation between established religion and my spiritual life. Even if I don't know my ultimate destination, or how many reincarnations are necessary before reaching it, I choose to be in the here-and-now, aware in this moment.

All weekend there was an extended metaphor, a symbol actually: the gathering of water and the holiness of water, our source. Samples were brought from rivers all around our country and from the Atlantic and the Pacific oceans. The final blessing was administered in pairs. We touched with fingers dipped in that holy water our partner's eyes, nose, mouth, ears, and crown, saying: "May this touch wash away all your pain. May you be refreshed in the life to come."

Sat Aug 22, 1981
In a Progoff Intensive Journal Workshop

I wonder again why most clergy are vehemently opposed to homosexuality. Is it because the possibility is always present? That they feel doubly guilty that, having eschewed women, they're attracted to and by men? Years ago, when Charles [my brother] was in the seminary, he said there were very strict rules against anything that looked like "fraternizing."

The last time I saw Father Charles, I gave him a hug, which he backed away from, a smidgeon. I wondered if he's afraid of scandal, of someone's reporting a priest being hugged by a woman? (No one would know I'm his sister.) I think Charles doesn't know how to hug, and I wonder how much he's been hurt by having dedicated himself to the Church and then being put down by his bishop. I'm surprised he's back from Rome so soon, considering that he was allowed to be gone until Christmas.

Fri Sep 11, 1981
At Saint Ann's Retirement Home, Visiting Mother

I had another terrifying dream, this one of spiritual warfare. The congregation, in taking Communion, was to keep strict silence for several hours. That's one of the many things I oppose in the Church–I mean, the prescription and proscription of behavior. I spoke two words, "I quit." When accosted, I pointed out to authorities that they'd used hundreds of words–during silence–in exclaiming against me and indicting me on the spot. When an authority figure flung me around at arm's length, I cried out, "Help! Police!" He laughed ominously and said, "I am the police." He warned that any scar tissue would be proof against the victim, not evidence of foul play by authorities.

His face was that of the priest here. He's so opinionated, prejudiced, and vehement that I couldn't help associating him with the great purges and purgers of history.

Thu Nov 5, 1981

I tossed in bed for hours last night, angry because I'd let Bart, a member of the Genesis II study group, use me as a target for remarks he was going to make anyway. He acted like a born-again catechist, spouting what he thinks Vatican II promulgated. One example: Bart, ostensibly asking for ideas about the celebration of Mass, gave *his* ideas, prefaced by the words, "Be forewarned that the music…" That's when I took the bait and replied, "Be forewarned that you are losing us."

Sat Dec 12, 1981

I concede there's a special significance in the words *I am*. Every time I say or think, "I'm hurting, I'm tired, I'm scared" or any such statement in the negative, I might better say, "I'm here, I'm alive, I'm aware." Further, "I am on my way to good health; I am on my way to sharing more completely with others; I am on the beacon set for me in spiritual life, even when turbulence hints otherwise."

Going beyond the title of the anthology I'm working on, *I Name Myself Daughter of the Divine*, is the realization that I share in the essence of the One known as Yahweh, I AM WHO AM.

Thu Dec 17, 1981

Last night at Communal Penance, the prayer we were to exchange was to be one of comfort and encouragement. What I said was, "May the Holy Spirit give you courage in all your undertakings." As I repeated it three times, I realized full well that this is the prayer I have for myself. Maybe all blessings are?

The Holy Spirit "brooding with oh! great wings" (as G.M. Hopkins describes it) is a mother figure. And in the sense of brooding, it represents the creative spirit and reassures me that, even when I feel the moody blues, it may be constructive brooding.

Oh, I so wish to experience the creative flow again, not just a sputter or a spurt but the Life Force!

Thu Jan 28, 1982

I woke from a dream, calling two or three times, "Elohim, save us!" I felt blah when I wakened, and later was distressed when I thought about the dream. In it I was not frantic, more like making an act of faith. The feeling was what I experience when praying to "whoever you are, whatever your name."

Presently I feel overwhelmed by Joe's wedding plans; Chas' and Stephen's biking plans taken over by their dad; my responsibility to the younger children; my having backed away from plans to attend the Women's Studies Convention on the West coast; and my inability to express needs or even to admit them to myself. "Elohim, save me!"

Sat Sep 24, 1983

There are two concepts (maybe challenges?) I want to think about. First is Bill's question in the Genesis II study group, "Do objects have a special energy in themselves, or do we project all their value onto them?" He was gesturing to objects of ceramic, porcelain, and clear glass. Oh, there was a white marble cylinder, too, that seemed to have an aura.

The second question is so big that I don't know how to phrase it. That Father K. left the priesthood after his mother died, for a woman who "needed his care" was a grave disappointment to me. Though "Thou art a priest forever, according to the order of Melchisedech" was a sacred contract, a *man* could be released from it. But what about persons caught in the marriage-is-forever policy of the Church when it becomes a mockery of a sacred contract? What is their release?

Fri Jan 20, 1984
One month after Mother's funeral

I'm recalling my godmother's singing at the funeral Mass. All that came through to me then was "One... One... One..." embellished in myriad ways. I realize now that when I address the Most Holy One, I'm also addressing Mother, or at least letting her tune in. This is what used to be referred to as the Church Triumphant (recognized along with the Church Militant and the Church Suffering).

I wonder how I will handle myself at the workshop on "Power and Sensitivity" today. John Sanford, in *Healing And Wholeness,* discusses Jacob's wrestling with the angel, "Here is the wounding of the ego by the Self. A deep encounter with the unconscious results in a wound through which pours the life and energy of the unconscious." Put more simply, the ego needs to become conscious of what is wanted from within.

"Who has wrestled with God" could have been applied to me several times in my life, but presently I don't feel this kind of struggle. What I am wrestling with now is: What work am I called to do?
I seek the greatness within me. If I am not a productive artist, then what is the source of my greatness? the evidence? the manifestation? What is the process?

Mon Jan 30, 1984

Maggie heard on the news that Father Fulcher (I still don't address him as Bishop) died in an auto accident last week, and the funeral had already taken place in whatever diocese he recently moved to. Stephen filled me in today that the accident was the result of a heart attack and Father's blacking out. The children had no idea that we were friends, or they wouldn't have told me so casually. He was a fine man, extremely intelligent, with a wonderful sense of humor, and was at ease in anyone's company, in a multitude of situations. Well this isn't the place to write a eulogy, yet I do praise heaven for his part in my life.

How is it that a person like Mother hangs on for years and years and a person like Father Fulcher gets stopped in his tracks, still in his prime?

Sat Jun 30, 1984

I'm debating about having a private session with the healer Eleanor Moore during the week that she'll be here in late August. Am I open to new experience right now when so much presses in on me? I've no intention of using the healer to salve my present wounds. My intent is to focus healing energy within me and eventually outward in a healing profession. I'm certified in Poetry Therapy and, through that internship and through participation in dream groups, I've experienced many therapeutic strategies. But I've only dipped into the master of social work program (MSW) and am unsure about pursuing it.

Fri May 17, 1985

I came across an antique card printed with the devotions to Our Lady Of Perpetual Help, devotions that Mother attended when I was deathly ill at age three (1935). The direct address is, "Mother of the Word Incarnate." A poet is that—a mother of words, incarnating the spirit of them.

If I could transform some of the Mariology that I've rejected since age 10 and incorporate it in an abiding faith in the Most Holy One, how much easier for me to be a yea-sayer to possibilities and to the future!

Sun Jun 15, 1985

At Mass, during the Gloria, I was following the musical line with embellishments, though people around me were singing the simple line. I wasn't actually singing at first, only shaping the words and mentally hearing the lovely music in its fullness. The Gloria I can still sing gladly, but I won't mouth the Credo again.

Wed Aug 28, 1985

I wakened laughing at a dream image. The scene was a university town in Germany–maybe Tübingen? The church and grounds looked medieval. I had to mail some letters or documents at a special station because they could not go regular mail. There I overheard, "At least 20 Cardinals were almost late to their next session because they had to hand-deliver their documents to this station first." The image struck my funny bone: 20 cardinals like 20 Rumpelstiltskins who think no one can outguess them. But there's a leveling effect socially when they must do as I have done!

In the dream, the sensibility of connectedness and continuity was so strong as to feel ongoing. And the medieval (middle-age?) setting allowed for a personal renaissance in me. A powerful image was the trees–brilliant, exultant–that reproduced the feeling I have when hearing a trumpet fanfare.

Mon Dec 23, 1985

What I thought was love was mostly hopefulness. I'm *feeling* again, and emotions are painful, similar to the return of circulation to my white fingers following the sharp pain of Raynaud's syndrome.

Micki drove me to O'Shaughnessy Funeral Home, whose atmosphere is truly homelike. There we met Molly and Kay [also members of Dreamtalk]. On the way home, Micki related a dream, and I thought, What a strong bonding we dreamers have! On an intimate level, appreciating one another, not analyzing or trying to change any one of us, yet encouraging each to become the person she envisions her Self to be. In addition to feeling close to these women, I feel close to the Most Holy One when I'm with these women.

Fri Jun 20, 1986

A dream of conflict about being outside the church (where, allegedly, "there is no salvation") or inside it. We women stood aside and waited while the Holy Name men lined up for procession. Most of the women wore summery dresses, floppy hats, and white gloves, but I was in navy blue. Oh well.

When we got inside the church, the choir was all women, simply because the men were in the procession, then in the front pews. I just mouthed the words of a couple of songs. Kezia, standing next to me, turned and looked daggers at me and even put her head near mine to hear if I were singing at all. So I sang loud and clear a high note, one that hardly anyone else can manage, and blasted her ear, even though my tone was pure.

Tue Dec 29, 1987

Why do dreams assail me near Christmas every year? Last night my piano was sinking rapidly, as if in quicksand. As one end was dropping, I pushed my shoulders against it–as if that might prevent more movement! But then the other end dipped and the whole piano was sinking. I called for help, but the only response was from my ex-husband, "You can appreciate what it did for you over the years." I was furious and shouted, "Don't talk to me about the past, and stay away from me in the future."

A piano hasn't featured in a dream for many years. But, since it relates to my spiritual journey, I need to pay attention to it. Surely my spiritual life is not sinking, but the Catholic foundation for it has been sinking for 10 years. "Appreciate what it did for you" is highly ironic coming from my ex, considering that the Catholic foundation did supremely well *for him* during the 31 years of our marriage. Even now a parish priest welcomes him, though knowing that my ex was married in a synagogue and attends there on alternate weeks from attending at Mass.

I did feel a loss this Christmas, especially when hearing some Gregorian chants. And I was angry when the Ohio legislature, in response to someone's having placed a menorah on the Statehouse ground, ruled that the Christmas tree standing there is not a religious symbol. Not a religious symbol? Paganism is a religion, if we want to trace decorated trees back that far.

Relative to the "sinking feeling" about the piano, which represents my spiritual journey, there are ups and downs along the way. What I rejoiced in 10 or 12 years ago can not be retrieved, and my "shouldering up to it" is not the appropriate response now. I need to explore a new way or ways to facilitate my spiritual journey.

Mon Apr 4, 1988

There was a verbal dream just before the alarm would have rung. It was emphatic: "Be aware of the word *awareness*. Be aware of the word *grace*." On waking I felt JOY and inferred that the message concerned not the words alone but the correspondence between *awareness* and *grace*.

I now have support in my attempts to reconcile old beliefs with new, because the counselor I'm seeing is himself a "recovering Catholic." He understands the intensity of my conflicts regarding spirituality and personal development. He also *feels* things and is open enough to say so.

– *Twenty-Five* –

Precognitive Dreams

I have experienced precognition rarely, and did not recognize it as such until after the event occurred. For example, in my junior year in the Music School, for a composition assignment in April 1971, I chose from the collection of 1775 poems by Emily Dickinson number 78, whose first line is, "I felt a Funeral in my Brain." The very day that I handed in my composition, I received a long-distance phone call that my father had died suddenly of a heart attack, after having exchanged storm windows for screens.

More often the dream warnings could be considered coincidences because they occurred at the same time as the event. An example of coincidence was my dreaming of a person's collapse in a piazza. I learned later that a friend had collapsed in Spain the day of my dream (and I was not even aware that he was out of the country). Another example was the dream "Earthquake Causes Joe's House to Fold" (Jul 8, 1986). I learned the next day that an earthquake (a 6 on the Richter Scale) had occurred in California, with tremors from San Diego through Los Angeles, at the very hour of my dream.

More specific was a dream (Mar 18, 1987) about my ex-husband, with whom I had little contact. I wakened myself calling out to him,"You've got to consider this! It's a threat to your life!" In the dream I was "trying to locate a Latin-sounding word. It could be an unusual form, like the future perfect passive–about to have been." When, after several unanswered phone calls, I finally reached my ex, I learned that he had in actuality misunderstood about a prescription and was having scary symptoms with his heart.

There have been times when disturbing dreams, especially those concerning one of my children in need or in danger, proved to be absolutely correct. But I had probably been given clues about their situation, so I did not consider those dreams about them as premonitory.

In a "Peanuts" cartoon, Snoopy, unable to sleep a wink, says, "When something bad is going to happen to you, there shouldn't have to be a night before" (Aug 12, 1981). Emotionally I agreed. Yet, no matter how much sleep I lost on account of foreboding dreams, I always paid attention to them. Following any warning dream about my house, car, or body–all of which related to my physical well-being–I acted promptly and made appointments with a doctor, dentist, or physical therapist, thereby forestalling a serious condition.

A Series of Warning Dreams

In early 1990, when I was almost 58, I had a series of warning dreams and, though I did not understand them as premonitions, I was alerted to possible danger. The first dream repeated a "same old, same old" theme of being criticized by my husband:

Jan 11, 1990
My Hand-Braking Saves Us

> Ed's biking friends have taken over the house. Disgusted, I go outdoors and get in the car to drive it. Now there are several people, including Ed, in the back seat and two in the front passenger seat.
>
> The accelerator pedal jams and I can't use the foot brake. There's no room for my knees and legs to move–they're twisted because the front seat has been pushed forward. I'm going to crash into a fence or tree.
>
> I use the hand brake and stop the car with a grinding noise. It sounds like stripping the gears. Ed criticizes me for this maneuver, even though it's saved our lives.

FEELINGS:
Outnumbered, disgusted, frightened, twisted, stripped, criticized.

REFLECTIONS:
1. My first spelling of brake was break, which was foreboding.
2. Sitting in the driver's seat suggests I have some control over the situation.
3. But I'm outnumbered and criticized by "back-seat drivers."

On the same night, another dream warned of a possible collision:

Jan 11, 1990
A Small Plane Drops Down into the Street Where I'm Driving

> It's a fairly wide street, and I am in the clear, no other cars around at present. As the pilot approaches, I'm praying the plane doesn't collide with me, doesn't crash or explode when it touches down.
>
> I can see the man in the cockpit. He's not a romantic stereotype with helmet, goggles, and silk scarf flying. He's bareheaded and not wearing a military uniform, just an ordinary brown jacket. He seems accepting of whatever may come. The expression on his face is not like a stunt pilot "defying death" or a flying ace "going in for the kill," [as in propaganda movies during the war years]. It's more like surprise.
>
> The plane comes so close to me that its left wing tip touches the hood of my car. Now lifts up over the roof. Now the tilted plane rights itself–I see this in my rearview. It doesn't scrape or even scratch me! The tap is almost like a salute to me. Or a blessing on my vehicle. The plane lands smoothly.

FEELINGS:
Deathly fear; relieved, saluted, blessed; uplifted by an unseen power, saved.

REFLECTIONS:
1. Again, as in the hand-brake dream, I am not in control of outside forces.
2. But the safe landing suggests that Fate isn't in control either.
3. Suppose the pilot + I = Conscious awareness, whereas the plane + my car = Unconscious awareness. These elements are seemingly destined to crash.
4. There is also a Super-conscious, whether guardian, guide, or God-power in action, following my prayers for intervention and the pilot's acceptance of whatever may come.

5. There is acknowledgment on the face of the pilot of the imminent danger of death. I link this with the desire on my part not to die through violence this time, in this incarnation.

Two weeks later (Jan 25, 1990), one dream scene was more specific, indicating "trouble with my car" and mechanics' attempts to fix it. That scene was so powerful that I took the car in for inspection of brakes, bought two new tires, had all the tires rotated, and replaced the muffler and tailpipe before my planned trip to Cleveland for a seminar by David Grove, "Metaphors We Live By."

I was optimistically looking forward in my life and also had tickets to fly to Greensboro, North Carolina for Reiki Attunements. (Information about this healing art is in the section "Surpassing All Boundaries.") That I was very excited about pursuing energy work was evident in a dream five nights after the dream of "trouble with my car":

Jan 30, 1990
Transfusion of Woman and Man

> As I'm facing them, she's on my left and he's on my right. They're on separate beds, set close together. There's one tube going from her to him and one from him to her.
>
> There is blue light, indigo to royal blue, more than shimmering, as if with thousands of brilliant stars/particles/atoms/surges/pulses. This light forms a current between the woman and the man.

FEELINGS:
With female energy and male energy connected, how invigorating and healing this transfusion must be!

While setting aside interpretation and focusing on appreciation of this dream, I felt its tremendous power. Gradually I understood that the loving connection between my male and female energies operated on the spiritual level as well as the more obvious physical level. So I pledged to reclaim, forgive, honor, and love my masculine attributes, roles, and lifetimes instead of cutting off their life force from my feminine.

But that loving connection was disrupted three days later (Feb 2, 1990) when violent dreams blasted through from my Unconscious, and I wakened crying, "No more testing for me! I've been through enough! I've had plenty of pain, I think I've learned my lessons about pain. If not, give me some clear clues. This is too much–eating shit, flooded by emotions, antagonized by infant and young adult, by daughter as well as son. NO MORE OF THIS STUFF!"

My protest was in vain. There was to be more, more, more STUFF. The very next day I was involved in a car crash with a near-death experience (Feb 3, 1990). And some of my injuries were like those in the hand-brake dream: My heels felt like they were jammed through the floor, my legs were twisted, and my right knee went through the car radio. I was stripped of many hopes, plans, activities, and any illusions about being in control.

The car crash was devastating. It differed from the precognitive dreams in two ways: I did not see the oncoming vehicle, and the fright did not overtake me before the impact.

The crash seemed fated. That very morning I had avoided a near-collision on a two-lane country road when two cars came directly toward me. A rural mail truck was too slow for a guy in a souped-up car, so he pulled around the truck directly into my lane. I dove for the ditch. After those vehicles had passed and I was breathing normally again, I got back on the road and turned at the next crossroad in order to get to a paved four-lane road. It was on that paved road, a couple of miles farther along, when I was turning into a shopping mall, that a big car plowed into my little one.

What registered was, *That's a hit!* The idea of fate was overpowering at the very moment of impact.

It was not until six weeks after the impact that a dream gave consolation about my survival.

Mar 19, 1990
Walruses and Wave

> I'm at sea–at a Great Lake or else an ocean. Water gets increasingly rough. I'm boating at first, next swimming amidst huge breakers and ice floes. I see walruses. I'll be killed by the breakers or the great animals!

> Now I see in the water words spelled in the churning froth:
>
> ≈ There's ≈ work ≈ for ≈ you ≈
> ≈ There's ≈ work ≈ to ≈ be ≈ done ≈
>
> And I know I won't die this time. The waves push me in toward land, and the water is warmer here.

REFLECTIONS:
1. "I'm at sea" = a feeling of lostness, and the repetition of "great" emphasizes that feeling.
2. The breakers suggest a breakup or a breakdown, certainly with the past, likely with my beliefs.
3. The icy fear that I'll be killed yields to a warmer feeling that I will not die a violent death in this incarnation.

The breakup or breakdown here, also the yielding to a warmer feeling, remind me of a passage from *Dreamtime and Inner Space* in which Holger Kalwait writes sympathetically of the state I find myself in the 21st century:

> Resistance to psychophysical change and a disintegration of the normal structure of existence has always been part and parcel of the transformative process . . . . True, existence itself is change, but the leap from three-dimensional to multi-dimensional perception and experience is the most fundamental change. To reach a translogical form of knowledge or realm of wisdom, celestial beauty, and spiritual essence is one of the most ancient experiential goals of mankind.

– Twenty-Six –

Beyond All Boundaries

The signature quality of dreams is the lack of boundaries. The dreamer can travel forward and backward through time and space, oblivious of geographical borders, historical eras, political institutions, social or religious constraints; impervious to pain, or triumphant over it; bouncing back from death if it occurs. S/he can play with identities, including sexual ones, give birth to extraordinary ideas and creatures, sport appendages at will, utilize x-ray vision, and out-perform any hero of mythology. The dreamer can converse with animals and inanimate creatures as well as spirits in various guises.

Dreams offer vast opportunities and tremendous freedom in responding to them. The dreams I have included thus far illustrate many of these features. In my NDE, however, I experienced a state of vastness that exceeded all previous conceptualizing. Infinity was no longer a concept but a reality and it was suffused with Infinite Love.

Some months after the NDE, I registered surprise that there had been none of the thrills of dream life, none of the colorful displays that had reassured me over many years, none of the old ecstasy of flying. Yet the near-death experience was more profound than all those dream features combined. I had difficulty writing about the event, yet continued making efforts, as follows:

My Near-Death Experience

I ascended, straight up, divesting first my physical body, then layer after layer of my aura. I did not look down or around, but was suddenly there, and realized that there was not a place but a state of being–without boundaries, yet all-embracing–immense, yet personally welcoming. I was suffused in a light beyond the known spectrum. Illuminated, yet without words or other sensory input. Full, complete, utterly perfect.

The experience itself was blissful, but the return to my physical body was tumultuous. This is how I described the sequence to my children a few weeks later:

> My consciousness whooshes down into a physical body, and I take a breath, strange and wonderful. I am aware of a Before, so this must be Now. I sense an Inner and an Outer, the tissues of my skin a boundary between them. Oh, I feel so heavy in this confinement.
>
> There's a voice calling me, but doesn't say my name, just, "Right... all right?" It's a woman dressed in white, with a pink sweater that I'd like to touch, but my hands feel frozen. I don't move, so she does. "I am a registered nurse," she says. But I know she's my Guardian Angel.
>
> "Would you like me to help you?" She unstraps what's choking me. Takes off my mittens, pulls down my socks, holds my wrist. "Pulse fast, but strong. Don't move... an ambulance is coming."
>
> Now different voices, too many questions. With another whoosh, my sensory apparatus kicks in, and I remember I was driving... Everything seems fated. Capital F, Fated.

The near-death experience (NDE) itself is inexpressible. Not only did words elude me, but I was afraid of diminishing the importance of the event in my attempts to describe it. The closest I came was through drafting the following poem, which I set aside for several years before calling it complete:

Translated

The Aramaic word for death translates as "not here, present elsewhere."
–P.M.H. Atwater

> No longer a song of the surreal,
> no more a metaphor for the ineffable,
> no traversing of the heavens

> in a multi-faceted balloon,
> no navigating the stars in a dirigible,
> no rising vertically on my own.
> This is realer than real,
> unexplained by the term NDE,
> uncontained in words or imagery,
> *of the Essence.*
> Unique, yet with cosmic oversight,
> not here, present everywhere:
> a scintilla of the Light.

Comparisons and Contrasts of Lifetimes

The year 1990 was a breaking point; it marked a life-and-death situation, a before and after, *that* incarnation and *this* one. In 1990 there were few books regarding the NDE, and some of those few I did not read until a year or two after their publication. My experience differed considerably from the classic stories about going through a tunnel and being greeted by relatives or friends. So I was relieved to find confirmation of my experience by Melvin Morse, M.D., a clinician who has interviewed hundreds of persons as soon as possible after their near-death experience.

> There is one aspect of the near-death experience that neuroscience hasn't been able to account for–the Light. Nearly every near-death experience of children (and about one-fourth of those of adults) has in it an element of the Light. Those who experience the Light say that it is more than just light. There is a substance that "wraps" them in a warmth and caring that they have never before felt. Where the rest of the experience is extraordinary, the Light makes it mystical. It is the "truth" of the near-death experience.

I need to emphasize that in the transfusion dream (Jan 30, 1990), discussed in "Precognitive Dreams", I *viewed* an energy exchange, whereas in the NDE (Feb 2, 1990) I *experienced* it. Yet there was a striking similarity between my notes on the dream and my journal notes on the NDE. Consider the "more than shimmering, as if with thousands of brilliant stars/particles /atoms/ surges/ pulses" along with, "I was a particle of the wondrous light, a scintilla of the warm, loving, totally, embracing, infinitely knowing brilliance."

Certainly my 1932 entry on earth was the opposite of my 1990 NDE re-entry on earth. The contrasts were extreme:

- oppressive blankness vs. expansive brightness
- my being held back by authority figures vs. embraced by The Most Holy One
- lassitude, to the extent of not trying anymore vs. rest in Infinite Love
- a sense of wrongness vs. a sense of perfect rightness

After the NDE, I was no longer opposed to the concept of reincarnation. For me it was a reality.

My belief that I re-entered this physical body "to do it right this time" remained unshaken. Yet I had questions, such as: Do other traumatized persons have to go through such an intense life review? Is this what born-again Christians experience, or are they relying on metaphor?

Beneficial Therapies

When I was allowed sessions in physical therapy, one of the modalities was gentle massage, to strengthen my kinesthetic sense and awareness of physical boundaries. Yet in the first session, within a few minutes, I was thrown into a scenario of violent struggle. I heard a scream without realizing that it was coming from me. If DR, the therapist, had not been in complete command of the situation, my body would have flown off the massage table. Similar spontaneous regressions, though not as fierce, occurred in the warm-water pool, and sometimes during the course of an uneventful day. The scenes were never about the car crash. I understood them as past-life events and, with proper coaching, learned not to re-experience the pain but to observe the scenarios and infer how my tactics for surviving them could apply in the present life.

Eventually those scenarios stopped. But they were followed by a replay, in dreams, of memory tapes from my 1932 birth onward, which seemed like adding insult to injury. What I needed were aids for living in the present; therefore, I sought help from a psychotherapist. I was not surprised that a "diagnostic dream" would occur prior to my meeting her, but I was unnerved by seven distinct dream scenes in a single night (Mar 13, 1990). Moreover, they amounted to a life review and provided a catalog of issues to consider in therapy, even though I believed that I had resolved several of them through previous dedicated efforts:

Focus of Dream	*Dominant Feeling of Dream*
1. X uses a vacuum cleaner on me.	1. Abuse.
2. A home honoring Our Lady Of Perpetual Help.	2. Idealism, disillusion.
3. Exploring F sounds: fiasco, philosophy, faith.	3. Need to make meaning.
4. Black thesis binders.	4. Deceit, entrapment, guilt.
5. Flying like a hot-air balloon.	5. Loveliness, awe, sense of purpose.
6. Ugly furniture of my past.	6. Anger, assertiveness.
7. Daddy's yearning and disintegration.	7. Death in life.

Of these seven dream scenes, only the fifth one displayed positive feelings. It was imperative for me to focus on positive feelings in 1990, and it is important to feature the lovely dream now, three decades later, as a counter-balance to the dreams precipitated by pain.

Mar 13, 1990
I'm Flying Like a Hot-Air Balloon

> First I see thousands of small hot-air balloons, the sky is filled with them. Each balloon has a person's name attached where the basket would be [in actuality]. Most names are of famous people. Now a few people, maybe eight from our area, are going up from their own back yards, somehow attached to the ropes below the balloons. Maybe these are helium balloons? They don't have hot air and a blower.
>
> Even when I'm allowed 3 to 8 pre-flight bounces, these are indoors, and I hit the ceiling on the first bounce. I need far more preparation for the outer-space cold, I want several scarfs and my pink sweater and mittens.
>
> Now I myself am going straight up–like a balloon, but without a basket and without adequate training. [I reason that] God has given me this gift and some experience already in a "maiden flight" and other flights. And when we arrive at another planet, God will show the way to shelter, food, clothing, etc. Yet I am handicapped by the cold and by people pulling on ropes and weighting me down.

FEELINGS:
Awe, loveliness, pleased to be in this adventure, a glorious calling, lift-off.

COMMENT:
The heaviness is not my own, but the pull of others–possibly my eight children.

Regrettably, the sense of loveliness and my inner glow were short-lived. Thankfully, in less than two weeks, my self-confidence was boosted by the following dream:

Mar 25, 1990
Boarding a Huge Plane or Space Ship

> I'm on time but not ready. I sort through a small day-pack and transfer a few things to my blue suitcase. I leave it unlocked and open on a counter and go looking for something else.

Now two little girls—age 5 and 3—run toward me, waving, smiling. They want to ride on an escalator at the airport. I set them next to each other on a step. But something is wrong—the treads catch their feet, their ankles, up to their knees. They don't cry out. It's as if they're two-dimensional, like paper dolls.

I'm terrified and push a big red button for emergency. The escalator stops, all the treads are flat now and loose. Paramedics arrive with a gurney. I say, "It's not that kind of emergency [not a collision]. They just need to have their legs released." The medics seem disappointed that there isn't something more dramatic to do.

I am drawn to the girls emotionally. Not responsible for them, yet very concerned. But I must leave, the space-ship departs soon. We must say goodbye. It's dusk and I'm worried about their getting home safely. I hunt for someone who might take them home . . . anyone. I find someone and now turn to leave.

I return to the space-ship's great lounge area in time for departure. I assume that my suitcase will reach the right destination, too.

FEELINGS:
Anxious to terrified, hoping for safety, expecting success, letting go of responsibility.

REFLECTIONS:
1. The large plane I think of as the next spiritual plane, anyhow my next destination.
2. Here is a progression from unreadiness to readiness for departure.
3. Yet, whether in the previous balloon-like ascent, when I was cold and unprepared, or in this large, warm, welcoming space ship, I do not know what my destination is. The former's way of desire leaves me most vulnerable, while today's way of trust allows me comfort.
4. The girls age 5 and 3 represent me at those ages, when I endured life-threatening illnesses.
5. The "need to have legs released" resonates to physical pain on most nights.

Even with the benefit of therapies, I still felt singularly alone:

June 1, 1990
Left on My Own to Float or Fly

> I'm being taken to a school on another plane! I'm getting very excited. I know excitement is risky in dreams, yet I yearn to go, learn, and understand.
>
> But something is hurting. I shift my position ever so slightly to relieve it, and immediately I'm out of the moving pattern and more consciously aware. I call to angelic powers, "Please come! Please support me!" My own voice wakens me.
>
> I was terribly disappointed about not arriving at the higher plane. In waking life, too, there was disappointment. I was not physically able to go to Japan, a trip arranged for by Hiroko's parents, and I had to cancel my plane reservations.

Attunements to Reiki

In July 1990, six months after the car crash, DR, my massage therapist, told me that Devonna, a local woman, had attained the Teaching Master (sensei) in Reiki; moreover, he had participated in her first classes. Reiki is a healing art that dates back at least two thousand years. A Level One student learns the ancient, traditional hand positions and places both hands on the client's body or a few inches above his body, for physical healing. A Level Two practitioner learns additional positions for emotional and mental healing, plus techniques for distance healing. Reiki also has efficacy when applied on oneself.

I signed up for the next available class! There Devonna counseled us, after each Attunement, to be alert for dreams or coincidences that resonated with the high frequency of Reiki. My dream offered powerful reassurance:

July 7, 1990
A Brilliant Display in the Sky

> Like lightning, almost reaching the ground, except this is a very wide band. And I see it as from an aerial view.

Now in the sky to my right is a brilliant display in a range of reds to bronzes—again wide areas, not like fireworks.

FEELINGS:
Sense of power/dynamo, yet also solidity—not something explosive or fleeting.

REFLECTIONS:
1. I could have dismissed this dream as simply residue from the 4th of July, except for my intense feelings of awe and wonder.
2. Resonating to New Testament imagery, the brilliant display is like a baptism or a transfiguration or an ascension, conveying an announcement. How I wish for a clear message!
3. If I were a Native American on a vision quest and had this dream, I would describe it to the elders, name it, and possibly take its name for my own. All right, I am on a vision quest, and I name this "Blazing Sky Dances" and vow to revisit it again and again.

I have treated myself with Reiki daily from 1990 onward, and know that it has been a major factor in my healing. One example: I had numerous appointments at the University School of Dentistry for oral surgery, grafts, splints, adjustment of the bite plane, and construction of an upper denture. Both my dentist and her supervisor were impressed with how quickly I recovered each time.

When I returned to my poetry groups, I wrote of progress this way:

Day In and Day Out

Life itself is all right for the time being.
–Elizabeth Bishop to Robert Lowell

For the time being,
since I have totaled my car
and fractured my sternum,
I take breath as life
and life as rightness itself.

For the time being,
the pulmonary therapist chanting
Inhale, Exhale,
my lungs expand
with the knowing:
I am all right with myself.

For the time being,
my spine realigned
and jaw back in place,
I am able to smile—
only once in a while,
but that is all right.

For the time being,
this hour of grace
with my poet friends,
life is *all right!*
Two words, long vowels,
exclamation point!

In November 1990, I received Attunements for Reiki Level Two, in the same class as DR. In December my insurance coverage ended. It had allowed only 10 massage therapy sessions and had not covered dental work, far less psychotherapy, so I was paying for those from retirement funds. Yet in the new year I chose to continue appointments with DR, at my own expense. Later he escorted me to a Chinese doctor for acupuncture. When that was not effective, DR took me through 15 sessions of Rolfing, which were effective.

One year after I had Reiki II Attunements, there came another dream concerning guidance:

Dec 19, 1991
Whispering about Guides

> I'm whispering to a man at the end of a lecture/demonstration and dinner. The man sits at my left. He's said something about the need for humans to be in touch with our

Guides, in order to save the world and build a healthy and flourishing civilization. I'm amazed that he confides in me this way. And I'm completely trusting when I respond, "I've been trying to get in touch with my Guides for about six months. I sense their presence and want images."

A woman speaker to my far right, at the end of our extremely long table (it seems half a block long), talks on and on. I'm very sleepy, can hardly keep awake. So look up, and am intrigued by gold swirls on the ceiling, and whisper to the man about their possible significance. He asks, "Do you like to solve problems?"

I say, "I love to! This is what I find most challenging." We are not talking about math problems. I don't know what area he specializes in, yet I'm game.

FEELINGS:
Confidentiality, relief to talk with someone who cares about Guides. With the man I'm attentive, intrigued, impressed by the artistic swirls, enthusiastic, challenged.

REFLECTIONS:
1. Two great things about Reiki for me personally are: having Guides and knowing that I can do no wrong with my hands during a healing session.
2. The occurrence twice of "at the end" suggests my personal end-time as well as Ann's. [She is a friend dying of cancer, whom I helped with life review and with compiling a book of her poems].
3. It has been a sadness to me that, with several of my children, I can not talk about Reiki, far less "whisper about Guides." I must respect the "areas they specialize in" and concede that their spiritual journeys and mine go along different routes.

In the novel *Mr. Gwyn* by Alessandro Baricco, is a passage that expresses how I felt then, and still feel as a Teaching Master of Reiki, concerning its practice:

> She did it in the light of a strange happiness that she had never felt before, yet she seemed to have carried with her for years, waiting. It seemed impossible that, in all

that time, she could have done anything except guard it and hide it. What we are capable of, she thought. Growing up, loving, having children, growing old—and all this while we are elsewhere, in the long time of an answer that doesn't arrive, or of a gesture that doesn't end. How many paths, and at what a different pace we retrace them, in what seems a single journey.

– *Twenty-Seven* –

Anniversary Dreams

Among dream researchers much attention has been given to precognitive dreams, but almost none to anniversary dreams. One's Unconscious, without prompting, often produces a special dream close to the anniversary of an important life event. Usually an anniversary dream brings reassurance, especially the first year after the death of a loved one.

I had anniversary dreams regarding my NDE for 25 years. I include only a few here. On the first anniversary of my NDE, I was blessed with this light-hearted dream:

Feb 3, 1991
To Make Me Feel Better

> A little girl puts her hands on me to make me "feel better." I encourage her and suggest that she put one hand on top and one hand under–this in my right pelvic area. She does, but almost jumps away in surprise, saying, "It tingles!"
>
> I can't just tell her, "This is Reiki," and I don't know what words might be appropriate. I say, "Isn't it nifty?" and hope she will put her hands on me again.

REFLECTION:
My Child Self likes the simplicity of Reiki and brings to it a much-needed playfulness.

On the second anniversary of my NDE, I was blessed with birds. Birds in my dreams are carriers of high energy; many times they represent bright ideas, and perhaps as often they represent spiritual Guides.

Feb 3, 1992
Two Rare Birds Visit Me

> A snowy owl goes out the back screen door of our family porch. Just pushes at the top left corner, and

> the door swings open. I go out and hope to induce her to come back. I set out some pie pans of water.
>
> Now a great pileated woodpecker approaches, swoops from a tree at the fence-line down to the back door. I see red on its breast, not on its throat or back of head. I wonder if it is blood. Is this great bird injured?

FEELINGS:
Surprised, concerned; awed, sense of mystery and majesty.

REFLECTIONS:
1. The pileated woodpecker has shown itself to me in waking life, in full splendor. When that occurred several years ago, I was told by someone in the Audubon Society that I could not have seen one because it was almost extinct. Yet I never changed my mind about it, and its appearance in this dream reassures me that I am free to "believe my beliefs."
2. The four occurrences of the word "back" resonate with life review, which has continued, consciously as well as unconsciously, ever since the car crash and NDE. Related to the dream birds' coming, I like to think in terms of a "come-back" and to focus on whatever forms of beauty and consolation are available to me.

The third anniversary of my NDE was a few months after I received the Reiki Attunement for the Non-Teaching Master.

Feb 4, 1993
A Special Shade of Comforting Blue

> A cylinder of soft light. I try to construe a human form but can't. Yet it seems a Great Being. In half-sleep I try to apply this color to my chest and shoulders [muscles hurting from the mammogram yesterday].

FEELINGS:
Comforted, vibrant.

REFLECTIONS:
1. This isn't the lapis lazuli that I associate energetically with a sky-to-earth pole.
2. It isn't the blue-white that people have noted in my aura.

3. Oh, I don't have to assign it a name, just be grateful for the feelings and apply the color along with Reiki.

On the fourth anniversary of my NDE, I had a flying dream . . . in a state of relaxation!

Feb 4, 1994
Reclining as I Fly

> It's daylight, but when I begin my take-off I sense a cloud cover that's stifling. Now I'm sitting in the air at about the angle that I have with my recliner exercise bike. I have a small pillow on my lap. By moving my hand positions on the pillow, I can change altitude.
> By exerting some pressure, I can accelerate.
> How can I maneuver? How can I brake?
> I rise over housetops and think about going out over the ocean, maybe find clear sky there. I'm taking great care not to get too excited because I know that will waken me.

FEELINGS WITHIN THE DREAM:
Resourceful, adaptable, delighted, excited, decisive.

FEELINGS UPON WAKING:
Regretful that I didn't reach the clear sky; aware that my hand was not in the splint last night and glad that I didn't hurt my hand while flying.

REFLECTIONS:
1. Flying dreams have been rare in the past several years, and none as expansive and intense as this.
2. My reclining position suggests that I can take it easy, even while adjusting the height of my goal (complete healing) and the speed for achieving it.

In early 1994 I flew to New Jersey, to a healing center just across the river from New York City, in order to observe a ninth-level Tai Do master. During two private sessions with him, I did have fresh insights about personal energy fields. But the *system* of Tai Do was too hierarchal for me and had too great an emphasis on its guru, including bowing to his portrait before each session. The inconvenience and expense of my longer stay in New Jersey were offset by a waking vision: I saw, in the midst of ice floes on the river, seven swans-a-swimming! I could scarcely believe my eyes.

Contrasted with the Tai Do experience was an intensive course in Juanji that I took a few months later, with initiation into the first level by Master Zhang Zhixiang himself. If I hadn't forsworn having a guru, and if I weren't 62 years old, I would have followed him in his itinerary across the United States. *I have never met anyone purer than he, or more powerful.* When he placed his hands on my head, the current down my spine felt like a cylinder of energy six inches in diameter.

My next trip inquiring about relocating to do healing work was in May of 1994, to the Gesundheit Institute in West Virginia, founded by Patch Adams, M.D. His master plan included cabins for persons devoted to the healing arts, but funds had gone only as far as to clear the acreage and to raise one building, which had a carpentry workshop on the ground floor and art studios above. So the answer to my inquiry about moving there was: "Not now and not in the near future. We are still in the fund-raising stage." So I stayed for only one week, participating in chores and taking in the philosophy that honored gardening as much painting portraits, cooking as much as rock-hauling.

Just before the fifth anniversary of my NDE, I tried to dialogue with a Guide who had appeared in a dream, "Responses from My Tutor" (Jan 31, 1995). That dream concerned my having chosen to drive to Detroit, Michigan to receive Attunements for Reiki Teaching Master. (A discussion of that dream is in the section "Angels and Guides.") Even though I was increasingly aware of helpers attentive to my prayers, I still longed for the love and joy I had experienced in the NDE.

Skipping to my eighth anniversary, after I had moved to Pueblo, Colorado, I described myself as "fully expectant about belonging and serving here. I'm being delivered on the spiritual level as well as a metaphorical level by a Guide who promised me this. Whether a Guide is an expression of my developing High Self, or an archetype (such as Wise Man or Wise Woman), or a unique entity assigned to help me, I cannot say at this time. I will say that he feels Other, in the sense of other-worldly" (Feb 3, 1998).

By my twelfth anniversary, I had a strong sense of guidance, which was illustrated in a dream:

Jan 29, 2002
A Grand Master Visits Me

> His title relates to something in conservation or preservation, and he says, "We will do it right in our city." He loves me, and I believe it. Yet I want him to prove his good intentions [in conservation or preservation].
>
> He carries something inside his pearl-gray suit jacket. I know if he tilts too much, that something will spill all over his suit. Yet he invites me to tilt–to embrace and hug and PLAY. I'm in awe that this could happen with me, for me.

FEELINGS:
Receptive; totally accepted, joyful.

REFLECTIONS:
1. I understand that this is a Guide because of the pearl-gray suit that's identified him in several previous dreams.
2. In the Emotional Freedom Technique, one of the steps is to say, "I totally accept and love myself, even though . . . " Following that, the qualifier is released. In this dream there isn't a qualifier!

Near the nineteenth anniversary of my NDE, in January 2009, I was caught completely off-guard by a siege of pneumonia. I was in the Intensive Care Unit for two weeks, during which I experienced a total black-out; in Specialized Nursing for three weeks; then was moved to a rehab center for six weeks. That was a siege, not just an episode. My children and their spouses came from around the country to say goodbye, and EJ, with medical power of attorney, went through my files relative to donation of organs.

Then I woke up! As if someone had turned on a bright overhead light! My sister, who had come from Florida and was with me through the whole ordeal, found it comical when I wakened and said, "Oh, hi Maureen" as if she had just been in the neighborhood and stopped by for conversation. Weeks later, she regaled me with what I had said during hallucinations–terribly funny.

Because no one would answer my questions about the missing time, I supposed I had been in a coma. Not so . . . the blackout must have been due to amnesia.

It was not until seven years later that I found an apt description of such an incident in a memoir, *When Breath Becomes Air*, by the neurosurgeon Paul Kalanithi:

> Severe illness wasn't life-altering, it was life-shattering. It felt less like an epiphany–a piercing burst of light, illuminating What Really Matters–and more like someone had just firebombed the path forward. Now I would have to work around it.

As for why I returned to consciousness, I still do not know. After much pondering, I decided that *why* questions are unproductive and that a more sane question is, *How shall I respond to this?* To this debility? To the need for more therapies? To keeping on keeping on?

A little more than a year later, at age 78, I had a hip replacement, and a year after that cataract surgeries. None of those surgical interventions approached the intensity of the pneumonia episode.

For the twenty-fifth anniversary of my NDE, my Unconscious provided a dream about traveling to a higher plane. Of great significance was that–for the first time–I disembarked there:

Feb 1, 2015
Flying to Terre Haute / High Land

> I'm flying to Indiana, if the stewardess ever lets me get on the plane. No one has checked my boarding pass, and I'm uneasy. Oh, it's one of those huge planes–I go through a long passage and down to locate my seat. At last someone looks at my ticket, which I've kept secure in a watch-locket on my left wrist.
>
> When we land I'm unsure about this place. I start walking. Now I am in a wooded area with tall, stately trees and little underbrush. I am at peace, breathing

the forest scent and admiring that it's well cared for.
Every tree has one or more bird houses and bird
feeders, some as large as a five-gallon drum.

FEELINGS:
Impatient to anxious; secure to insecure; peaceful.

REFLECTIONS:
1. The watch-locket = the Lifeline bracelet I wear, which represents security regarding emergency or death at home.
2. An important message is: I am at peace when breathing deeply and appreciating that I am well cared for.

Most of these anniversary dreams reflected on my life changes, sometimes in startling ways. For instance, an old dream story about returning to the university in unusual circumstances developed a new twist: I was not only looking backward with knowing but also looking forward in unknowing–even to the extent of doubting any negative statement declaimed by an authority figure. To alleviate my uneasy position of knowing/not knowing, I condensed several of those dreams into a poem:

Sonnet: On the Sense of an Ending

Blithely I return to the university–
to three of them, each in a different state–
yet can't find my place in history,
or the building, or the class where students await.
Burton Tower is here, and there the Oval,
the Showalter Fountain, the Lilly Library.
But as part of the Blossom Music Festival
I need directions and serendipity.

Non-performance isn't a problem unless
there's been a dearth of well-earned publicity
and the audience doesn't show. I can express
myself as well as the Whiffenpoof Glee.
So what's this notice from the dean's secretary:
TOMORROW HAS BEEN CANCELED.   Seriously?

– Twenty-Eight –

One Template Laid upon Another

For a very long period I projected my concept of Playmate Lover onto a professional man who was doing his best to help me heal. DR was a massage therapist to whom I was assigned following the car crash and near-death experience in February, 1990. Within months of his ministrations, I realized that I was, in dreams, laying his features, manners, and voice on a template I had made for my Playmate Lover. Time proved that my assessment was correct–both concerning his sterling qualities and my projections. Over the next seven crucial years I had 24 dreams featuring DR, and there was a farewell dream in 2014.

Two years prior to the NDE and my meeting the massage therapist, a dream had set up that template in this manner:

May 23, 1988
Image of a Healer-Teacher

> A light-haired young man, maybe in his thirties, stands almost in profile a few feet in front of me, slightly on my left. He holds a length of fabric–several yards, perhaps, but not a bolt of it–to demonstrate something with the flow of it. Not exactly shaking it out, but almost, and there's a curving motion in mid-air before it drapes or settles.
>
> The material has an iridescent quality. It's a vibrant color, not quite jade and not quite teal, and pure, even though the fabric is heavier than silk. The abilities to flow and to drape and to rest, along with the brilliance and purity, are a joy to behold.
>
> There is a sense of four levels. Or is it four forces? I am on the third level or else dealing with the third force. This all relates to healing somehow. The feeling is similar to the dreams of instruction in Night School.

REFLECTIONS:
1. The flowing fabric represents generally the fabric of my life and specifically the goods/material available to me at present.
2. An inference I made this morning was "healing as a lifestyle."
3. I have for a long time associated cranberry red, shining through a blown-glass pitcher, with a healing ministry, and jade green with healing myself. As if these were separate functions!

Two months later came a dream so vivid that I entitled it "A Visitation," and I construed it as "a sexual initiation that is part of the healing process." I was sleeping lightly, naked, with legs apart. A man leaned over me, breathed over me, and bestowed almost-kisses that were mere breaths on my lips, cheeks, and neck. The result was "a sense of peace that amounts to joy. Joy!" (Jun 23, 1988).

Five months after that, I had more than a glimpse of a healer-teacher (Nov 25, 1988). I met a young, tall, sandy-haired man whose first words were, "Tell me how I appear in your dreams and what my work says to you." I felt drawn to him more by his voice and intonation than by his good looks. I was so surprised when he approached me with his question that "I wanted to find a quiet corner and explore these questions and some of my own. How does he know that he appears in my dreams? Do I appear in his also? His question could mean: How does it come about that I appear in your dreams? Or: In what situations, or in what manner, do I appear? Or: In what guise or manifestation do I appear?"

This enigmatic person manifested in waking life in February 1990 a few days after the NDE. My first appointment with him was at a clinic adjacent to the hospital where the ambulance had taken me. Knowing my condition, he applied a very light touch. But something came over me. I heard a scream, not knowing it came from me, and, without volition, almost flung myself off the massage table. But he was right there, in command of the table and reassuring me. When another therapist came running to help, he said very calmly, as much to me as to her, "We're all right." That he said *we* established my trust in him. If he had stood there in his impeccable white jacket and referred to me as *she*, the way doctors and nurses often did in my presence, I might have withdrawn from him.

Over time, other regressions occurred when he worked on different areas of my body, but none as dramatic as that first one. Because this therapist disliked his given name (based on a town in France where his father served during World War II), he used his initials, DR. Within a few months of my meeting with him, I had a dream whose story was so cohesive and true to my situation, that I include it here at length:

May 24, 1990
A Charming Man Speaks to Me and Mother in a Hotel

> I don't know why Mother and I are at this lovely hotel, maybe for a banquet. We're sitting in a great lounge where upholstered chairs have been placed close together. A tall, well-built, young man [late 30s or early 40s] sits next to me. Our arms rest on a mutual arm-rest and, as he's talking, we touch. It's so electrifying that I wonder if my hand twitched, but I don't withdraw, just sit there, pleased. He's in casual conversation, I don't recall the subject, when Mother, in a chair on my left, leans over me and asks him where he's from. "Connecticut." She says, "We've stayed there, in _____." He beams, "That's close to my home. Do you know Kentbrook?"
>
> Now Mother is making up to him, she's so impressed because she just knows he's in the Social Register! Mother behaves like the rich woman in "Rebecca" making over the rich man played by Laurence Olivier. And I feel like the plain, naive woman. Except this man is holding my hand, and he's being affable to her because he likes me, not the other way around.
>
> He rises to go to his assigned table, and we go to ours. Mother says, "Don't double-face with me. You know who he is, don't you?" No, I don't. "He's _____ and very wealthy. And he's married, you know that." No, I don't. When mother says how rich he is, I say, "I can tell by his suit–it's fine wool and fits him perfectly."
>
> While we're still at our table, he comes past me very slowly, smiles at me, and touches my left hand. I curl my

> fingers to press his a few seconds. Our hands are warm
> and smooth and fit perfectly. He doesn't look back at me,
> yet I feel we will meet again, he will tell me his name and
> status, and we will touch again. I know he's very smooth
> and probably very sophisticated, but I'm not afraid of
> his taking advantage of me or making me feel foolish.
> Gentleness is the feeling–a true gentleman, I think, not just
> a playboy. His confidence [in me] is reassurance that all is
> well and that there will be good times in the near future.

FEELINGS:
Appreciated, admired; confronted by Mother and her value system; hopeful, warm, reassured.

REFLECTIONS:
1. Even within the dream, I thought about the puns "well-suited" and "fits." This morning I infer that Connecticut = a state of connecting.
2. From the first time I met with DR, I recognized his confidence, felt his gentleness, and was blessed by his reassurance.

It was DR who connected me with Devonna Simpkins, a woman in Columbus who had just achieved the level of master teacher *(sensei)* in Reiki. (I had made attempts for a year to find a teacher, and held airline tickets to North Carolina to attend classes there, when the car crash occurred.) After I received the Attunements for Reiki One, I ordered a massage table. When DR learned that it would not arrive for six weeks, he loaned me his portable table for that period, so I could begin channeling Reiki for other persons. Students at that time were expected to do 90 sessions, including some sessions on other persons, before applying for the Reiki II classes. In the interim I had this encouraging dream:

Sep 16, 1990
A Wonderful Hug from DR

> We meet at a Reiki event, probably at Devonna's house.
> There are hugs all around, and his is the first. He comes to
> me with that rare smile. He speaks while holding me, "It will
> be like this every time we meet, now that the structural work

> is finished. You know there had to be professional distance before. You might not know that your body is attractive, so I'm telling you. I want you to know and be happy."

FEELINGS:
Pleased, blessed.

When DR moved from the hospital clinic to work at a spa, he allowed time to drive to my house to continue our sessions. When I was able to drive again and to replace my car, one of my first jaunts was to an appointment with him. Later, when DR positioned his work at the far side of a suburb, I was able to drive that far.

Coincidentally, he and I took the Reiki II classes at the same time. He encouraged me to participate in the peer group sessions, even though he could not, due to other commitments. About two years after the car crash and my first meeting DR, I had the next dream about him:

Jun 7, 1992
Surprised by DR at the Pool

> Many youngsters and teenagers—a whole class or busload of them—are playing, not swimming, and no one else can swim laps. Now I see DR on a lounge chair at the side. I toss a wadded-up towel at him to get his attention, but it misses. When he does see me, he waves and pulls another chair over next to his. I dive in gracefully and glide quickly on a diagonal to where he's sitting.
>
> He welcomes me, then says something like, "About our appointment tomorrow . . ." [but is interrupted]. The odd thing is the way he's dressed—in baggy pants and shirt, like a cartoon of a prisoner. He looks husky, not slim and graceful. He looks lonely, and his posture is awkward.

FEELINGS:
Surprised, welcomed; puzzled about his interrupted message; concerned about loneliness.

REFLECTION:
In the night I thought, Any dream with DR is important to me. But this morning I haven't a clue.

In waking life, I remember being surprised when I saw DR one day in the pool where I did therapy exercises. There was no way that I could know he had a membership there. More surprising was that he called to me and later came over to talk for a minute before leaving. In the next two years or so, at several workshops, DR explained what I didn't understand. Later he introduced me to several healing arts practitioners, including one who utilized essential oils.

After I had made considerable progress physically, DR took me to a Chinese doctor for the experience of acupuncture. After ten sessions the doctor said, "And now we can begin." I said, "And now we can stop." It may have been in the third year that DR offered Rolfing sessions. I agreed to the full 15 sessions and, even though they were intense (also expensive), I felt improvement after each session.

DR was himself a mentor in several areas, including knowledge of the Eastern paradigm of Five Elements and the System of Meridians. More important in the long run, he taught me the basic principles of Polarity Therapy, which expanded the traditional hand positions taught in Reiki.

I was consciously aware of the necessary professional distancing between us, but that did not stop my Unconscious from inserting DR in dreams. I became aware that I was projecting a lot onto DR when in a dream I saw him projected on a movie screen!

Much later, there was a strong sense of farewell, with no understanding on my part:

Oct 8, 1992
I Ask DR for a Kiss

> We've been at some event. I'm exhausted and lie on my bed for awhile. He comes into the bedroom and says something about "2:30 in the afternoon." I'm out of it. He leans over me to repeat the message. I say [in a slurred voice], "Kiss me." He stiffens, and I'm instantly aware on some level that I've said something wrong.
>
>   DR puts a hand on top of my head. Or? Now I think he's kissed me on top of my head, saying goodbye. For

how long? Confused, eyes still closed, I waken enough to murmur, "What's 2:30? When's 2:30? Where?"

Now he's on the edge of the bed, at my left side. He puts his hands on my face, stroking, and now kisses me deeply. There's no speaking and no heavy breathing. I trace his body as far as I can reach [like a blind person tracing another person's features]. There's delight for me, but now increasing heaviness. Does this mean our relationship has changed? Will he never touch me again? Is this his idea of a final farewell? What's going on here?

FEELINGS:

Exhausted, confused; sexually aroused, delighted; conflicted, worried.

REFLECTIONS:

1. There's a Prince Charming motif at first–that he will return at an agreed-upon time and that I can sleep meanwhile. That's probably why I ask for the first kiss–to seal a pact.
2. The other kiss, though, when he decides not to leave after all, is the awakening kiss of a fairy tale. If anything of the sort were to happen with DR, I doubt that I'd ever see him again.
3. I see how DR is a stand-in for the man I expect to meet soon. That man will need to have some of DR's finest qualities, including a healthy body. And he must accept me totally as I am, even when recognizing my inadequacies.
4. I'm surprised how swiftly the dream's action went from business to romance to sexual arousal.

Actually I got no closer to a Playmate Lover in waking life. Meantime, my dreams of DR increased, "sexual dreams in which he comes to me" (Nov 13, 1992). In my notes, "I dismiss the idea and the voice as wishful thinking, fantasy, compensation, all those fancy psychological terms. Yet this kind of whispered voice is powerfully real when it happens. It has a distinctive quality and feels as though I'm meeting the person on the dream plane."

The next dream of this extended series was a simple diagram of two circles with spokes. There was one word, HUB, and the explanation: "The two circles with purple rims represent DR and me. The clouds surrounding them/us may be the astral plane" (Mar 23, 1993).

About a year later, a dream had DR and me dressed in white again. In the midst of playfulness, "I fully realize that this is DR and that our relationship will always be on a professional basis. Professing what? I love him and believe that he loves me, but not in a sexual way. What man does love me that way? A dilemma. This feels like an assignment in an acting studio: Do it as if you are so-and-so. Do it as if you feel such-and-such" (Aug 3, 1993).

The next dream was two years later, five years after my car crash. I had found a doctor who did osteopathic manipulations and was blessed with other healing modalities, too. Friends going through certification programs in Trager and in Polarity Therapy gave me free sessions, and the Reiki peer group met at least twice a month. I believed that I was not in a dependency relationship with DR and continued having appointments with him about once a month. I acknowledged (on my dream tablet) that I had projected my desire for a Playmate Lover onto the most important relationship of this new incarnation, writing, "That's not fair to anyone and counter-productive for me. DR is modeling what I can only hope to find in a Playmate Lover." While waiting, waiting, I did Reiki daily and had the Attunements for the Teaching Master of Reiki in 1995.

Fortuitously, I came across the concept of Task Mate as distinguished from Soul Mate, and inferred that Task Mate was my relationship to DR in this lifetime. With that in mind, I concluded, "I need to appreciate that, with our mutual respect, we are close to unconditional love. Also that I have had many lifetimes of light and love, not always of sickness and violence."

In the next dream that featured DR, he was showing affection for me in public. Even in my morning notes I did not know how to handle that idea. "Here he is, in an aspect that he's never implied and one that I've consciously repressed. I mean, imagining what those wonderful hands and the Reiki Energy and his great heart might bring to me! I know what I could bring to him. A phrase rings in my ears, "Too late, too little known." That I most likely have known DR in several lifetimes doesn't ease the tension now. I know that most of these dreams are projections, yet this one feels as though we met on the dream plane—mutually lovable and loved" (Oct 15, 1995).

In autumn of that year, I labeled a dream "An Encounter with DR on the Dream Plane." In the morning, after writing the details, I was still puzzling, "There's very little tension sexually. I don't know if it's physiologically possible to reach orgasm without sexual tension first, but that's how this seems. I go rapidly from liquid warmth to gasping, and DR goes rapidly from unawareness of me as a sexual being to total acceptance of me this way."

REFLECTIONS:
1. I don't for one minute assume that humans have sexual intercourse on the dream plane. My guess is that our Essential Beings commune, perhaps in the manner portrayed in the movie "Cocoon," when a high-level Guide agrees to "show" herself to the young captain through electrifying lights. He says in awe, "If this is foreplay, I'm a dead man."
2. This I do know: I had a peak experience during the night and offered thanks for it. What I'm circling about in this writing is the spiritual uplift I've been feeling. I recall Jeremy Taylor's assertion that explicitly sexual dreams are often spiritual dreams. Anyhow, this encounter is important for the feeling of heightened awareness.
3. The past few days I've been thinking of the wrench there'll be when I leave Columbus. One of the most difficult goodbyes will be to DR.

In fact, when it came to my leaving, my last stop at the edge of town was to say goodbye to DR. It was 17 years later when a dream about DR seemed final (Mar 22, 2014). "I see DR across the room. We make eye contact, but he seems to be warning me not to move toward him. I'm puzzled. Later he's almost covered the distance between us, and I take a few steps to stand at his right side. Now he faces me and touches my face. A bolt of energy goes completely through me. I can't touch him. It's not sexual energy or anything like a romance novel in physical sensation."

The bolt wakened me to "a feeling of terrible loss. I wonder about the possibility of DR's passing. There's a momentary joy with the thought that he cares enough to let me know. But if he's still alive, what could our meeting on the dream plane signify? Or accomplish?"

No one could ever match the mentoring that I received from DR, or the unique friendship that developed over seven years. Yet, when I moved to Pueblo, I was able to locate a Trager practitioner, Valerie Spencer, who was an answer to prayers. Valerie is certified in several of the areas that I so appreciated with DR. She has attained advanced levels in Dr. Upledger's cranio-sacral therapy, developed her intuitive skills, and invested in providing a center, Life's Sanctuary for Health and Transformation. For over 20 years I have been blessed by her expertise and caring.

– Twenty-Nine –

Epiphanies

The dream themes that I have traced thus far indicate that an "aha moment" can come in any situation, concerning oneself or any person, and in totally unexpected ways. A particular instance can amount to an *epiphany*, which means *manifestation* and carries with it a sense of revelation. Though it may seem to be a sudden occurrence, it may have been long awaited. Epiphanies are what most people call "big dreams." They are memorable and appreciated for years after their occurrence.

Moments of Illumination

Nov 18, 1988
Everything Is Illuminated

> The first sign begins in dusk. Suddenly the world lights up, as far as the eye can see. And there are no shadows! Everything is illuminated. Someone says (or maybe I do), "It's like 250 watts over each of us, over everything, everywhere." The sky itself is a brilliant blue.
> Crowds have gathered, gawking and exclaiming, and now another wonder: a loud, resonant Voice that surrounds us. It doesn't echo but is equally loud and resonant wherever anyone stands. I'm sure this is happening all over our Earth. What does the voice say? It sounds like something from the Bible, but I don't pay enough attention to the words to get a message. The reason is: I'm aware of a Divine Friend coming to me, and this Presence has me topsy-turvy with joy. While other people are shouting, quaking, kneeling, responding in awe, I'm saying a big, warm "Hello!"
> I'm sure the second sign will be rain and wind. Yet I'm eager for Mother to witness the brilliant sky and bright world. She disbelieves and asks, "Well, what's the message? What did

he say?" I admit, "I can't recall, and if I get into a logical mode of thinking, I may lose the memory of the event itself, the way I've lost some dreams." Now I wonder why I didn't stay with my Divine Friend rather than run home to alert Mother.

I think the third sign will be snow. Thousands of crows darken the sky, but I'm not afraid of them.

Jan 17, 1992
Light Patterns that Comfort Me

> Lights are like banners unfurled. Now, other movements, rotations. The sense is in-going movement, a boring down into the ground or into some grounding surface.
>
> Now light patterns are on a horizontal surface—on a circular disk about two feet in diameter. The sense is out-going movement. It's slow enough that the brilliant colors do not blur together.

FEELINGS:
From being exalted to being grounded; from being centered to expanding outward; overall a comforting.

REFLECTIONS:
1. A diagram I made during the night reminded me of the Reiki symbol for "Put the energy here."
2. The "boring into a grounding surface" resonates with Kundalini energy when it traverses a person's spine.

Aug 21, 2011
A Vision of White Lights

> Several small white lights are [when I study them] globes the size of a basketball. Or else they are at a greater distance than I supposed? I sense them as not just balls of Energy but as Angelic Beings, extending love. I feel expansiveness and JOY.

FEELINGS:
Gladness. Whether the dream images are a symbol of Angels, or an actual manifestation of them, I am glad for this event. And just as I give thanks for blessings during the day, I give thanks for the blessing I received during the night.

REFLECTIONS:
1. These lights resonate with photos that I saw in the waiting room of my massage therapist–photos of Beings that [allegedly] range from garden sprites to Archangels.
2. These lights also resonate with Polaroid snapshots that have captured energy around friends' faces or bodies.
3. More powerfully, on a feeling level, the lights are welcoming... as if I am one of them! That astonishes me now, as I write this.

Ecstatic Openings

Beyond illuminative dreams are ecstatic dreams. These lift me out of mundane concerns in ways that music, art, literature, and Olympic medalists sometimes do–letting me feel a part of a greater picture, a greater harmony, a finer humanity, and poetry-in-motion. Even inanimate objects in a dream can reveal something essentially spiritual. Here is an example:

Jun 26, 1992
Tetra Plates

> I'm in a small room of a church–very crowded, stifling, not enough elbow room, not enough breathing space. I attempt to teach a mixed choir how to sing but am thwarted every which-way. At last I'm "saved by the bell."
> I'm willing to leave. But someone comes in and, with a flourish, sets new dishes, fresh out of a fortified packing box, on the table. This is an invitation for me to stay, like a Communion meal. The plates are pure, sparkling white yet translucent, porcelain I think, though I exclaim, "Tetra!" [as if that identifies them]. They exude or emanate light.

FEELINGS:
Frustrated; relieved; welcomed, awed.

REFLECTIONS:
1. These few lines do not convey the brilliance of the plates or my awe.

2. In my unabridged dictionary, tetrarch means "one of four joint rulers or chiefs of a province." I infer that the four plates in this dream represent four levels of awareness–physical, emotional, mental, and spiritual–and that I am communicating through them.

INFERENCES MUCH LATER:
1. In a workshop led by Ken Kelzer at the ASD Conference in Santa Cruz, he spent an hour on this dream. And participants encouraged me to make affirmations, such as: "I take my beauty off the shelf, permanently. I take my art off the shelf, permanently. I take my Self off the shelf, permanently."
2. *But the tetra plates weren't on a shelf;* they were in a fortified packing box and were presented with a flourish. So my affirmations should be related to my moving on, unpacking/revealing my best qualities, and recognizing myself as a Light Being.

A second instance of an ecstatic dream, which occurred six years after my NDE, included persons as emblems of the Divine and artistic objects as having sacred nature:

Mar 26, 1996
Every Day a Mystery as Well as a Documentary

> A girl younger than 10 helps me with a skit or some other presentation. It feels like a scavenger hunt. When we arrive close to our goal, she announces it in terms of "hugs and kisses." This sounds so childish that I write it down as "love and protection." In an excited voice, she gives the final cue or clue, "a great doll for hugs and kisses." Or maybe it's "a doll great for hugs and kisses," meaning renowned for this. The doll we're seeking feels Oriental, like a Buddha.
>
> Now indoors, I see a long wall with shelves from floor to ceiling. The room is a shrine, with much gold, also brilliant colors. The shelves are packed with boxes of incredible materials and artistry, expensive books with fabulous bindings, and porcelain urns that I assume contain ashes of important personages. There's a feeling of ancestor worship.

The urns line the lower three shelves. I feel the "great doll" figure, or else the ashes of a great personage, can be found in one of the urns. The girl and I have only one chance, can make only one selection, concerning the great doll and what it represents.

As I ponder how we'll make our selection, I choose to write the skit or story thus far. There are elements of beauty and artistry in it that I want to recall, even if we don't win [the scavenger hunt]. Looking for writing materials, I glance at a window. Its frame makes the scene beyond look like a medieval painting.

I'm aware of early morning mist and feel a sense of mystery.

Now this thought strikes me: Every day a mystery as well as a documentary!

FEELINGS:
Seeking, playful, cooperative; scrutinizing, awed; challenged and pleased with the venture.

REFLECTIONS:
1. The little girl = my Creative Child, eager and excited. She gives the cues/clues relative to reaching the goal.
2. My Adult is more deliberative, even while savoring the beauty and mystery.
3. The skit resonates with grand-daughter Crystal's involvement in "Odyssey of the Mind," also with the creativity and cooperation necessary for those skits and for the problem-solving later.
4. To the extent that I am the "great doll," what I'll be remembered for is hugs and kisses, love and protection, not for being a memento of an historical period.
5. The ashes in the porcelain urns suggest my past lives and the honor given them.

REFLECTIONS THREE MONTHS LATER:
I have done free-writing about this dream, five pages on a legal-size tablet. Here are some of my inferences:
1. I see and hear the dream as a story about my healing ministry. The girl younger than 10 represents the years I've been doing hands-on healing work.

2. The "great doll for hugs and kisses" resonates with a doll I have used in Inner Child work. That doll has been hugging my talisman polar bear for six years.
3. In a scavenger hunt, the clues and objects have little monetary value. The chase and chance are key elements, along with playfulness and the beguiling of persons whose doorbells are rung.
4. The shelves in the shrine resonate with my bookshelves, which presently hold 16 boxes of dream notes, several boxes of the *Opening Night* manuscript, my published books, and an array of books about healing.
5. The shrine in the dream also suggests the Temple of the Akashic Records.

Numinous Dreams

There are some truly exceptional dreams that expand boundaries to infinity and somehow convey infinite love. Rare as these openings are, I have had several in my lifetime, but presently can find no record of them. I must have placed the notes regarding them in a special folder, one that was overlooked or lost when I moved from Ohio to Colorado. The best description I have read of such expansiveness appeared in a novel, *The Dream Life Of Sukhanov*, by Olga Grushkin:

> In anyone's life there can be only a few such moments—moments when a long, ringing hush fills your hearing, the world stands still as if under a magic spell, and thoughts and feelings course freely through your being, traversing the whole of eternity in the duration of a minute, so that when time resumes and you return from whatever nameless, dazzling void you briefly inhabited, you find yourself changed, changed irrevocably, and from then on, whether you want it or not, your life flows in a different direction.

In the numinous dream related below, 10 years after the peahen story (given in the section "In Awe of Dream Animals"), the energy presented itself as male, in a down-to-earth setting. The dream's title was "Enormous Prehistoric Horse Weaves through the Forest" (Feb 13, 1986). Even when transposing the dream into a poem, I was still in awe, to the degree that I distanced myself from the vision by using a third-person narrator:

Out of the Woods at Last

She steps into a clearing,
    stands where sunlight is bright,
    stares at an enormous creature
        weaving through the forest.

The creature is sleek. It's gray, like pewter.
Tall, unbelievably tall. The forerunner of a giraffe?
Not a dinosaur, yet something ancient—
prehistoric and very like a horse.
    How can that belly, those hindquarters,
        follow the path made by forelegs and withers?

Bigger than Bigfoot or the Abominable Snowman.
    Have other sightings been reported?
    She's heard nothing of it on "All Things Considered."
It's 30 or 40 feet tall. An anachronism.
    She hopes it's a vegetarian.
    She stands in the open and stares.
As if her eyes make it take notice,
the browsing animal lowers its gaze,
    appraises her
        as one might a butterfly.

>   Now and again she remembers to breathe.
> Her voice is a long time coming. "Naturalist!
> You've got to see this!" No answer.
> "Someone, anyone, hurry!
>   I need this creature verified." No answer.
>
> It smiles (can a horse smile?) bemused,
>   sees through her into the future . . .
>   She gasps, *Ancestor.*
>
> The magnificent being sizes down
>   to a carousel animal,
>   to a gray plush donkey,
>   to a piece of fuzz in her mending basket.
>
> It dematerializes
>   to an abiding memory
>   of a god incarnate.

The following example of a numinous dream was so expansive as to convey musical voices from several eras. Here are the feelings, reflections, and a transposed poem:

Dec 3, 1987
Presenter in a Multi-discipline Seminar

FEELINGS:
I have the feeling that what I heard weren't recordings as such but the actual voices of the poets, still preserved, out in the ether and time-traveling. The voices are as clear as on compact disks, actually more so, as if the poets are actually in the room with Kezia and me. Or maybe I have been astral traveling and have somehow intersected with their audio beams! That would account for my being in the presence of the poets, as in the presence of the musicians, without seeing them.

REFLECTIONS:
1. While noting comparisons of voices, and trying to understand history, I fall into a logical mode. This terminates the dream.
2. In an imaginative leap, I ponder about Kezia's and my voices. Were we once upon a time Anonymous?

In a Multi-Discipline Seminar

I open my lecture by reading
paired poems, medieval and modern.
Surprised by accompanying sounds
of mandolin, oboe, and saxophone,
I wonder, Who are these musicians?
Yet I choose not to glance around,
unwilling to break from communion.

Do the grad students hear it . . .
this infusion of the Spirit?
Well, that's not my affair—to guess
whether they appreciate
or are even aware.
The sublimity of this moment *is*,
regardless of inattention.

Now more voices enter,
with exactly the right pitch and rhythm—
the very poets I have chosen—
as clearly as if recorded on CDs.
Or am I the only one to hear them?
Have I intersected with their beams,
like visual holograms but auditory?

William of Aquitaine's voice resounds
like that of Dylan Thomas,
and Anonymous (who was a woman)
has the cadence of Mona Van Duyn.

Awed, I dare imagine who in the future
might intersect with me
while reading my poetry.

A recent example of a numinous dream focused on relationships:

Jan 21, 2015
Self-Teaching and Theory

> I've found a book that answers all my questions. It's a book of revelations, also of relationships, that I never understood before. Things are so clear that I could conduct the theory class myself! I'm expounding on the tonic [key note] and I am eloquent.
>
> A prof now stands in the doorway, nodding approval. I'm so excited that I don't feel embarrassed. He asks, "How do you know all this?" I say, "I should have understood years ago," and refer to the University of Michigan, to Ohio State University, and relationships here in Pueblo.

FEELINGS:
Enlightened, reassured, excited, eloquent, approved of, encouraged.

REFLECTIONS:
1. Music theory helped me in writing poetry. I understood how notes on paper could elicit feelings in an audience, how important sequencing is, also cadencing (punctuation) and silences (end-stops).
2. Yet this dream concerns more than music theory; it's "the theory of everything." There's a new emphasis here, on the importance of relationships in my life and how they help me understand life as a whole.
3. The tonic = key note. My "expanding on it" relates to my adapting to different persons and situations in different ways—not as a denial of the essential Self but as a method of extending boundaries.
4. *Theoretically*, the three periods of my life (in Michigan, Ohio, and Colorado) are linked by my intense desire for fulfillment—through music, writing, and healing work.
5. "The book of revelations and relationships" resonates with the Akashic Records. No wonder I'm so excited about how people and things work together as part of a master/mastery plan.
6. "I should have understood years ago" *that* people and things all work together, even when I didn't understand *how*.

– Thirty –

And Let Perpetual Light Shine

There is a significant difference between those dreams that occurred prior to my near-death experience and those that occurred after it. For at least a year after the car crash, however, what possessed me was *how* it had come about. Here is an example of my questioning:

Mar 4, 1991
Woman in Black Blocks My Progress

> She's in a slinky black dress, driving a shiny black car, and stops across from me–in my lane–blocking my progress. It's as if she expects to make a left turn, but her lane is *NOT* one for left turns. She tries to stare me down.
> I am in a through lane. I decide to go around the woman and then get back in my lane to proceed. I'm clearly in the wrong doing this, yet more concerned about a policeman's seeing this than about the imminent danger.

FEELINGS:
The whole traffic scene is so artificial that fear is not a strong element. I'm mostly puzzled. Why oh why would I put myself in danger just to avoid the sitting-still dilemma? Why didn't I wait for the woman to make her own necessary re-routing?

QUESTIONS AND INFERENCES:
1. Maybe the woman's appearing so unreal and outside of my expectations is the point of this dream? I feel she is not a self-image, but is Other. She may represent the woman whose car hit me; I think that woman changed lanes and pulled around another car just before crashing into mine.
2. The woman resonates with a magazine picture I've been playing with [for collage]. It advertises a perfume called "Knowing" and has the slogan "Knowing Is All." In this dream, I am up against my old neediness to know what is Truth.

3. The woman, when trying to stare me down, is like the wicked step-mother in "Snow White" and, by extension, like my mother. Am I still blocked by enmity with my mother? Still trying to get around her for always putting me in the wrong?
4. This dream warns that there can be obstacles not of my own making, that I can be blocked temporarily in an unjust manner, and that my lane/path/course will be cleared sooner or later *if I stay put and remain in control of my vehicle*; i.e., myself.
5. Aha! This dream is an illustration of a "rite/right of passage." As such, it gives reassurance that in the coming years I will be more right with myself than during the past terribly difficult year.

In the next death-and-dying dream, there is a miraculous revival, albeit a temporary one:

Oct 18, 1995
Pieta Woman

> The mother of a friend dies in my arms. This takes about 20 minutes. Now I keep holding her while others are making plans about the funeral home. My mother goes on and on about "not taking candelabra this time." I say, "The funeral home will send a car to pick her up" [meaning the body]. Mother insists, "NO, you carry her yourself." She means for me to walk a long block, past the florist's, with this burden.
>
> The woman is getting stiff. She's in a Pieta position, and I try to lay her body more flat. Angelyn brings a folding chair so I can prop up my legs to hold the woman. After an hour the woman revives! She talks to us. I see the sparkle in her eyes and realize how much I've loved her, for several years. Truly, dearly.
>
> But now she gasps. I think she's choked on something and may vomit it. This time she's dying for sure and she knows it. This time she's not just "passing away," there's some struggle. She's like a child in delirium–reaching out, murmuring, jerking occasionally. But the struggle is to get there [to heaven], not to stay here with us.

FEELINGS:
Displacement, bewilderment; honored to assist at her death; pure love and appreciation.

REFLECTIONS:
1. Assume that the dying woman is my Self. That she revives long enough to talk about the process encourages me to share my NDE with more friends.
2. Here's the usual conflict between Mother's valuing things and my valuing friendship and compassion; between Mother's insisting that I carry the whole burden, and my wishing to let it go.
3. I still haven't let go of an overwhelming desire to *get there*, to heaven. And the struggle itself makes it more difficult to *stay here* on earth.

I was still here 15 years later. At age 78 I had two dreams with almost the same title. The first focused on my destination; the second, on my moving toward it.

Aug 17, 2010
Time to Go Home

> The scene is in lowering darkness: time to get home, be home. But where is home? I approach on foot, on the left path, toward an exclusive enclave for rich people. But I know that I'll be going in circles or cul de sacs interminably. So now I take the right path, which leads to a second area that has neo-Gothic buildings. One building that feels like a castle is an art museum and others are university buildings. One, which must be an important library, I am able to enter by ascending wide and steep steps.
>
> Inside, there are obstacles, such as a reflecting pool that seems to go the entire length of the library and prevents me from exiting the tall doors. Determined, I walk right through the pool and proceed outdoors.

FEELINGS WITHIN THE DREAM:
Lost, stopped in my tracks; in awe, reflecting, sensing mastery.

FEELINGS UPON WAKING:
My feeling of mastery evaporates, and heaviness overtakes me.

REFLECTIONS:
1. While writing, I get a chill when trying to describe the neo-Gothic buildings, especially the important library, which represents an entry level on a spiritual plane. Its steep steps = a steep learning curve.
2. Going home = finding my place in the afterlife.
3. The lowering darkness = my approach to death.
4. Though in this dream I take the right path, there are still obstacles, and I feel as lost as ever. I infer that the answer to *overcoming* is simply *to keep on keeping on.*

Oct 28, 2012
Leaving for Home

> John Wayne is working on a ceiling. He's drilling a hole and can get his hand in, but not his whole arm, to reach something.
>
> I tell John I'm leaving for home. He comes down off the ladder and just stands there, wordless. I lean my right side against his chest, and now turn toward him and put my arms around him, saying, "Just give me two more minutes." He doesn't embrace me, but stands at ease, and the warmth of his body is consoling.
>
> I go out the side door, but first decide to lighten my load. I exchange my white purse for my black purse, but decide against that weight, too. I don't even take my billfold [for I.D. card and credit cards], far less a book, and start walking.

FEELINGS:
Slight reluctance to leave; comforted, relieved of burdens; familiar with the neighborhood, generally okay.

REFLECTIONS:
1. Attention to *hole* and *whole* = personal wholeness.
2. John Wayne resonates to Jay, who once told me, "In another lifetime we can be lovers." Also to John Kneisly, who gave me hugs when I needed them. (I've had three incarnations with him.)
3. Leaning against John, I receive support. Yet he does not insist on holding me to the physical level or even to the emotional level.

4. This leaving for home feels like leaving for heaven. To go there, I must lighten up.
5. Leaving possessions behind, also leaving attachment to my identity in this lifetime, I go–minus burdens–toward home.

Over the years the heaviness and the struggling waned considerably. When they recurred, there was usually a transition to a more serene state, as in the following dream:

Jan 11, 2012
A Possible Death Scenario, in which I Can Still Think for Myself

> [Following a bizarre surgical dream scene] I get up groggily, heavily, but without assistance. I stagger, fling my arms out for balance, feel myself flung backward and then catapulted forward [as when I had the Meniere's episode]. I wobble toward my red raincoat, which is in a heap and wrinkled. I put the coat on and lean against a wall, exhausted, and think, If I ever see an old lady in a state like this, I will not think ill of her but will sympathize.
>
> I see a small globe made of metal strips, which looks like an emblem of UNICEF. I tuck a loose edge of a continent into the empty center of this globe shape, and begin to put the whole thing in my purse. It collapses neatly, with a tinkling sound.
>
> Now a gray-haired woman, slightly unkempt, comes by. I guess she is an attendant and I ask her, in the first words I've been able to utter, "Where are my shoes and socks? I can't leave here in these slipper-socks."
>
> To this moment I've been essentially numb. But now I feel Reiki at my heart center, and gradually realize that I've been dreaming. Yet I can't open my eyes. Also my breathing is almost still. Is this how dying will be for me? In my mind's eye, I see a pearlized area a few feet above me, toward my left. No people, no voices, no music, only the sense of Reiki spreading in concentric circles from my heart.

FEELINGS:

Dead-weight, anesthetized, wobbly and unbalanced; sympathetic, goal-seeking, reassured by the globe and the coat; gathering my wits; suffused with Reiki and at peace, even when I can't frame questions or when they go unanswered.

REFLECTIONS:
1. The globe relates to many of the visual symbols in the movie "Thrive." For me personally, it's mostly a symbol of reassurance, which I'm pleased to carry with me.
2. My shoes and socks represent the ability to move safely, which is missing here.
3. My red coat represents the continuity of my lifetime as Margaret and now as Maggie. The coat's good fit over the years resonates with old ways and new ways of looking at daily living.
4. The "pearlized area" and "no people, no voices" resonate with the plane I reached in the NDE.
5. Do I think of myself as an ill-kempt, wrinkled old lady?

In spite of my nightly prayers to be delivered to heaven, there were more challenges to overcome here on earth, as suggested in the following:

Jan 6, 2013
Preview of My Passing

> I'm having trouble breathing. I use Reiki but it seems slow in taking effect. I tell myself *NOT* to go into fear when I feel I'm sliding that way. I ease into a better breathing pattern—not erratic but not fulfilling either.
>
> Now I'm floating a foot or two above the bed. Just suspended. I realize I'm frowning and choose to smile instead, which is how I hope to be discovered at my death. And now an inner smile comes with this thought: Deb is coming today and my body will be discovered soon.
>
> I marvel that there's time for thoughts at all and time to say, "Into your hands O Lord, I commend my spirit." But now there's vertigo . . . instead of flying. If I had a choice I would fly. But I'm trying to be cooperative,

not directive. HA! I thunk down onto the bed. Now I
know that this has been a dream, not the real thing.

FEELINGS:
Fear to imposed calm; disappointment to reassurance that my death can be this easy.

But the very next night there was no ease; the feeling in a dream was frenzy.

Jan 7, 2013
Dis-Integration

[Around 3 a.m.] Snatches of dreams are like a life review in bits and pieces, seemingly unrelated and extremely puzzling. How do I even have this Stuff in my memory bank? Dis-integration, no connecting threads, far less a plot line. All middles, no edges, therefore nightmarish. All the techniques I've learned over half a lifetime have not changed this visual onslaught.

[At 4:30 a.m and 6 a.m.] I'm trying to explicate–one Persona to another Persona it seems–and to make some sense of the images, to make meaning.

FEELINGS:
These images play like the multi-screen blasts in a theater complex. They change so rapidly, they leave only a vague impression and a frenetic feeling in response.

REFLECTION:
This dream reminds me of the major programming that occurred just after the car crash. It seemed I was "transferring all my files" from Margaret Persona to Maggie Persona. I do hope there's no significant life-changing event in my near future! Death I can accept graciously because it will be gentle this time, but any onslaught, the very idea of such, I find terrifying.

One year later, the setting of my death was unusual and the tone analytical:

Jan 20, 2014
My Death and Autopsy

> In a well-lighted laboratory, a researcher is analyzing my remains. My body has been cremated, yet he is interested in the ashes—sifting them, weighing them, etc. On a shelf above the counter where he's working are some glass containers. One is like a small aquarium and has something like spaghetti wriggling in it.
>
> A lab rat that is not caged looks into the glass tank. I wonder, What's the attraction? In another glass container are some larger round pieces in shades of pink-to-red that might be from vital organs. But surely not from mine because of the cremation.

FEELINGS:
Curiosity, awe related to scientific process; annoyance with the lab rat; detachment while observing.

REFLECTIONS:
1. Death + research relate to my year-long experiment in 2013, living as if it were the last year of this lifetime.
2. The well-lighted laboratory = illumination concerning my labors.
3. Analyzing my remains = life review, including bequests.
4. Lab rat = another version of the researcher, except the rat is sticking his nose where it doesn't belong.
5. Cremation = cream rising to the top, the richness of my life presenting itself.

In *Dreams at the Threshold*, Jeanne Van Bronkhorst, who has worked for 20 years as a hospice social worker and bereavement counselor, summarizes my situation:

> There is so much ending at the end of life. It is a daily, sometimes hourly, procession of loss and goodbyes. Every day brings a new physical frailty and another small, potent ending . . . . Each change reminds [the patient] that everything they have ever known will end, in fact is ending a bit at a time—first their work and hobbies, and eventually their strength, balance, and

endurance. Dreams help put the emotional experience of loss into a manageable, physical form.

A little over a year later, at age 83, I had a reassurance dream regarding my eventual death.

Apr 25, 2015
Images and Sounds that Suggest My Passing

> First is Reiki. I'm wakened by someone calling out in the next room. I go there and find Mother in pain. I ask, "Do you want Reiki?" and she says, "Yes," which amazes me. Now I learn that son Joe has been giving her Reiki for quite some time. I'm glad to continue.
> Second is bell-ringing. I ask some students who are alternating playing jazz with performing opera arias, "Where can I play the bells? Doesn't your Music School have a tower?" They look puzzled. "Well, many schools do," I tell them.
> I'm confusing handbell-ringing and rope-pulled bell-ringing and electronically-programmed carillons.
> Third is stained-glass windows. The reverberation of bells through my body is akin to the bright colors of stained-glass windows, which I notice now. I'm not aware of images in the windows, only the brilliance of the colors–several reds and blues, including royal blue.

FEELINGS:
Greatly surprised about being allowed to do Reiki for Mother. Accepting, even when I can't find the right place to play the bells. Thrilled, physically and emotionally, by the sound of the very large bells and by the brilliance of the stained glass.

REFLECTIONS:
1. The ringing of bells refers to my poem, "Ringing the Changes," which affirms success in my life as a whole, and is a eulogy at my death.
2. That I am the bell-ringer suggests active involvement in my passing, as expressed in the "Departure Prayer," by Marcia Beachy,

especially this verse: "May my departure occur in its own perfect timing."
3. That Mother would accept Reiki might be a comment on forgiveness–hers and mine. On two nights of the preceding week, I was arguing with Mother in dreams, something I never did in waking life, and I felt bitterness upon waking. So there's more work for me to do on myself before I die.

Again, regarding my passing or crossing, I was intrigued by Jean Van Brockhorst's observations of persons pausing before they cross a threshold into a new arena. Here is her distillation of hospice patients' dreams of passing:

> Dreams of journeying and traveling can occur at any point in life. They are most common when people are facing major transitions such as changing jobs, graduating, marrying or divorcing, or having children, to name a few. At the end of life, however, journey and travel dreams become more common and take on a new emotional resonance.
>
> In their dreams, people pack for travel, close up shop, and wait in line. They buy cars, cross bridges, and board trains, ships, and airplanes. Their dream landscapes fill with airports and train stations and windows and doors. They cross oceans, walk down passages, and step over thresholds into a place still unseen.

There seemed no end to delays concerning my departure from this lifetime, as illustrated in the next variant:

Jan 24, 2016
A Two-Phase Journey to Arrive Home

> I'm visiting friends in a city about two hours away by train. I've been here awhile, it's now Saturday or Sunday, and I should return home. But I can't find my return ticket for the train, my plane ticket for home, or an itinerary.
>
> I don't remember which airline I've booked. I decide to call Southwest first, and United second, if necessary,

to confirm my flight and time. But there's no phone directory in my friends' house and no help from this host family. They [the family] are scattered on jaunts of their own and ignore me, except for assuming that I'll cook and wash dishes for everyone when I do for myself.

I ask at neighbors' houses for a directory, but they are all disagreeable. I re-pack my suitcase and am ready to ask for a ride to the city [from which I came] or at least to the train station, so I can embark. I'm terribly afraid of missing my plane and feel that time is a high priority, of the essence.

FEELINGS:

Anxious, at a loss, confused, ignored, dismissed, afraid; yet goal-seeking.

REFLECTIONS:

1. Suppose the first phase of the "journey home" was the years from 1990 to 2009 (i.e., from the car crash and NDE to the pneumonia episode, when everyone thought I was dying).
2. Suppose the second phase is the years since 2009, about which I told son EJ, who is my executor, "I'm just putting in time."
3. Southwest is where I reside now, and United—with the Divine—is where I long to be.
4. The plane that I've booked = a direct route to home/heaven.
5. There's no one, and no map, to direct me. Very frustrating.
6. That "time is of the essence" indicates my belief that it's nearly time for me to move on.

Yet the idea of my being tied to Time has persisted, as in this dream scene:

> In my bedroom is a life-size cuckoo clock.
> Kevin Kline offers to wind it up for me,
> but I decline. I can't endure any more
> ticking or tocking than what's already
> going on in my limbic brain. Nevertheless,
> on the hour, out the clock's door
> comes Jose Carreras ... *cuckoo!*

Luciano Pavoratti . . . *cuckoo!*
Placido Domingo . . . *cuckoo!*
each trying to upstage the other,
moving clockwise or counterclockwise
on a whim. My romantic daughter
applauds the din: "This clock
is more than musical, it's positively lyric!"
My delayed response, *sotto voce:*
"The prevailing tenor of my day
is slapstick, tragi-comic."

When I'm working on any project, there's always anxiety about whether I'll live to complete it. Yet this book endeavor, *Dream Encounters*, is both retrospective and prospective; it can continue to the day of my death. Ergo, I need to focus on the affirmation: *I am enough and I have enough time.*

– *Thirty-One* –

Angels and Guides in Dreams

I can almost hear someone objecting, "Supernatural Beings belong in the section on personal myths." But I need to address angels and guides in a section dedicated to them, because their energy is of a higher vibration than that of myths; consequently, their images are brighter, their visitations more reassuring, and their impressions longer-lasting.

As a child I had a strong sense of my guardian angel, but I did not attribute the name Caritas until long years later. From my catechism days, I understood that angels are pure spirits. In contrast, guides are likely to have had incarnations on earth. As an adult I had many occasions to exclaim, when one or another of my children had a close call, "Your guardian angel was certainly looking out for you!" Or, "Mercy, your guardian angel must have been working overtime!"

Around age 42, when I began to connect a dream image with guidance, I tried to discern whether it represented a person I knew, was an angel accompanying me on life's journey, or was a guide helping me with a specific project such as writing, editing, or gardening. Sometimes a name came to me right away, but most times not, so I began capitalizing Angels and Guides as if they were proper names.

I recall the first time that I sensed a Guide. It was in 1989, when I was taking the first level of Transformational Kinesiology®, the life work of Rolf Hausboel and Grethe Fremming. In Columbus, Ohio, they introduced their work at the Unitarian Church. At one break in the intense weekend, I was at a water fountain but felt transported elsewhere by someone awesome. I stood there for quite a while, oblivious to my surroundings. That visitation assured me that I was on the right track with this healing modality, which relied on carefully worded statements and muscle-checking for information from one's Unconscious. When the weekend was over,

I asked for the Being's name and arrived at it by using an alphabet chart.

In my dreams the most consistent image of guidance has been two men dressed in tailored suits, usually pearl gray. These Guides have helped me up ladders, through tunnels, past obstacles, and have shown me that I have choices (plural) about the house I live in and the work I engage in.

There have also been singular Beings who epitomize love, and these I regard as Angels. They are most often represented by shapes from plane geometry or solid geometry, in astonishing brilliance. I feel them as Other, their essence so powerful that a dream in which they manifest stays with me for days. Their hints, nudges, warnings, and encounters in special dreams have proved true and valuable, and I give thanks for them.

As to whether they are messengers or messages, there are convincing arguments for both. On my dream tablet I have found notes on Geddes MacGregor's *Angels, Ministers of Grace*, in which he alluded to Emanuel Swedenborg's experience:

> In the latter part of his life he lived in a world peopled with angels. It was a world strangely like the one with which we are familiar, yet one in which the spiritual state of the inhabitants dictates the whole scenario. It is the combination of the familiar and the unfamiliar that at first startles us as we come to grips with Swedenborg's writings about the angelic world.
>
> The angels do not only speak; they write. Angelic writing is very different from human writing; for example, he tells us, in the inmost or highest heavens the angels express affection with vowels; with consonants they express the ideas that spring from the affections; and with words they express the total communication that they wish to make. He assures us that in angelic language a few words can express what it takes pages of human writing to say.

From this passage I better understood why I loved the names Caritas and Ovidelia, with their warm vowels. More importantly, I was confirmed in my belief that Angels and Guides express affection as well as inspire, console, and protect.

Another way of perceiving Angels comes from Jean Bolen in her book, *Close To the Bone: Life-Threatening Illness and the Search for Meaning*:

> I could envision white cells as millions of microscopic guardian angels who protect me by circulating through all the tissues of my body, able to recognize and rid my body of what should not be there. Maybe this image comes close to what really happens: maybe an angel is a quantum of subtle energy that we can influence or direct by our visualizations and prayers to heal and protect us. Maybe they are the messages that activate or energize the immune system of white cells to look after us.

I see no conflict between these perspectives, and am comfortable with both.

I do make a distinction between "the band of angels watching over me" and the group that I regard as my Council/Counsel. The latter have been with me through all my incarnations. They have helped me to frame the purpose of each lifetime and to make choices about the family and situations most appropriate for my learning in each lifetime.

Whatever I have written about Angels is an understatement, yet I need to include some descriptions here. To my astonishment, there were three eminent visitors on a single night whom I associated with Reiki:

Sep 1, 1991
Three Angel Visitors

> The first Being is composed of brilliant blue crescents—two of them in my left visual field, almost peripheral vision. The effect is two asymmetrical stars.

> The second Being appears also at my left, in a viewing range about the height of my nose, is composed of crisp black lines set in motion—a spiral or a swirl that produces a soft gray star shape, as if seen from above. The feeling is fluidity and is comforting.
>
> The third Being presents as a cube of light that becomes more and more intense, to a dazzling whiteness. It appears in front of me, three times, at the level of the pupil of my right eye. I open my eyes [during the dream] to check if I'm dreaming or if this is an optical illusion. I infer that I'm dreaming, otherwise this light would destroy my eyes.
>
> I am awestruck and at the same time desirous of learning more.

My Guides appear more down-to-earth than Angels, yet have a special aura, like these:

Jul 1, 1990
Two Men with Bright Eyes Guide Me

> Both men are dressed in trim-fitting, tailored suits—the one dark, perhaps a uniform, the other pearl gray. The feeling I have about the first man is safety, a safeguard. He escorts me on a dark street. I trust him because of his bright eyes, which I believe indicate an Old Soul.
>
> He brings me to another man, who is on a sidewalk. This man is talking to a group of people about having just purchased a double-house. "I don't know why I've done this. I'd like to refinish it completely, but it needs too much work for beautification right away. I may make some tenants happy."

FEELINGS:
Relieved, safe, trusting, happy about the possibility of beauty.

REFLECTIONS:
1. With the first Guide I felt reassurance; with the second, aesthetic pleasure.
2. The several instances of doubling indicate that this dream is important. The two men in tailored (bespoke) suits, who often appear in my dreams, represent Guides.

3. Supposing house = my physical body, more work needs to be done. Yet, if I don't insist on completing the refinishing right away, I can be a "happy tenant" in my Dear Body during the process.

The next two encounters, within a four-month period, introduced a singular visitor:

Jun 4, 1993
Introduction to Blaze

> There's interweaving of blue ribbons and white ribbons wound around a ✢ frame. There are four parts eventually, making the emblem *ojo de dio*, "the eye of God." The blue is a representation of a high Being I've felt close to me recently.

REFLECTIONS:
1. This particular brilliant blue is an example of another entity's lowering his vibrations to meet mine, to manifest on the material plane.
2. Why wasn't I weaving lights? Surely in imagination I could weave lights more readily than material ribbons. Does this suggest that I need to work at something material? Or is it agreeable for me to let things work out on a spiritual plane, even if I don't carry a message into waking life?

Oct 8, 1993
Another Manifestation of Blaze

> This pure blue is more important than hundreds of other images and dozens of scenes. The setting is formal, maybe purely decorative. There's a pillar about elbow high on the left and on the right [of my visual field]. In between is the pure, brilliant blue. Is it air? water? sky? Oh, light-rays this time. The intensity is important, and the feeling of depth. The blue is related to a belief that I hold and want to keep holding on to: that I am guarded, guided, and comforted every day, every night.

Two months later, I made an inference about another Angel:

Dec 14, 1993
A Priceless Pitcher Representing an Angel

> The first pitcher to catch my eye has several facets that reflect light from a glass showcase. It's violet, almost amethyst, and its brilliance is the most important feature. I choose to believe that this pitcher represents an Angel of healing, the one I call Amethyst.
>
> I wonder if, when I get home from San Francisco, my healing work must go into a more public "showcase"? Is that necessary for me to best reflect Divine Light? I do not want my ministry to be complicated.

One of the first times I tried to dialogue with a Guide who had appeared in a dream was after I had chosen to drive to Detroit, Michigan to receive Attunements for Reiki Teaching Master. I intentionally chose from William Rand's schedule the weekend that was the fifth anniversary of my NDE, thus honoring both my past and my future. When I wakened from the dream, I recalled no images but much information, which I wrote down immediately:

Jan 31, 1995
Responses From My Tutor

> Responses from my tutor included these.
> - There have been some consistent cues/clues, only a few of which can be found in dream notes of the past.
> - Now be alert for recurrence of a particular scene or setting, most likely outdoors, with a Presence. No need to analyze this.
> - It is wise and well to bring more material to consciousness this way.
> - Do not worry, there will be enough sleep–and "quality sleep"–to function well in the daytime.
> - Do not overload the Reiki weekend with a great metaphorical or symbolic valence. It is a turning point, and it can be joyful.

REFLECTIONS:
1. Throughout the five years since my NDE, I've had a strong pull upward, toward participating in the glorious Light and an equally strong pull downward, of being grounded, but in its negative sense.
2. I am grateful for the prompts of the past few days and nights relative to preparing joyfully for death; not grieving; saying goodbye to Planet Earth; and transitioning–wherever, however, whenever–in glad anticipation, not burdened by fear or other negative ballast.
3. I am grateful for the tutoring in dreams. And I welcome whatever helps me understand, appreciate, and carry through with counseling from this Guide.

Though I have longed to see Angels and Guides, I have never developed clairvoyance. So I am glad for the lovely dream images associated with their presence. Though I was increasingly aware of helpers attentive to my prayers, I still longed for the love and joy I had experienced in the NDE. There is nothing like it. Years before, in Symphony Chorus, we sang the "Songs of Kierkegard," one of which proposed, "Thou in the longing, *the longing*, hast given us the highest gift." Well, I am here to say that the longing is also a great trial.

An aid to my zeroing in on an issue pictured in dream life, and in better understanding the guidance therein, was the use of muscle-checking for information, which I learned in courses of Applied Kinesiology. Also, after my entering in 1996 the apprentice program of Resonance Repatterning®, the masterwork of Chloe Wordsworth, and being certified in 1999, I had at my fingertips eight of her books. Each book contained lists of statements–as many as a hundred statements for each topic in a particular Repatterning–that could be muscle-checked for personal non-coherence or coherence. Because many of those statements concerned spiritual development, I utilized them in dialoguing with Angels and Guides. Within a few years I developed a signal system for asking questions of my Self and later for asking questions of Angels and Guides (mostly evaluations of a carefully worded statement, on a scale of zero to five).

My experience has been that Angels and Guides do not give directions in the sense of 1-2-3 or a-b-c, but do offer prompts when I am at a loss for words or hesitant about actions. Angels and Guides always leave decision-making up to each person.

In the dream that follows, some High Beings offered reassurance after a person had trivialized my ideas and goals:

May 21, 1999
Assessing My Aura

> I'm in someone's spacious apartment. It has one wall of glass, giving a view of a far vista. A woman makes a remark that seems to dismiss me or to trivialize my ideas and goals. Yet she allows for others' opinions.
>
> At this juncture, two or more Beings come from afar–right through the glass. They stand next to the woman and declare to me, "You are white except for this shoulder." Then, as an after-thought, "Also a little violet."
>
> Now a stranger sight than their coming through the glass is, they want to "show" themselves to me [as in the movie, "Cocoon"]. One says something about the need for green, and I infer that means green in my energy field. First they show me their faces without a trace of green. They look red, feverish, almost raw. I cry, "Oh stop! Don't hurt yourselves just to illustrate something." I'm aghast that they would go to such lengths to instruct me. I remain puzzled about the relationships among the crotchety woman, myself, and these High Beings.

REFLECTIONS:
1. I've come to understand that these beneficent Beings are Guides relative to the initiation I'm involved in, and all have had human incarnations. It is these Guides who have been activating the energy patterns in my feet, also balancing and smoothing my field.
2. Today I had an appointment with Valerie Spencer, for Trager massage. Without my saying anything about the dream, she decided to use many crossover moves, for integrating left-to-right sides of my body. I felt I was being sewn together, not with stitches in a line but with loops over and over.

3. When processing afterward, Valerie said, "The white light was clear, yet soft, not brilliant, and there was a little light blue." (I've been told this several times by healers and by clients.) "When I was working on your shoulder, lots of gold–liquid gold–came through. My Guides told me not to touch your feet today, that your feet are sacred." My response was, "I believe the previous five days or so have been in preparation and that today's session was/is the initiation." But neither of us had a clue–initiation into what?

Oct 9, 2003
Conferring with an Advisor

> We are in a small room used for interviews. It has only a table and chairs, no books. The advisor, a woman, tells me casually that arrangements are being made for me at this place of higher learning. I'm puzzled and question, "Now? I made requests two or three years ago, and got no response then, so I gave up on the possibility." She gives a one-sentence reply, "Now is the opportune time."
>
> Quietly and gradually, other women come into the room, which seems to expand with each new person. There are always enough chairs (and eventually a sofa), so there's never a sense of crowding. I catch the name of the woman on my right, Estelle. I write it in my too-small notebook, with the pen I use for dream notes. It bothers me that I don't catch the other names, don't have enough empty pages to write in, and mostly that I don't know what is of significance to jot down. The advisor makes a point of saying that two or three persons present have a master's degree already. I'm puzzled until she clarifies, "Masters in Night School."
>
> I am welcomed here, respected, and accepted. No curriculum is stipulated, and I won't be just fulfilling requirements until I can study what truly appeals to me.
>
> Only a few men enter this interview room, and they are wearing tailored suits [like my Guides in many dreams]. One makes a request for help. I wonder if this is a test, like an advanced placement test in college on Earth. I do

> not volunteer, I sense that I am free of encumbrances. No one is pressuring anyone else. There is something more than collegiality here, and more than camaraderie.

FEELINGS:
Because of the casualness and calmness of this encounter, I almost didn't examine the dream. Yet the reassurance was so deep that I lay pondering for a while.

REFLECTIONS:
1. This wasn't an awards ceremony or an offer of a scholarship. It wasn't a response to my request of a few years ago but an invitation in the here-and-now.
2. It wasn't recognition for anything I've said or done or endured. It wasn't a test to see if I would volunteer or pledge myself to a cause.
3. It was an introduction to a new phase of expansiveness. But even this sounds vague. I take it to mean that I'll be asking for help and wisdom and prompts regarding more important things than what I've asked about to date.

Jan 18, 2015
Returning To Symphony Chorus

> After a long absence—years—I don't need to audition. I go forward in a long line, as if for Holy Communion, and receive my packet of music from a tall blonde woman. She greets me by name and says I may take the last package, even though several persons are in line behind me. It's a square box, maybe five inches on each side, and gift-wrapped.
>
> Maestro Evan Whallon [often a Guide in my dreams] is dressed spiffily in a three-piece suit. When he takes off his jacket, his vest is fitted and he looks trim.
>
> I look for the alto section. It's behind the men's rows. Now an organ plays a hymn and I look to see what number. But I don't have my glasses, and can't see others' hymn books, and can't read the index in my own.

> There's a lot of talking all around me. As more people enter, I see several are in extravagant costumes—gold lamé—and infer that they've come from a dress rehearsal or a performance.

FEELINGS:
Welcome, special, gifted; limited vision; annoyed by the talking; surprised at the costumes, joyful on seeing Evan; optimistic.

REFLECTIONS:
1. Hopeful aspects of this dream are: Holy Communion, my going forward and being welcomed, and the presence of Evan.
2. Evan's vest suggest vestments, and the fitness suggests his appropriateness in the spiritual realm.
3. Although the church or cathedral setting is not incongruous, because we did rehearse and perform in several of these (also a synagogue), I infer that this dream relates mostly to my spiritual level. Though I am welcome, I sense that my performance is not of the highest quality (not gold lamé).

In a recent dream, a Guide—whom I readily identified by the suit he wore—indicated that my progress could be easy:

Oct 17, 2015
A Man on a Tractor Gives Me Directions

> I've driven onto a narrow dirt road and feel lost. I stop the car, waiting for a tractor that's approaching [south] to come alongside. Now I wave to the driver. He gets off the tractor and comes to me, so I get out of my car. He isn't a farmer, is wearing a business suit, no hat, wire-rimmed glasses. I say, "I want to get to Ann Arbor, can you direct me?"
> He says, "That's easy. Turn around and go to the road you just crossed—that's Connecticut. Make a right turn and the next road is in eye distance. Make a right turn there and follow that road." [It is parallel to the road we're on presently.] I thank him, and now we're embracing. We kiss. The kisses are sweet—like whispers between our lips.

I start driving. But after I've turned my car around, it stalls. So he gives me a push, gently with the tractor, to get me started. And that charges my battery as I move along.

FEELINGS:
Bewildered, friendly, thoughtful, relieved, reassured, totally accepted.

REFLECTIONS:
Because the feelings are so strong, I don't want to settle for metaphors. But that seems the first step in understanding the Guide's directions, so here goes:
1. *Tractor* suggests a tutor keeping track of me.
2. *Connecticut* = not a shortcut but a connection between where I am and where I want to be.
3. The *second road*, parallel to the one I'm on, is the one I wish to follow, and it is within sight. Oh, this refers to my book! I need to go back the way I've progressed and make some right turns.
4. *Stalls* = unconscious resistance. Although *Dream Encounters* has much about death-in-life, that's not to be the focus. It's more about joy. Enjoy juxtaposing very different elements. Be joyful in the process, and the product will convey joy.
5. The *Kisses/whispers* are more than reassurance, possibly messages in themselves. Unfortunately, I did not recall any words upon waking.

QUESTIONS AND RESPONSES:
I've carried the good feelings for almost two days before asking a Guide for clarification.
1. Is the parallel road related to my desire to have a spiritual intention when making new collages and possibly hiding Reiki symbols in them? Yes.
2. Were you prompting me with some of the recent collages? Yes, the diptych, the boy scribbling on a wall, and the golden sphere with sunflowers.
3. Are you also "keeping track" of me during the writing of *Dream Encounters*? Yes.

I conclude with another demonstration of the versatility of Angels and Guides, one that both startled and reassured me during the eighth month of sequestering in the Covid-19 pandemic:

Oct 30, 2020
An Encounter with Clowns

> In a crowd, outdoors (it may be a fairground), I see the most striking clowns ever. They're dressed not in plaids or stripes or motley, but in tailored suits—the fabric, a pattern of sparkles. No, finer, like mist.
>
> I'll call the one Lionel—because he is taller and seems the leader—and the other one Leo. They come directly to me, Lionel a few steps ahead of Leo, first with smiles, now with a few encouraging words.
>
> Here's what's amazing: When Lionel gets within three feet of me, magnetism takes over, and the climax is on an energetic level. He seems to glide into my arms, into my very being. He does not overwhelm me. We rest easy in an all-encompassing contact undefined by time or space. This is not a sexual contact or a romantic one, this is fulfillment. Leo stands by as witness.

FEELINGS:
Surprised that I am singled out; welcomed; amazed; fulfilled.

REFLECTIONS:
1. Most importantly, they approach me.
2. The whole encounter is understated—no fireworks, circus band, or even a drum roll—yet powerful beyond measure.
3. Their smiles melt any resistance I might have, and initiate an open-arms gesture on my part.
4. I'm about to step forward, to close the gap between us, but magnetism takes over, annulling any effort I might make. Now I understand that I do not have to move forward, even in small ways, during these trying times, for Grace to operate on me and within me.

– Thirty-Two –

The Interrelatedness of Dreams

This section provides a sampler of themes already discussed, as viewed from a different perspective since my NDE: schooling at various levels, artistry, flying, sexual coupling, music theory, rehearsing, performing, and healing. I trust that these samples convey not only the complexity of dream work and play but also the relatedness of stories that recur over a long period of time.

Since 2018, when I was 86 years old and diagnosed with a rare lung disease (its acronym MAC), I have been blessed with supplemental oxygen at night. Two noticeable results that concern dreaming are: I sink into a deeper level of sleep than previously, and I am disinclined to write notes during the night (even after a bathroom break). I believe that the frequency of dreams is the same as before, but their intensity may have diminished.

New Renditions of Old Themes

Having referred to the Contents pages of this memoir, I am prepared to make generalizations about some of the themes and motifs as they appear in my advanced years. My rehearsal dreams now are in the spirit of the early Mickey Rooney films, when youngsters exclaimed, "Let's put on a play!" I write the script and direct the production and, wonder of wonders, my students are completely engaged and the audience is totally receptive, as in the following dream:

Dec 8, 2011
Being of Service to the Story while Directing It

> The audience is smaller and younger than anticipated. The play is outdoors, with threat of rain. But sunshine comes through.

> Some well-rehearsed child actors freeze, but extemporaneous actors do not. [Functioning as narrator] I recap the action for the audience and provide segues, continuity, some interpretation. Two themes are introduced at the start: love interest and a need for adventuring.
>
> There's an interruption by a group of women, singing. I stop them and lecture against political messages here. Another woman sings a different song, solo. It's clear and classical but still inappropriate for this story.
>
> The men who've gone adventuring come back successful, and both themes are completed: love interest and adventuring.
>
> After the show I am neither artificially high nor wiped out. In an assessment–a circle discussion with several adults, some of them actors–I tell them, "I wish I could hear what I said to the first group of women and how I said it. Did anger come through? or some other quality?" A woman to my left–her name is Joy–says she taped the whole show and can locate that part for me. Now she gives me a CD or DVD in a sealed envelope. How diplomatic she is, and respectful of all concerned! She leaves the final judgment of my words and my delivery to me.

In my advanced years, other artistic endeavors in dreams have pleased me greatly; they most often involve diaphanous fabrics or brilliant light displays with colors beyond the known spectrum.

It may be significant that in dreams I am no longer a wayfarer. Also, with the exception of the dancing and swimming that I long for, I am increasingly accepting of physical limitations. It's a relief that competition is neither a threat nor an attraction to me now.

Animals have all but disappeared, and my awe of them has been transferred to my awe of Angels and Guides. Brilliant birds still appear, bringing reassurance and sometimes a message.

My love of flying continues, though rarely in solo flights. There is a communal sense now, with many people embarking–without baggage–on their final destination in huge space ships. I do have frustration dreams about being prevented–at the last minute!–from embarking on my flight home. Flying has become closely associated with healing, and that "my craft is self-propelled by desire" (May 31, 1991) reassures me that my desire to be completely healed can be realized.

Anxiety dreams are minimal. Though I am still subjected to being tested, even in Night School, I am given more information, and sometimes tutoring, to succeed. Nightmares are rare. I attribute this to the increasing chaos in world events, which requires me to adapt–consciously and almost daily–in waking life.

Though erotic encounters are few and far between, they are still intense. But I no longer have romantic or have sexual affairs with movie stars. (Sigh).

Goodbyes to friends are poignant because I am aware within those dreams that I have outlived so many of my contemporaries.

I no longer wrestle with religion, though I sometimes fight against fear itself. A few dreams contain rituals that I might never have thought of in waking life. In one ritual my friends and I make a formation "with five persons like a star in the center, and eight persons in an outer circle. We move inward and outward three times, sending Universal Energy to others and receiving Universal Energy from others. Wonderfully simple and direct" (Feb 2, 1992). As for numinous dreams, the feelings in them seem to have been supplanted by feelings during Reiki sessions in waking life.

An Entirely New Theme

After my NDE a new theme appeared–that of graduating, often followed closely by a dream of being initiated. One of the early graduation dreams seemed superficial, when "I wonder if I'll have a two-tone graduation robe? or two different robes–one for class night and the other for graduation ceremonies?" (Jul 16, 1993). Yet that dream held a deeper element–my being healed in two areas.

Most graduation dreams pointed to a greater ease when doing healing work. Many were set in another dimension or realm, where I participated in Night School, often shown as a university with an infinite supply of subjects to study. I understood Night School to be on a plane that is just as accessible as the dream plane, and believed that its spiritual instruction can be applied to waking life.

The concept of Night School is wonderfully important to me. It contradicts and surpasses everything taught by a nun when we first graders were being prepared for First Communion. Her threat could be summarized by paraphrasing a song that we children knew:

> You better watch out, you better not cry,
> You better not pout, I'm telling you why:
>> God the Judge is always looking down.
>
> He's making a list and checking it twice,
> Setting two columns: Naughty and Nice.
>> Don't give God the Judge a cause to frown.

When we reached sixth grade, the nun who was preparing us for Confirmation declaimed, "How much goodness you store up before you die determines what state you will be allowed in heaven. There's no more learning there and no more chance to earn grace." A static heaven went against my nature, and I knew that grace was a freely bestowed gift, but I didn't dare say so. That would have been anathema.

It was years before the assertiveness training I'd had during Poetry Therapy internship found expression in a graduation dream:

Oct 5, 1999
From Art School to Night School

> Here are intricate designs with feathers, and here is a
> piece of sculpture made with several woods and finishes.
> It looks wobbly, not exactly top-heavy but unbalanced
> somehow. I wonder if that's intentional? The prof's attitude
> seems to be, "If it isn't broken, don't fix it. If it seems
> imperfect, cheerfully lay claim to intent." How refreshing!
>   I handle many pieces and ask many questions
> without a raised eyebrow from him. Even though
> there are several people milling around, he is
> totally present to me and, I feel, to everyone.
>   Now we are in and out of a bright yellow bus aimed
> for Night School. It's filled with young women as well as
> young men—all talkative and sounding knowledgeable.
> At the first stop, the art professor and some advanced
> students go around telling new students and reminding

the others, "Lean on one another for support, so you don't tire easily." This does work in twos or threes. Eventually we form circles of a dozen or so persons and feel the support and energizing effects. All this leaning while looking and learning and drawing our own conclusions!

A dream so rare that I have had only one other of similar character, involved a dear friend from whom I had been parted for about 10 years:

Aug 25, 2001
I Am Set Free

> Right after we uncouple [sexually], Jay says, "Now I have freed you." I think he means freed my inhibitions, but DR has done that, if only in dreams.
> I ask, "What do you mean?" Jay doesn't answer me. He speaks to a psychologist, "Not without pain for either of us, but it's been such a long time we've waited." As if that explains anything. Then he drifts or dissolves.

FEELINGS:
Intercourse was so complete that when I wakened I felt sated–a first for a dream union!

REFLECTIONS:
1. Even in the dream, I know this is goodbye, but neither casual nor dismissive. I sense that he's already said goodbye to his wife and that his coming into my darkened room is a transition state.
2. I haven't dreamed of Jay for many years. But this is more than a dream, I believe a passing. If his wife is a survivor, I pray for a blessing on her.
3. Maybe this encounter frees me from my sense of unrequited love.
4. Even if this is not actually his passing on, he could have come to me on the dream plane just to help me clear any blockage to love and joy. Now I can negate that double negative–"not without pain"–and focus on freedom for both of us.

In recent years during waking life, I've had graduations from physical therapy and a rehab center following surgeries. From a constellation of dreams that concerned rehabilitation, I shaped a poem:

Tripping the Light Fantastic

12 a.m.   Reprise
I try to dream up a way to pay
for the $210 prescription
not in my insurance formulary ...
Drive a shuttle bus to the State Fair?
be a greeter at Wal-Mart,
even though I don't respect their policy?
or stand at 29th and Dillon,
wearing a sign that pleads
    WILL WORK FOR DRUGS ...

1:30 a.m.   Repetition
"There's no sense in crying
now the needle is out,"
the doctor says, to stave off my tears.
The doctor says, "No sense in tears.
Don't cry out
when I'm needling you!"
The doctor shows me his six-inch needle,
saying, "Don't cry, it's out."
And I'm outta here.

3 a.m.   Rounding Out
I feel like a circus elephant with gout,
goaded to stand and pirouette.
The doctor is not my trainer but
some yokel on a pharmaceutical circuit
whose cure-all elixirs don't.
His prodding rankles me.
I wonder when "Reverse Psychology"
(his know-it-all sound track)
will take a break?
Right in the midst of the drum's pat-a-pan,
I'd like to do a can-can
and kick him up the grandstand.

4:30 a.m.   Recompense
The therapist is smooth and limber—
as graceful as Marcel Marceau
climbing an invisible ladder—
his pelvis tilt and roll a pleasure,
keeping his patients enthralled.
My performance is another matter.
I see myself as the Pink Panther
or (worse!) the bumbling Inspector Clouseau
sucked into quicksand or treading water,
catapulted, sprawled.
But despite my fumbling incognito,
clues emerge from the midst of pratfalls.
Now a brass band plays the "Marseillaise"
as I tilt and roll across the great hall
to accept a medal for solving the case.

6 a.m.   Restoration
no fight in me now, no resistance
to breakwaters, boulders, or fate
the current warm, without turbulence
otters draped in seaweed
tossing tidbits in their mouths
seagulls in perfect harmony
the end of the world golden
over the peaceful waters
as I float and drift to nirvana

Even when in waking life my mind was fuzzy from pain, my education continued, as indicated in the following three dreams:

Aug 26, 2005
Reading a Math/Philosophy Book in Night School

> It's a slim volume, maybe 6 inches by 10 inches, hard-cover edition, vintage. The text is in paragraph form and there are no formulas standing alone or diagrams, still it seems this is a book about higher math. The math explains the

> principles of our universe in a straightforward way, without religion or mythology or attempts to explain either of them.
>
> There's a wonderful feeling when a tall man standing to my left actually encourages me in my reading. Even when I'm ready to set aside the book and admit defeat concerning the high-power concepts, he supports me in that decision. As if my having been exposed to the text has assured my understanding it at some later time in my life!

FEELINGS:

Inquiring, intrigued; overcome, defeated; encouraged, supported, blessed.

REFLECTION:

The message may be that inquiries are valuable of themselves. I recall reading, many years ago, Teilhard de Chardin's *The Phenomenon Of Man*, and knowing, chapter after chapter, that I had only an inkling of what he was saying. Yet I was drawn to his ideas and read several more of his books before purchasing *Hymn To the Universe* for many re-readings.

Dec 9, 2012
First Day of Graduate-Level Courses in Music

> I remind myself to "play this close to my chest" [a caution Mother gave about playing a hand of bridge that was bid at a high level, then doubled and redoubled]. I hold a book tightly against my chest as I'm walking outdoors to, and in, a crosswalk.
>
> Indoors again, I move fluidly from one class to another, even make some notes as to the room numbers, also descriptors of the profs, the size of the rooms, the number of persons enrolled. When I get to Gertrude Kuefuhs [prof of Music Theory], she tries to persuade me to take Photography instead of Voice. But I stick to my plan and tell her, "I'm not taking electives, I've had scads of those. I'm here for graduate courses in music." More, to emphasize the urgency I feel, "I've lost a whole semester already." My intensity may surprise her, and she agrees. I don't know any of my classmates, yet I'm fairly at ease, considering this is the first day.

FEELINGS:

Accepted, confident, elated; ready, eager; intense, joyful.

REFLECTIONS:
1. There are no auditions or entrance exams this time and no requirements that I'm unable to fulfill!
2. A prompt for this dream was my holding a stained-glass angel "close to my chest" on Friday, when I crossed the street to an artist's studio to have it repaired.
3. I hear puns in *bridge* and *crosswalk* relative to bridging to another plane and crossing over to my heavenly home.
4. Here the crosswalk is at an intersection, which implies that I still have decisions to make. I hold many thoughts close to my chest/heart concerning my desire for a happy death.

Apr 15, 2013
Enrolled in a Graduate Linguistics Course

> It's the first day of class. The prof is a middle-age woman. She's stocky, wears glasses, could be a nun or ex-nun, stodgy, and I don't respect her highly. But once she's into her topic, her face is animated and her motions are enthusiastic. I believe I can do well in this class.
>
> At first I take notes, but gradually focus more on her presentation. It seems I'm the only student asking questions. I wonder if she will disregard my raised hand, but so far so good. She lectures for a full hour, then suggests we stretch while waiting for the guest speaker. My friend Barb sits next to me, undecided whether she is going to stay or drop the course.
>
> We wait and wait. Finally a young man who's just received his PhD begins a spiel. Then two men and one young woman arrive and occasionally toss in a remark. Now it's useless to take notes, the speakers ramble so I ask for a context, "I don't even know what century you are in!"
>
> The speaker's attitude is, "Well, duh…" Then he says, "The theme, if you must have one, is man's journeying."
>
> "Okay, something like Chaucer's Canterbury Tales?"
>
> "You might say so. Are you able to read Middle English?"

> "Sort of." Now I think of the Peer Gynt adventures, which must be based on an old legend, but I don't say anything more, don't want to be annoying.

FEELINGS:

Happy to be enrolled, optimistic that I can learn the material, pleased that I could say Yes about Middle English; concerned that I'll be disregarded or considered a nuisance; puzzled why the young woman defers to the men.

REFLECTIONS:

1. At first I thought that males dominated: three on the panel, also Chaucer, Peer Gynt, and "man's journeying." But for emotional content, the female professor and the questioning student (myself) are strongest, with Barb and the young woman mostly observers.
2. Of course I transpose *man's* journeying to *human's* journeying, thence to my own life's journey. And I think of my book *Take Fire*, based on Dame Alice's story and covering my marriage in my 20s, 30s, and 40s.
3. A basic question, deeply felt, is this: How much longer is my journey?
4. *Middle* is a motif here: middle age, stopping in the middle of the class, and Middle English. Am I only in the middle of transition to the after-life? As I type this, what I feel is muddle.

When I reached the grand age of 82, a very physical dream had an intense spiritual component:

Sep 30, 2014
Astral Gymnastics

> I'm aware of floating and that I haven't had a flying dream in many months, so I tell myself to relax. This elevates me more, and I wonder, Is deep relaxation actually high relaxation?
> Now I see to my left some buildings and—yes!—I rise to an altitude where I can see most of a city, most of its moderately high buildings of tan and russet colors. I'm at about the same height as the buildings, 8 or 10 stories possibly, without vertigo or fear. Is this Grand Rapids?

> I experiment very carefully so I do not pull out of this elevated state. Now I'm standing, I mean I'm positioned, vertically. Is this the experience of astral traveling that I've read about? I don't see or feel any cord, gold or otherwise, that links me to my physical body, but I don't look back or down to inspect.
>
> There's such buoyancy that I'd like to do somersaults or hand-springs. Anyway there is weightlessness and a sense of playfulness.

FEELINGS:
Floating, relaxed, elevated, curious, at ease, playful.

REFLECTIONS:
1. I don't know what led into this dream, what took me out of it, or why I didn't fly.
2. Upon waking I almost scolded myself about selfishness. Some people use astral journeys to help heal others, and here I was just having fun. Then I reconsidered: I'm healing myself. And that's what stayed with me all day–the possibility of light-heartedness even while in the physical body.
3. Grand Rapids [my birthplace] might have been a time-marker, except in this dream I'm not looking back. If only I'd gone into flying, the words "grand" and "rapids" could have been descriptors of the flying.

Dec 11, 2016
Graduation Celebrated in Song

> At the kitchen sink, looking out the window, I've finished washing dishes. Maureen says, "We have to leave in 10 minutes for graduation." I take off the apron covering my good dress and reach for my graduation gown and cap.

FEELINGS:
Complete, encouraged, relieved.

REFLECTIONS:
1. In the dream I realize that this is a major transition, and wonder what to expect in my next phase.

2. There's no excitement, but this isn't ho-hum either. Maybe this marks my graduating from extreme mood swings to a state of equanimity? I hope so.

CONTINUATION OF THE DREAM:
I turn off the alarm, fall asleep again, and dream up a Broadway musical called "Graduation":

> This musical has vignettes of several persons, not stereotypes but somehow representing many approaches to learning. There are some men along with the women as backup to the soloist.
>
> In each of the three acts, a woman sings about a clergyman, "He likes me!" It's first a priest, then a bishop, then a cardinal. Each time the chorus members counter, "But do you love him?" She sighs in a downward glissando, "Ah, no."
>
> An androgynous person complains, from blues to scat-singing, "No jobs to be had." The chorus responds, "No, no."
>
> Now I see myself discard the black graduation gown and stand in a spotlight in my sparkling white dress. I'm singing, almost shouting, "Let this be my last big step!" The chorus responds, "Who knows?"

REFLECTIONS:
1. In this dream I acknowledge the dark side as well as the bright side of both my primary roles: standing in my kitchen as a homemaker and standing in a spotlight as a performer.
2. My wearing the sparkling white dress and the black graduation gown together indicates awareness and acceptance of my Shadow.
3. Ever since the near-fatal pneumonia episode in 2009, I have been pleading that it be my last big step before release from this incarnation. Yet in this dream I am not looking backward but am stepping forward into the unknown.

Later there came a dramatic dream concerning Night School, "A Very Large Area for Staging" (May 28, 2017), which portrayed great expansiveness. From it I excerpt the following:

FEELINGS:

Expansiveness, colorful vibrations, eager expectation.

REFLECTIONS:
1. The vast rooms do not lead off a corridor, as in many dreams, but lead one to another; not a single unit but complements. I infer that the rooms = the sections of *Dream Encounters*.
2. The wardrobe = a variety of roles that I've played in this lifetime.
3. The lighting, particularly when it's a rosy, almost golden, glow = spiritual direction.
4. Two elements are new to me: the vastness of the rooms and an implied invitation to set the stage, this final stage of my life, however I can imagine it. The emphasis is on creativity more than on production.

Two months later a dream presented opposite feelings, which prefigured the total lack of communication during my next hospital episode. Here are excerpts:

Jul 13, 2017
A Graduate Course Supposedly in My Mother Tongue

> The books are printed on yellow paper. Publishers found original works yellowed with age and copied that, but the effect is ugly. I knew the readings would be voluminous but supposed they'd be in my mother tongue. Some seem to be in Old English, some I can understand from Middle English, but there are too many passages in French and Latin. Of the six students, I'm the only one who can't read French.
>
> I'm in over my head. It isn't sufficient that I got in on day one if I can't understand the language. I come across the words "i tongue." From the context I infer that it means "I speak."
>
> I'm worried. Do we have to write a paper on each of these books? Someone says No but doesn't explain what is expected beyond the reading at home and discussing in seminar.

FEELINGS:
Accepted, timely; not fully informed; overwhelmed, worried.

REFLECTION:
Relative to "i tongue," I think of Caesar's declaiming, "I came, I saw, I conquered." It's not sufficient for me to declaim, "I speak, I read, I write." I need to understand.

In my waking life, mis-communication and mis-information were rife among doctors. When I went to the emergency room after I had fractured a vertebra, the scans also showed a lung problem. Told that "it looks like t.b. but isn't t.b.," I had to wait for a specialist to counsel me, and what he said was not in my mother tongue.

The hospital allowed me extra days, even though my status was *observation* until someone would come with a back brace. But when I expected a referral to a rehab center, the hospital could not give it because I had not been *officially registered* as a patient.

Long story short, the hospitalist referred me to a pain specialist, who couldn't see me for four months; then he referred me to a neuro-surgeon, who did only major surgeries and opined that I could heal by myself in time; the hospital's e-mail portal did not convey test results and soon shut down completely; a woman in the Records Department refused to help us, saying in a stage whisper, "Those records are confidential"; my PCP, a medical internist who was notorious for being unavailable to calls from specialists, had no interest in my case. At long last, when the fracture had widened instead of healing, the pain specialist, who had years of practice as an anesthesiologist, performed a kypho-plasty in the Outpatient Clinic.

In the meantime my four sons cared for me. Coming from East Coast and West Coast, they rearranged their schedules–for four months–in order to alternate weeks of care. I never would have dreamed of such a thing! I will be ever thankful for the love they displayed. They were unstinting in their care; they bought groceries and cooked the main meals, helped me get to the toilet in the middle of the night, assisted me in tapering off pain meds that were causing grief, and took me for more scans and lab tests.

I sincerely hope that the following dream is the last example of my being tested:

Apr 30, 2020
Two Final Exams

> For the first test I ask to have an Incomplete grade, supposing I can cram for the test a few weeks from now. The prof refuses. I exclaim, "This F is the first in my life. Can't something be done?" Silence.
>
> The second final is in math. I show up late, while the prof is in mid-lecture about DOs and DON'Ts. He lets me come in and find a seat. Now I have no paper or pencil. He looks daggers at me. I ask him if he has some old papers that I can write on the reverse.
>
> At the end I realize there's been an underlying factor not obvious in the equations: It's the years and years of experience that help a person to arrive at a solution. In lit studies, it's called the sub-text, and in today's jargon it's referred to as the back story.
>
> The prof asks a Q. that no one answers. I raise my hand halfway, and he calls me by name. I say, "This amounts to an equation, probably for advertising: x = good for now and good for always. It's short and snappy."

FEELINGS:
The emphasis on final is reassuring. I choose to believe that I am safe at home and will never go to the hospital again. I'm pleased to be called by name and to answer the Q.

REFLECTIONS:
1. This dream resonates with the test of sequestering during the Covid-19 pandemic. I am more able to tolerate this than most people are, and less likely to complain.
2. But there is no quick solution to the pandemic. Few tests are available and no serum for vaccinations.
3. Both the Incomplete and my lateness are unsettling. Yet there may be a pun concerning "write on the reverse," implying that I can continue right on in spite of reversals.
4. I construe the "good for now and good for always" as referring to *Dream Encounters*.

– *Postlude* –

Reckoning the Bottom Line

To summarize this endeavor, which extends over 50 years, I list how the recording and the processing of my dreams have aided me. The recording phase fosters a closer relationship between my Unconscious and Conscious on the continuum of day-time events and night-time responses. The discipline of writing dream notes requires total honesty about the stories and my feelings; it also demands clarity and conciseness. Additionally, my perseverance in writing dream notes has helped me when I have had writing blocks in other endeavors.

The *processing* phase often reveals practical applications to problems—some immediate, others longstanding. They merit subdivisions here:

First, the processing of dream notes has helped me to arrive at other major decisions, as to:
- audition for the Poets-in-the-Schools Program
- quit the degree program for Master of Social Work
- travel for conferences in the United States and abroad
- leave my marriage of 31 years
- schedule surgery without procrastinating
- expand my editing to a small-press operation
- set up a healing practice
- change the focus as well as the title of this book to *Dream Encounters*.

Second, the processing of dream notes helps me in daily, conscious living to:
- discover the source of a current problem or a recent one, and deal with it
- uncover the cause of a nightmare whose setting is in my past, and recognize what triggers my reactions in the present
- re-enter a dream consciously and change a specific action and/or the outcome, which leads to resolution of conflict

- prevent actions that exacerbate physical symptoms
- do creative maintenance of my physical body and physical surroundings
- phone or write a person who figures in my dream; if positively, as encouragement to re-establish contact; if negatively, in hope of resolving any misunderstanding or hurt
- express myself in group settings and demonstrations with increasing self-confidence
- enhance my creativity by incorporating dream images in poems and collages.

Third, the processing of dream notes aids me in the exploration of conscious dying to:

- let go of negative judgments of my Self that I've internalized since childhood
- confirm the knowing that occurred during my NDE so I can maintain serenity while putting in time until my final departure
- remember, especially when physical setbacks occur, that progress is not charted in a straight line but along a wandering path
- share my NDE experience with others, rather than fearing that talk might diminish its significance
- re-connect with the expansiveness and joy of the NDE, especially when I have slipped into feelings of abandonment
- develop an image bank now, that I can call up during the death process
- connect with the Angels and Guides who support me
- show gratitude to the many helpers along the way, before I leave this life.

That I live at home today, not in an extended care facility, is due chiefly to two factors—the provisions that my children have made for my comfort, and the dreams that I respected and heeded. In parting, I include a poem transposed in December 2019 from what seemed the most visionary of all my dreams:

Dreamer

Last night there came a four-folded dream,
like a mandala come to life,
three parts extolling the feminine;
one, the masculine.
My Creative Child, who at birth speaks clearly,
within hours performs with timbrel and dance.
My Womanly Adult, wearing conservators' gloves,
codifies scrolls on shelves in a vault.
My Kingly Adult searches highway and byway
for folk disposed to enjoy a great feast.
I am in the midst of it all,
unsure in my role as an elder,
yet ready, willing, and able to partake.
> Everything here is serenely white:
> window-frames have damask draperies;
> sills of Carrara marble display
> fragrant white roses in crystal vases;
> Oriental carpets, patterned in ivory and cream,
> muffle any extraneous sounds
> while a woodwind ensemble plays Brahms.
> I glide to a grand, expandable dining room.
> China gleams on tables set for eighty,
> and caterers stand at attention,
> leaving to me only finishing touches–
> the centerpiece and the lighting of candles.

And here comes everybody!
They enter one by one, in their Sunday best,
believing this is the day the Lord has made,
being glad and rejoicing in it.
They nod or bow and mingle at ease,
while I roam through the gracious rooms,
acknowledging each person:
Make yourself at home . . .
It's been a long time . . .
You are ever so welcome.

– Addendum A –

Themes and Motifs Not Discussed in This Book

The following *themes* were listed several times in my dream concordance, but less frequently and/or with less intensity than the ones I chose to feature in my memoir:

Accusing, Accused
Apologizing
Balancing
Bleeding
Changing, Exchanging, Making Change
Climbing
Creating, Composing, Inventing
Criticizing, Critiquing
Dancing
Driving, Driven
Entering, Exiting, Leaving
Facing the Void
Freezing, Frozen
Gardening, Landscaping
Losing the Way
Making Movies
Opening, Closing, Ending
Rescuing
Sewing
Struggling

THEMES AND MOTIFS NOT DISCUSSED IN THIS BOOK

The following *motifs* were listed several times in my dream concordance, but less frequently and/or with less intensity than the ones I chose to review in my memoir:

Apartment, Condo, Garage
Architectural Features
Characters
Clothes, Closet
Colors
Construction, Destruction, Renovation
Craft, Craftsmanship, Witchcraft
Electricity: Current, Shock, Wiring
Family: Origin, Generation, Extended
Festivities
Frustration
Furniture, Furnishings
Geometric Designs
Gifts
House: Rooms, Stories, Additions
Marriage
Ministry
Musical Composition, Musical Instruments
Nakedness, Exposure
Persons by Relationship, by Occupation
Return, Reunion
Sacraments
Signs: Directional, Symbolic
Vehicles
Words: Argument, Unusual Vocabulary

– *Addendum B* –

Citations in the Order of their Appearance

Epigraph
> Ullman, Montague. *Appreciating Dreams: A Group Approach* (Thousand Oaks, California, Sage Publications, Inc., 1996), 243.

Prelude
> Moore, Thomas. *Care of the Soul: A Guide for Cultivating Depth and Sacredness in Everyday Life* (New York: HarperCollins, 1992), 14.

One: Sorting Roles and Works
> Domhoff, G. Wm. Interviewed by Andrea Rock for *The Mind at Night* (New York: Basic Books, 2004), xiii.

Four: The Genesis of My Creative Child
> Sowton, Christopher, *Dreamworking: How to Listen to the Inner Guidance of Your Dreams* (Woodbury, Minnesota: Llewellyn Publications, 2017), 296–300.

Five: The Dreamer as Artist
> Shuman, Sandra. *Source Imagery* (New York: Doubleday, 1989).

Nine: A Rude Awakening
> Houston, Jean. *The Possible Human: A Course in Enhancing Your Physical, Mental, and Creative Abilities* (New York: Jeremy P. Tarcher/Putnam, 1997).

> Swedenborg, Emanuel. *Journal of Dreams*, commentary by Wilson Van Dusen (New York: Swedenborg Foundation, 1986), 21.

Ten: The Give-and-Take of Dream Notes

Ullman, Montague. *Appreciating Dreams: A Group Approach* (Thousand Oaks, CA: Sage Publications Inc., 1996), 24–27.

Mellick, Jill. *The Natural Artistry of Dreams* (Berkeley, CA: Conari Press, 1996), 51.

Bogzaran, Fariba and Daniel Deslauriers. *Integral Dreaming: A Holistic Approach to Dreams,* (New York: SUNY Press, 2012), 32.

Jung, Carl G. *Man and His Symbols,* ed. Marie-Louise von Franz (New York: Dell Publishing Company, 1964), 160.

Eleven: In Awe of Dream Animals

Hillman, James. *The Dream and the Underworld* (New York: Harper & Row, 1979), 158.

Saunders, Nicholas. *Animal Spirits* (Alexandria, VA: Time-Life Books, 1995) 51, 78.

Hillman, James. *Dream Animals,* illus. Margot McLean (San Francisco: Chronicle Books, 1997), 43–45.

Vaughan, Alan. *The Edge of Tomorrow: How to See and Fulfill Your Future* (Santa Fe, NM: Sun Books, 1985), 52–54.

Twelve: My Love of Flying

Cather, Willa. *Death Comes for the Archbishop*. Everyman's Library. 1992.

Fourteen: Anxiety Dreams

Garfield, Patricia. *The Healing Power of Dreams* (New York: Simon and Schuster, 1991), 27.

Windsor, Joan. *Dreams and Healing: Expanding the Inner Eye* (New York: Dodd, Mead & Company, 1987), 179–180.

Kalweit, Holger. *Dreamtime and Inner Space: The World of the Shaman* (Boston and London: Shambhala Publications, Inc., 1988), 103.

Fifteen: Nightmares

Garfield, Patricia. *Creative Dreaming* (New York: Simon and Schuster, 1974), 107–111.

Interlude

McPhee, Charles, *Stop Sleeping through Your Dreams*, 85.

Gilbert, Elizabeth. *Big Magic: Creative Living Beyond Fear* (New York: Riverhead Books, 2015), 223–225.

Seventeen: Erotic Encounters

Renshaw, Domeena C. "Sex, Intimacy, and the Older Woman," (Women and Health, Vol 8/4 Winter 1983).

Eighteen: Personal Myths

Moore, Thomas, *Care of the Soul*, 223–224.

Nineteen: Me and My Shadow

Jung, Carl G., *Man and His Symbols*, 160 and 200.

Ostaseski, Frank, *Discovering What Death Can Teach Us about Living Fully*, 35.

Miller, Alice. *Pictures of a Childhood*, trans. Hildegarde Hannum (New York: Farrar, Straus & Giroux, 1986), 15.

Perry, Christopher. *The Society of Analytical Psychology*, https://www.thesap.org.uk/resources/articles-on-jungian-psychology-2/about-analysis-and-therapy/the-shadow/

Twenty-Four: Wrestling with Religion

Sanford, John. *Dreams: God's Forgotten Language* (San Francisco: HarperCollins Publishers, 1989), 152.

Sanford, John. *Healing and Wholeness* (New York: Paulist Press, 1977), 34–35.

Twenty-five: Precognitive Dreams

Dickinson, Emily. *Final Harvest*, ed. Thomas H. Johnson (Boston: Little, Brown and Company, 1961), 42–43.

Kalweit, Holger. *Dreamtime and Inner Space: The World of the Shaman* (Boston and London: Shambhala Publications, Inc., 1988), 89.

Twenty-Six: Beyond All Boundaries

Morse, Melvin. *Closer to the Light* (New York: Villard Books, 1990), 115–116.

Baricco, Alessandro. *Mr. Gwyn* (San Francisco, McSweeney's, 2014), 166.

Twenty-Seven: Anniversary Dreams

Kalanithi, Paul. *When Breath Becomes Air* (New York: Random House, 2016), 120.

Twenty-Nine: Epiphanies

Grushkin, Olga. *The Dream Life of Sukhanov* (London: G.P. Putnam, A Marian Wood Book, 2005), 94.

Thirty: And Let Perpetual Light Shine

Van Bronkhorst, Jeanne. *Dreams at the Threshold: Guidance, Comfort, and Healing at the End of Life* (Woodbury, MN: Llewellyn Publishers, 2015), 63.

Van Bronkhorst, Jeanne, *Dreams at the Threshold*, 72–73.

Thirty-One: Angels and Guides

MacGregor, Geddes. *Angels, Ministers of Grace* (New York: Paragon House Pub., 1987), 88.

Bolen, Jean Shinoda. *Close to the Bone: Life-threatening Illness and the Search for Meaning* (New York: Touchstone Books, 1998), 149.

– *Acknowledgements* –

That this book has become a three-dimensional reality is due to the encouragement, support, and problem-solving abilities of two persons–Catherine Atwood and Joe Honton.

Catherine Atwood is a librarian whose specialty is conservation and restoration of documents on paper. In addition to scientific articles, her credits range from slave narratives of persons who had been freed and then were captured by bounty hunters, to maps of the Lewis and Clark expeditions. When Cathy is not in the lab, she can be found, along with FEMA, alleviating effects of fire or flood on historical documents.

Back in 1970, when I conceived of a five-year project in recording my dreams, Cathy and I were at The Ohio State University at the same time. She showed interest in my project, recommending acid-free paper for the notes and providing resources for acid-free folders and storage boxes. Though Cathy's career led her to reside in seven States, we kept in touch, and eventually she read every draft of my dream book and proof-read the galleys of *Dream Encoounters*.

When my manuscript was not set in the program that literary agents required, and my idiosyncratic choices of two wildly different type fonts caused problems for transcribing, Cathy called Joe Honton in California, asking if he would take on my project.

Joe graciously agreed and, during the Covid-19 pandemic, has functioned as my literary agent, editor, and publisher. As a published author of technical articles and books, he has considerable knowledge of the publishing industry.

That may have led to his asking as many questions of me as I asked of him. His extraordinary patience when correcting difficulties that I had got myself into is worthy of highest praise. Joe's efforts in designing large computer programs for businesses and civil authorities is evident in his meticulous design of *Dream Encounters*.

www.ingramcontent.com/pod-product-compliance
Lightning Source LLC
Chambersburg PA
CBHW031402290426
44110CB00011B/238